ima
COMICS P

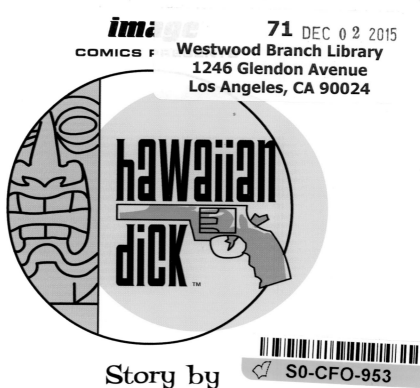

hawaiian dick™

Story by
B. CLAY MOORE

Art by
STEVEN GRIFFIN

Book production
and design by
STEVEN GRIFFIN

Story fonts by
blambot.com

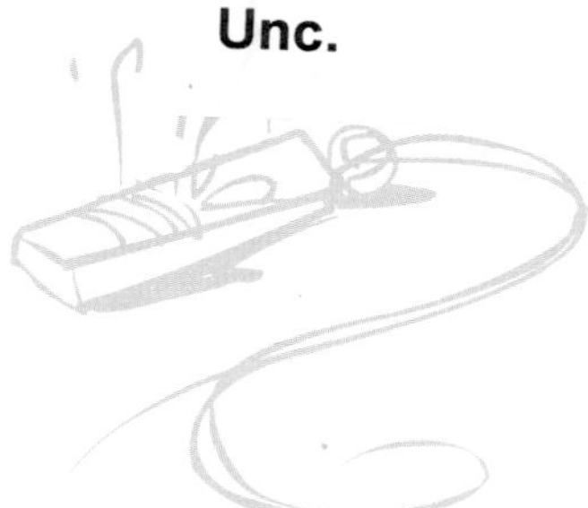

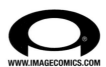

WWW.IMAGECOMICS.COM

FOR IMAGE COMICS:
JIM VALENTINO • PUBLISHER
ERIC STEPHENSON • DIRECTOR OF MARKETING
BRENT BRAUN • DIRECTOR OF PRODUCTION
TRACI HALE • CONTROLLER/FOREIGN LICENSING
BRETT EVANS • ART DIRECTOR
ALLEN HUI • WEB DEVELOPER
CINDIE ESPINOZA • ACCOUNTING ASSISTANT
TIM HEGARTY • BOOK TRADE COORDINATOR

HAWAIIAN DICK VOL. I: BYRD OF PARADISE.
AUGUST 2003. FIRST PRINTING.

Published by Image Comics.
Office of publication:
1071 N. Batavia Street
Suite A
Orange, CA 92867

Originally published as Hawaiian Dick #1-3 in single magazine format.

PRINTED IN USA

INTRODUCTION
by James Sime

"You want another, buddy?"

It's a mid-summer Tuesday afternoon in San Francisco, one of those days the tourists love, with clear blue skies and a light breeze blowing in off the ocean. But I'm not outside seeing the sights with the tourists or soaking up the sun with the flower children in Golden Gate Park. I'm sucking down Mai Tais in a secluded tiki bar on the edge of Chinatown.

My bartender's name is Keoni, an aging sour-faced islander who looks as if he might have been born behind that bar, and is most assuredly well on his way to dying behind it. I've seen Keoni at this bar before and he always has the same routine - watch infomercials on the tiny tv, eat his sandwich, and glare at you during the commercial breaks unless you have a pair of tits or brought a pair with you.

I once witnessed Keoni eliciting squeals from a couple of young girls with a yarn about losing his wallet and an eye at knifepoint and a joke about garnishing their cocktails with his glass replacement. Back when I was slinging drinks rather than comic books, I worked with any number of bartenders who attempted this kind of aphrodisiac alchemy of tall tales and stiff drinks, but Keoni takes the artform to an all-time low. The old man is so full of shit, even his "glass" eye is brown.

Today he's glaring at me so hard it looks like that eye of his might pop out and give him another story to tell the ladies. He doesn't exactly appreciate me using his bar as my office and tap-tapping away on my laptop.

But I don't care.

Because I'm writing about Hawaiian Dick. And as the off-duty cops start to roll into Keoni's five and dime tiki paradise from the station house across the street, I can think of no better place to set the stage for the book you now hold in your hands.

Hawaiian Dick is a kick-ass comic book.

B. Clay Moore's story has all the makings of a classic; a murdered beauty, a web of organized crime, bumbling two-bit thugs, and a hero with a mysterious past. But Moore makes this classic all his own with shadowy glimpses into the nether regions of island mysticism and the Hawaiian spirit world. The mood for this noir tale is infused with color and set from the first page through Steven Griffin's gorgeous artwork and terrific sense of pacing. Griffin's versatile palette is at moments gritty and menacing, smooth and soulful as 1950's jazz, and as glowing and colorful as a Hawaiian sunset.

Like I say, a kick-ass comic book.

You just can't go wrong with hard-boiled 1950's tiki noir... especially when you add a generous amount of sexy island girls, angry Polynesian gods, vengeful zombies, and an explosion of tropical color. Anyone with a modicum of style and taste will understand when I say that Hawaiian Dick is so undeniably cool it hurts. Books like this are the reason I traded in my cocktail shaker for a comic book store and am damn glad that I did.

"Hey, buddy," Keoni grumbles pointing his sandwich crust at my empty glass. "You want another or what?" Hell yes I want another. B. Clay Moore and Steven Griffin had better get to work.

And Keoni can get me that Mai Tai, too.

And also, one of these...

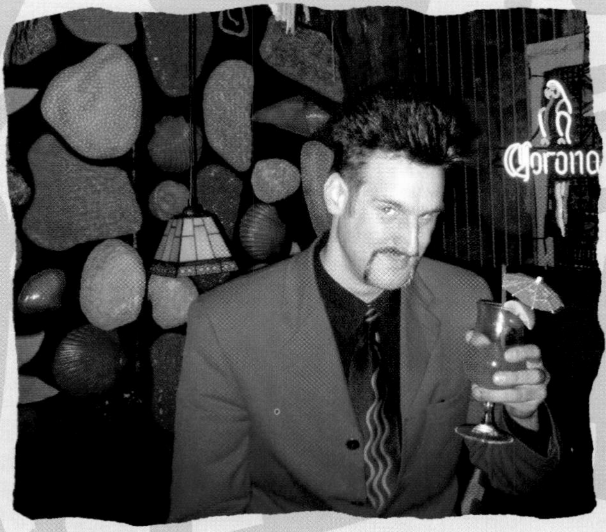
Corona

James Sime is a former bartender who spent nearly a decade mixing adult beverages and holding court in swank bars, upscale restaurants and trendy watering holes the nation over. Armed with a fistful of quick cash and a closet of Italian suits, James brought his new vision to the comic industry by opening the sexiest comic store on the planet, Isotope the comic book lounge in San Francisco.

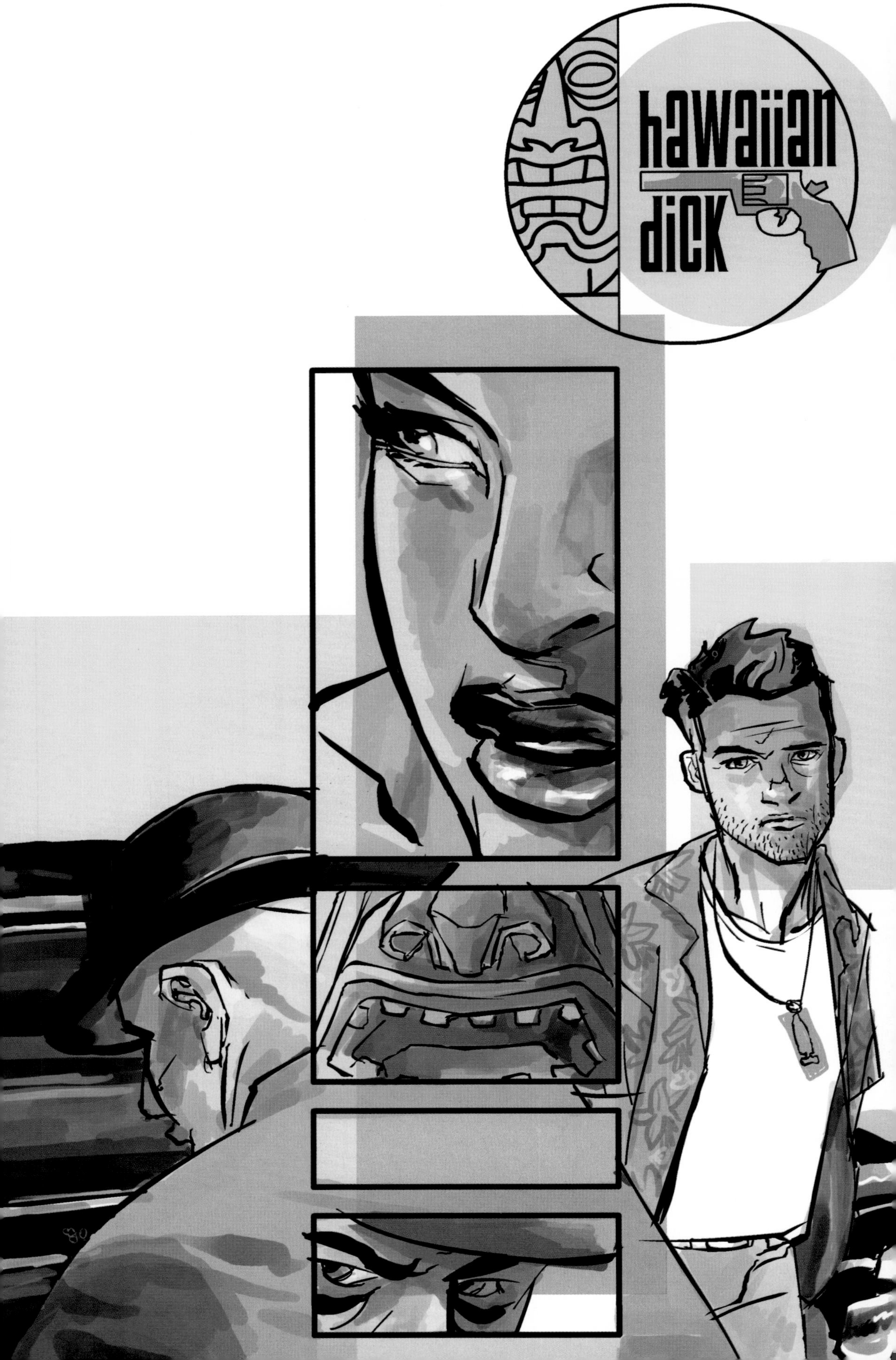
hawaiian
dick

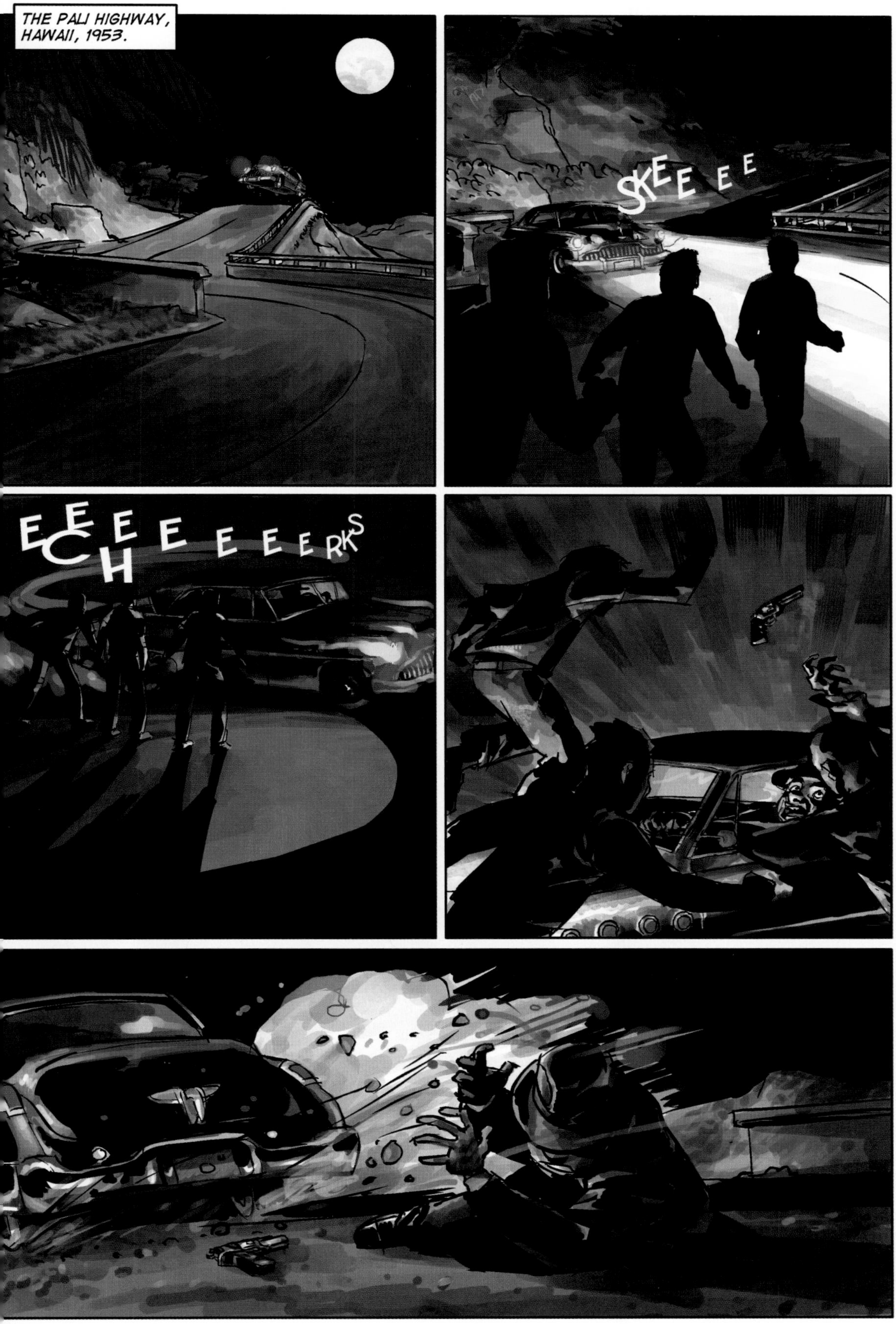
THE PALI HIGHWAY, HAWAII, 1953.
SKEEEEE
EECHEEEEEERKS

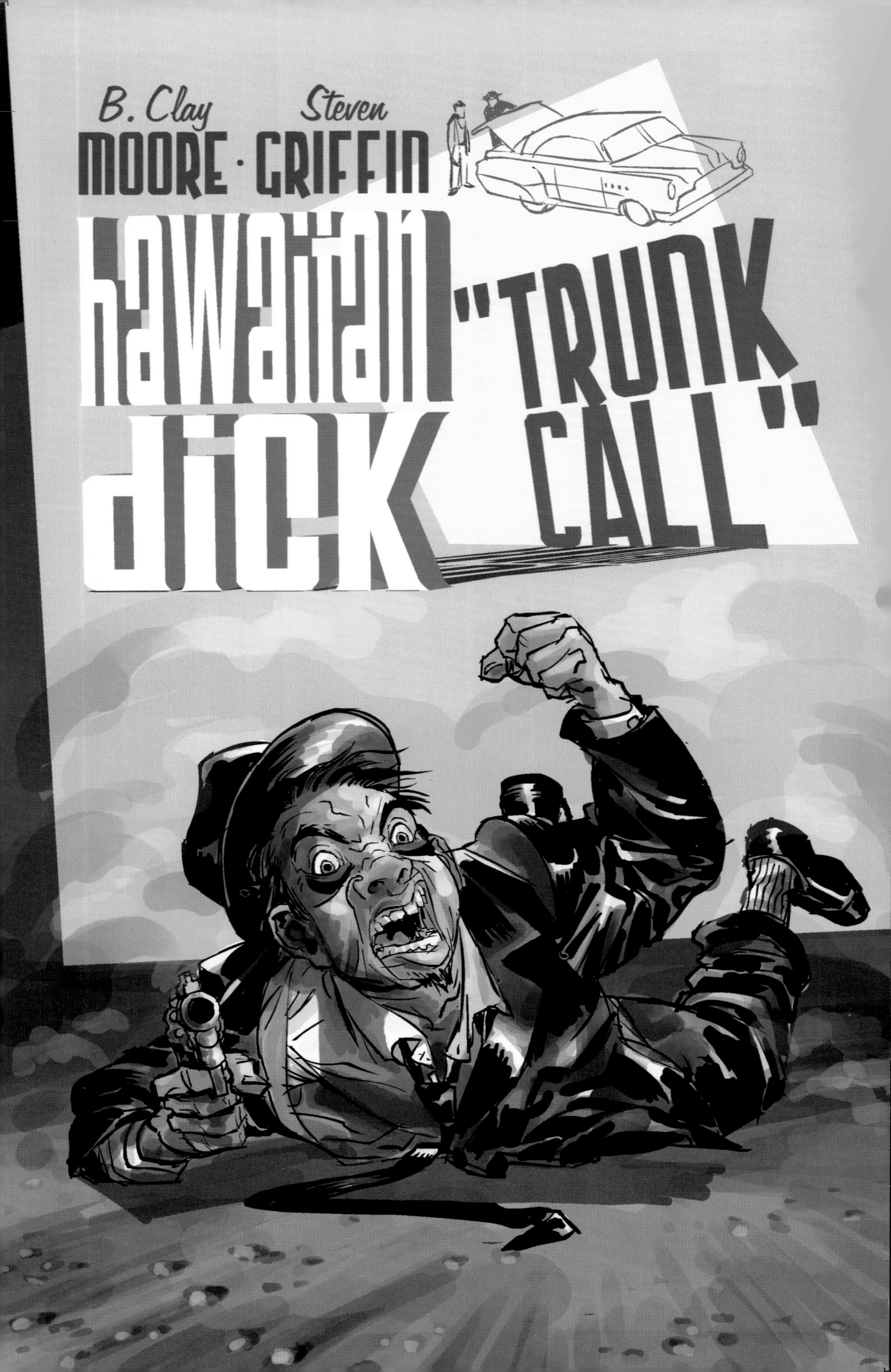
B. Clay
MOORE · Steven
GRIFFIN
Hawaiian
dick
"TRUNK
CALL"

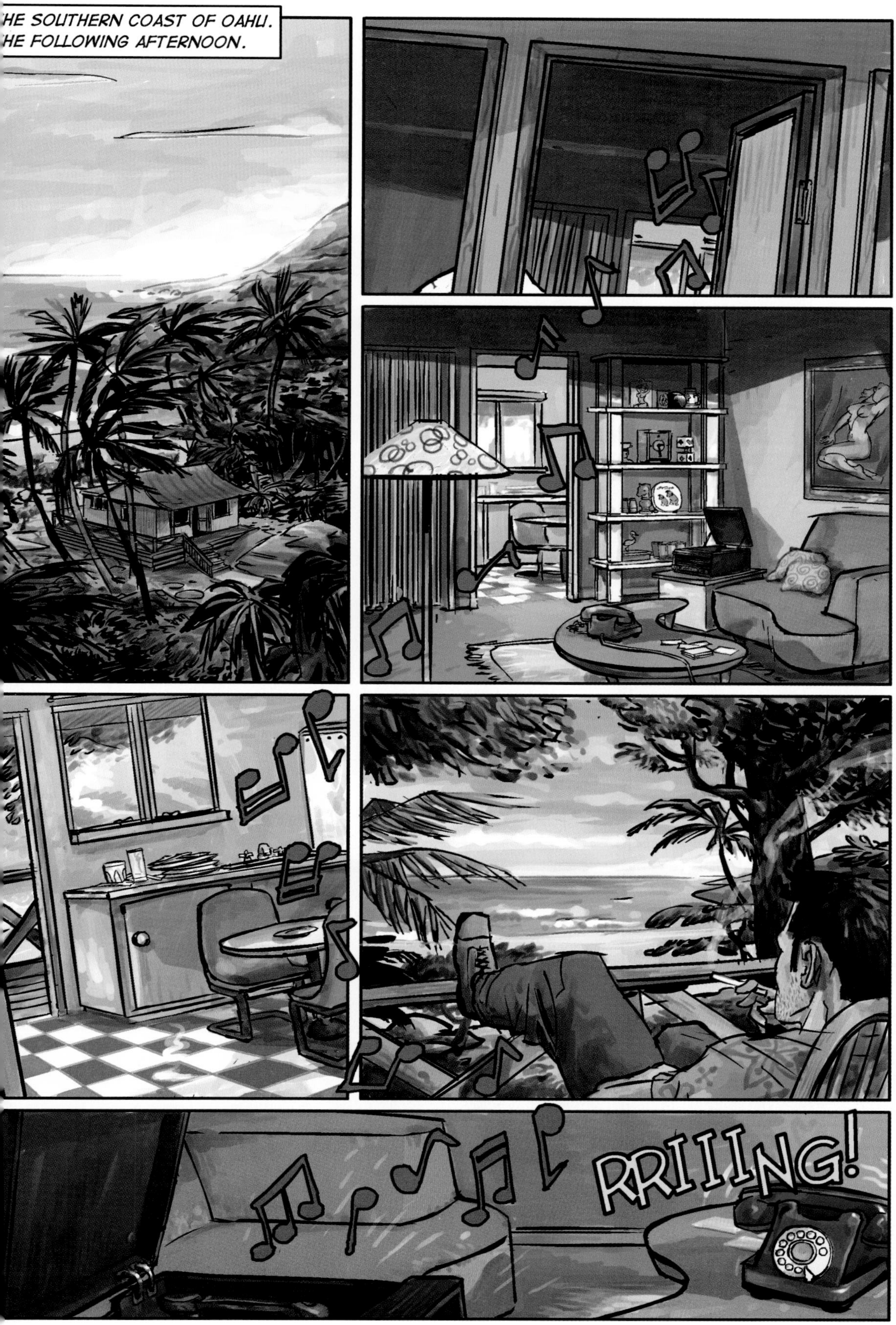
HE SOUTHERN COAST OF OAHU.
HE FOLLOWING AFTERNOON.
RRIIING!

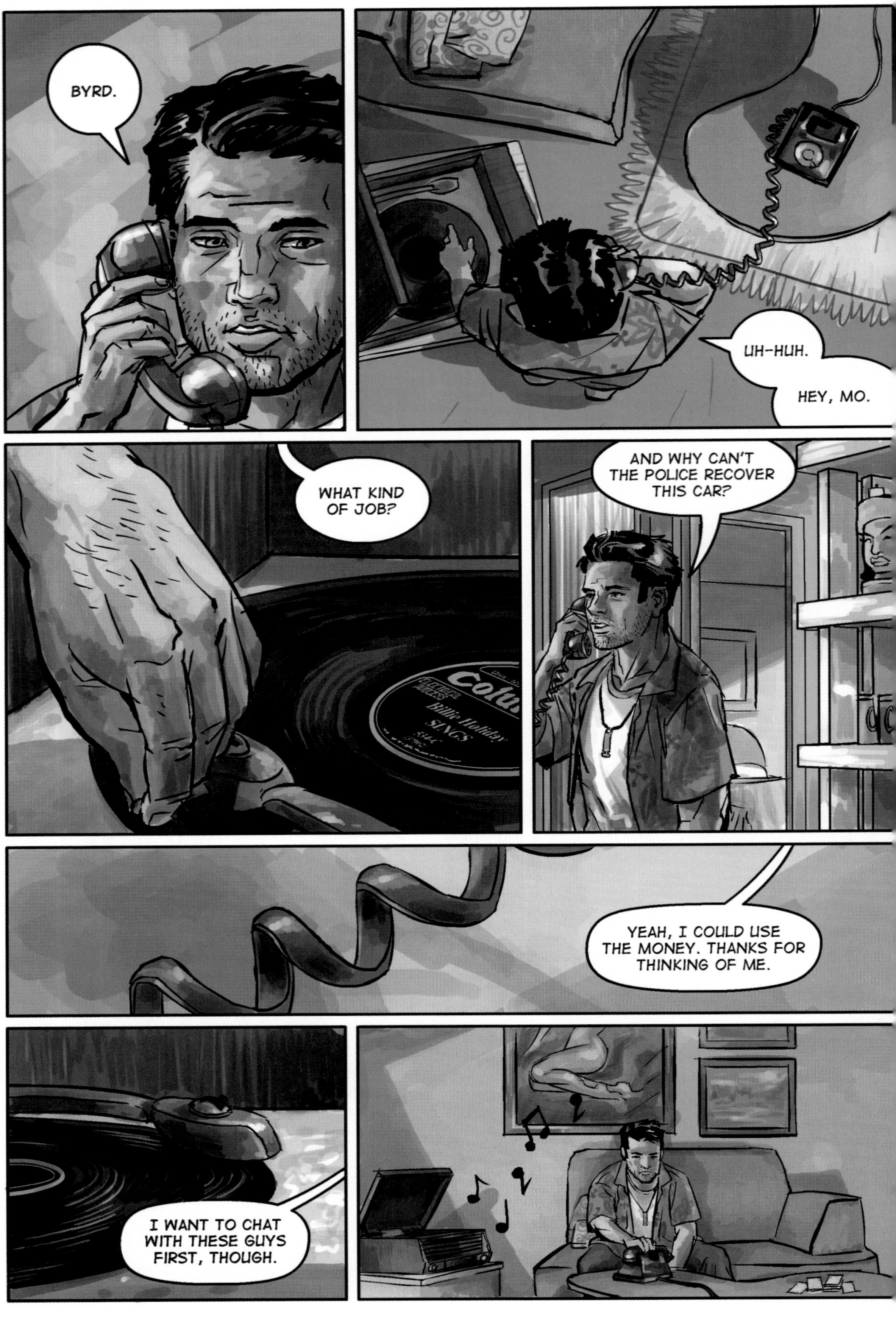
BYRD.
UH-HUH.
HEY, MO.
WHAT KIND OF JOB?
Billie Holiday
SINGS
AND WHY CAN'T THE POLICE RECOVER THIS CAR?
YEAH, I COULD USE THE MONEY. THANKS FOR THINKING OF ME.
I WANT TO CHAT WITH THESE GUYS FIRST, THOUGH.

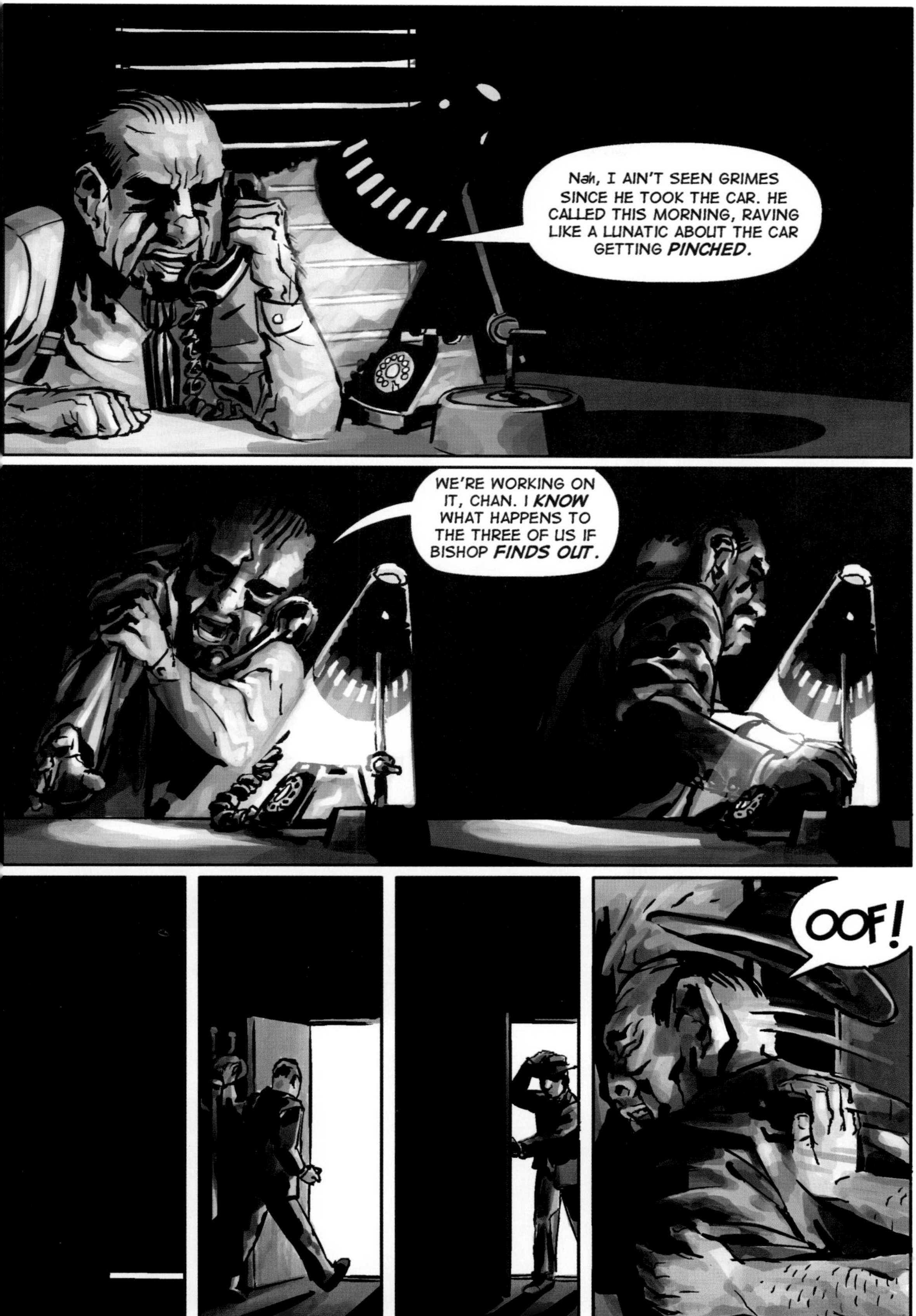
Nah, I AIN'T SEEN GRIMES SINCE HE TOOK THE CAR. HE CALLED THIS MORNING, RAVING LIKE A LUNATIC ABOUT THE CAR GETTING *PINCHED*.
WE'RE WORKING ON IT, CHAN. I *KNOW* WHAT HAPPENS TO THE THREE OF US IF BISHOP *FINDS OUT*.
OOF!

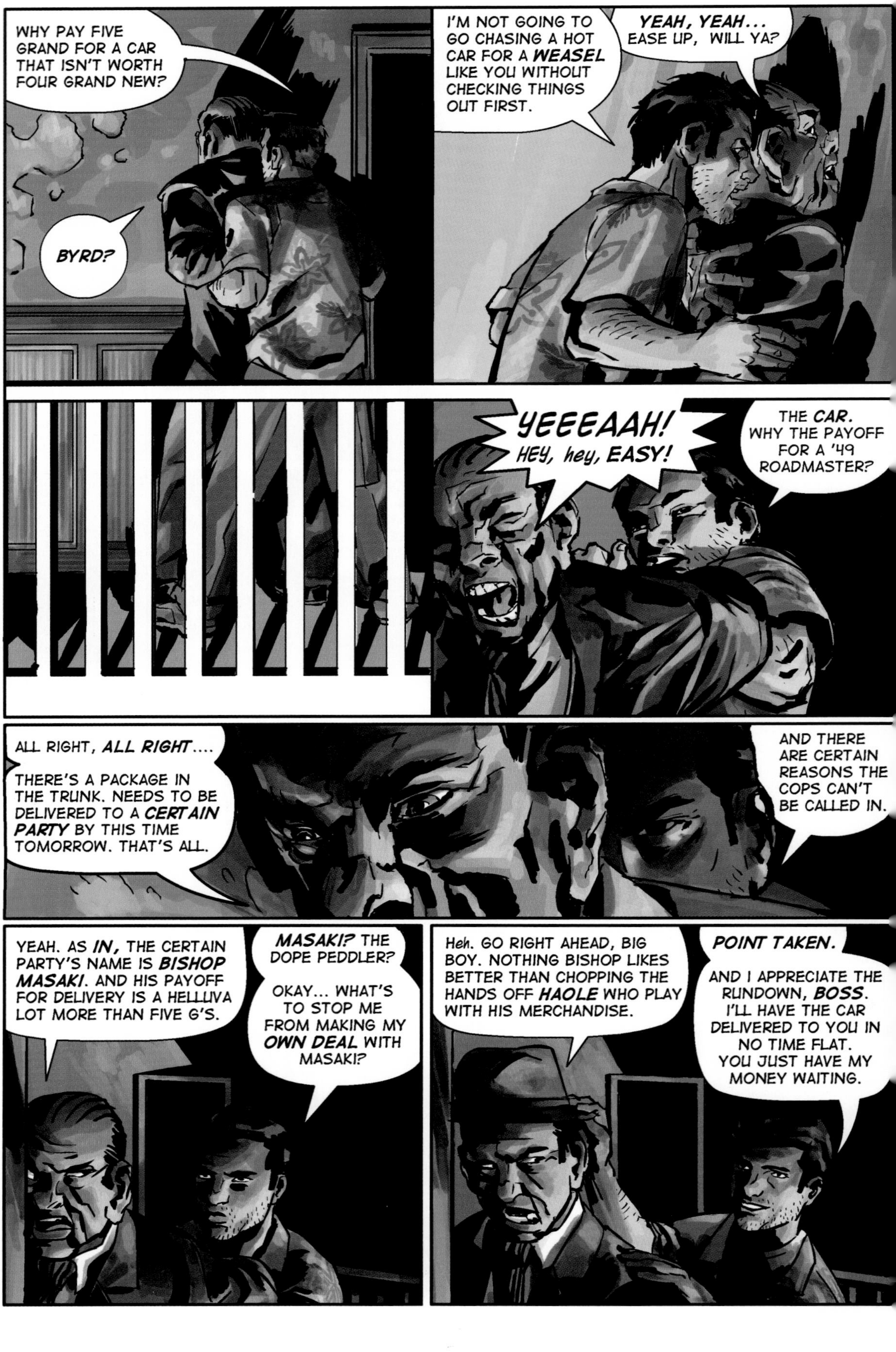
WHY PAY FIVE GRAND FOR A CAR THAT ISN'T WORTH FOUR GRAND NEW?
BYRD?
I'M NOT GOING TO GO CHASING A HOT CAR FOR A WEASEL LIKE YOU WITHOUT CHECKING THINGS OUT FIRST.
YEAH, YEAH... EASE UP, WILL YA?
YEEEAAH! HEY, hey, EASY!
THE CAR. WHY THE PAYOFF FOR A '49 ROADMASTER?
ALL RIGHT, ALL RIGHT....
THERE'S A PACKAGE IN THE TRUNK. NEEDS TO BE DELIVERED TO A CERTAIN PARTY BY THIS TIME TOMORROW. THAT'S ALL.
AND THERE ARE CERTAIN REASONS THE COPS CAN'T BE CALLED IN.
YEAH. AS IN, THE CERTAIN PARTY'S NAME IS BISHOP MASAKI. AND HIS PAYOFF FOR DELIVERY IS A HELLUVA LOT MORE THAN FIVE G'S.
MASAKI? THE DOPE PEDDLER?
OKAY... WHAT'S TO STOP ME FROM MAKING MY OWN DEAL WITH MASAKI?
Heh. GO RIGHT AHEAD, BIG BOY. NOTHING BISHOP LIKES BETTER THAN CHOPPING THE HANDS OFF HAOLE WHO PLAY WITH HIS MERCHANDISE.
POINT TAKEN.
AND I APPRECIATE THE RUNDOWN, BOSS. I'LL HAVE THE CAR DELIVERED TO YOU IN NO TIME FLAT. YOU JUST HAVE MY MONEY WAITING.

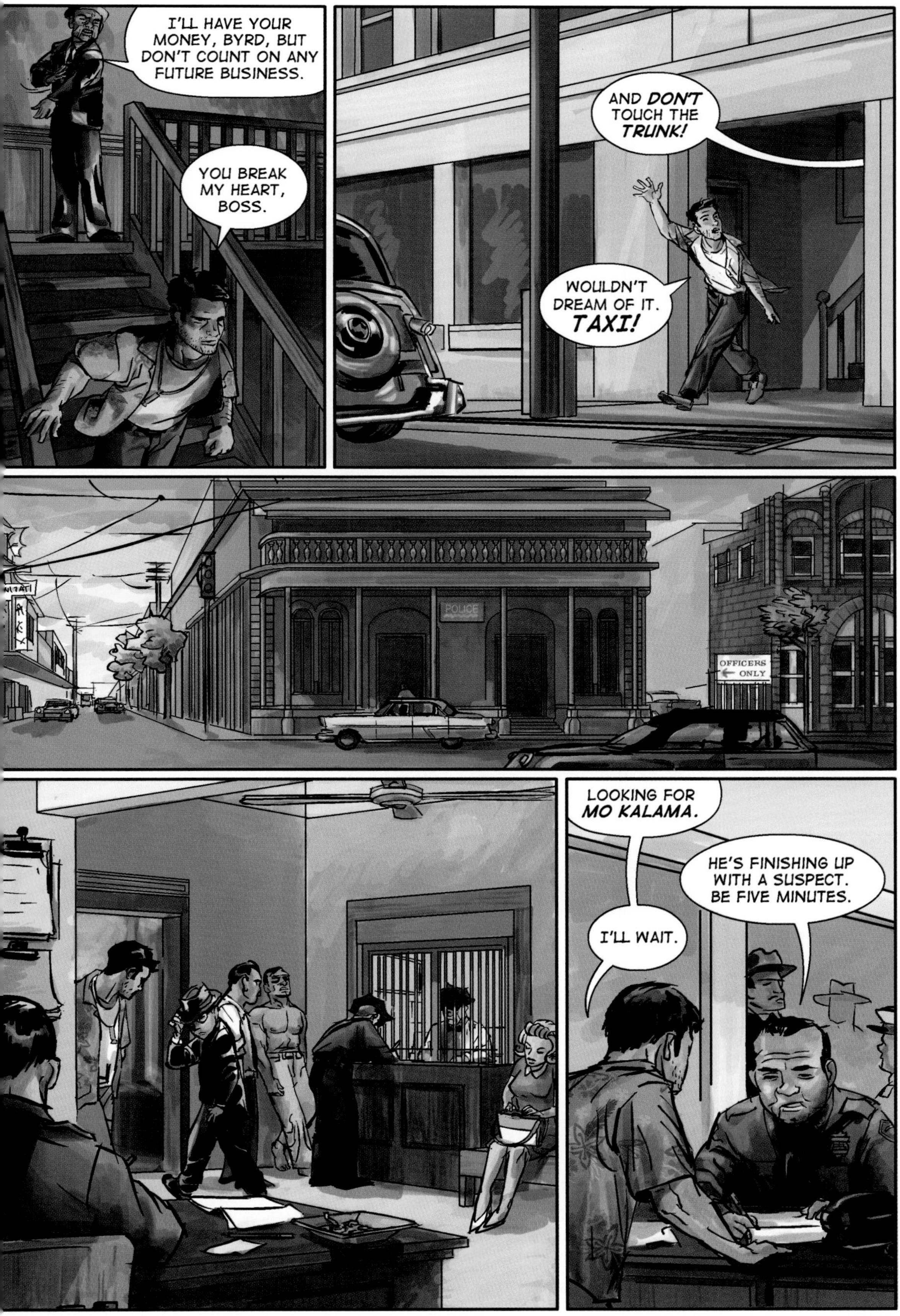
I'LL HAVE YOUR MONEY, BYRD, BUT DON'T COUNT ON ANY FUTURE BUSINESS.
YOU BREAK MY HEART, BOSS.
AND *DON'T* TOUCH THE *TRUNK!*
WOULDN'T DREAM OF IT. *TAXI!*
POLICE
OFFICERS ONLY
LOOKING FOR *MO KALAMA.*
HE'S FINISHING UP WITH A SUSPECT. BE FIVE MINUTES.
I'LL WAIT.

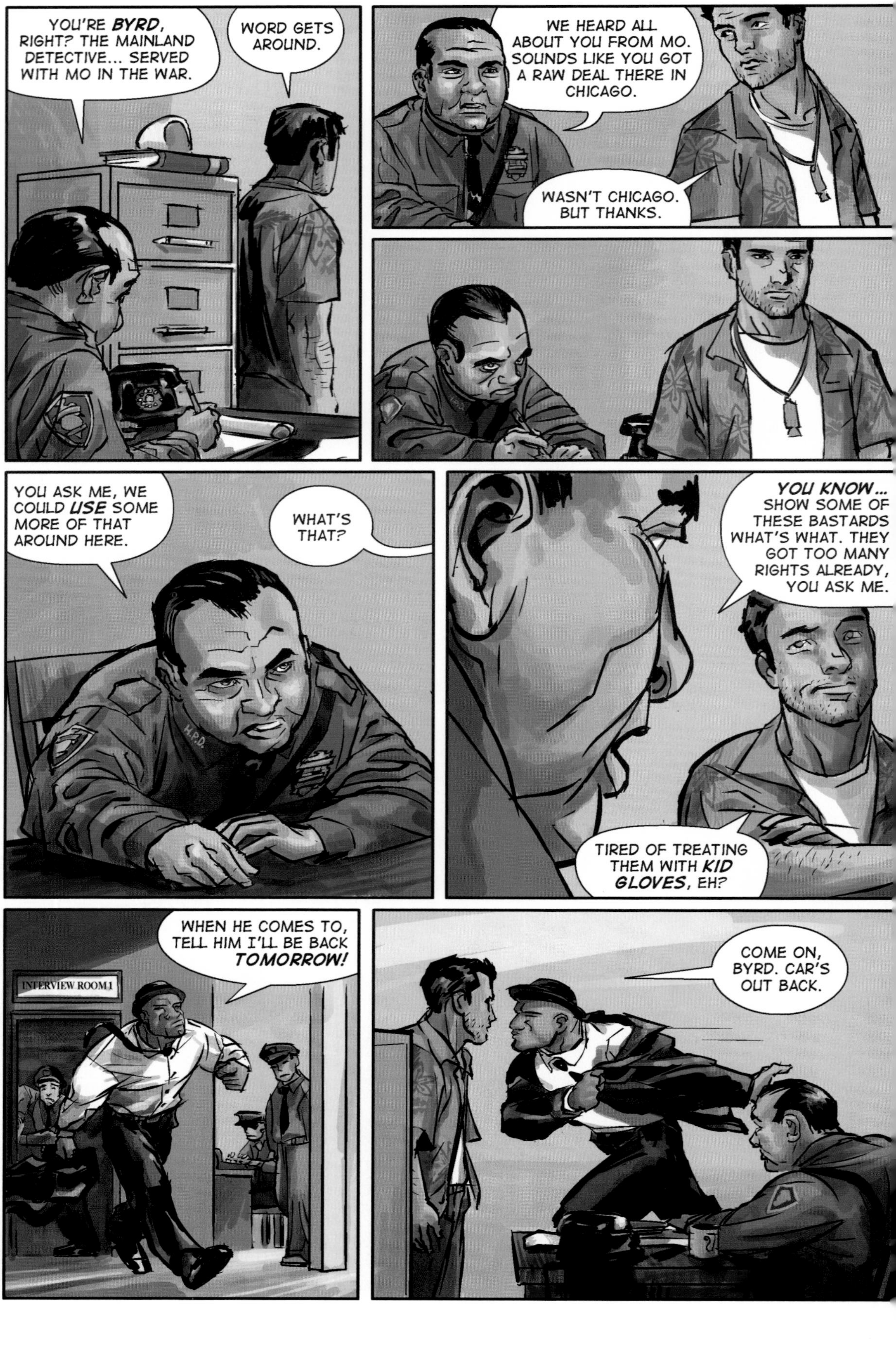
YOU'RE BYRD, RIGHT? THE MAINLAND DETECTIVE... SERVED WITH MO IN THE WAR.
WORD GETS AROUND.
WE HEARD ALL ABOUT YOU FROM MO. SOUNDS LIKE YOU GOT A RAW DEAL THERE IN CHICAGO.
WASN'T CHICAGO. BUT THANKS.
YOU ASK ME, WE COULD USE SOME MORE OF THAT AROUND HERE.
WHAT'S THAT?
YOU KNOW... SHOW SOME OF THESE BASTARDS WHAT'S WHAT. THEY GOT TOO MANY RIGHTS ALREADY, YOU ASK ME.
TIRED OF TREATING THEM WITH KID GLOVES, EH?
INTERVIEW ROOM 1
WHEN HE COMES TO, TELL HIM I'LL BE BACK TOMORROW!
COME ON, BYRD. CAR'S OUT BACK.

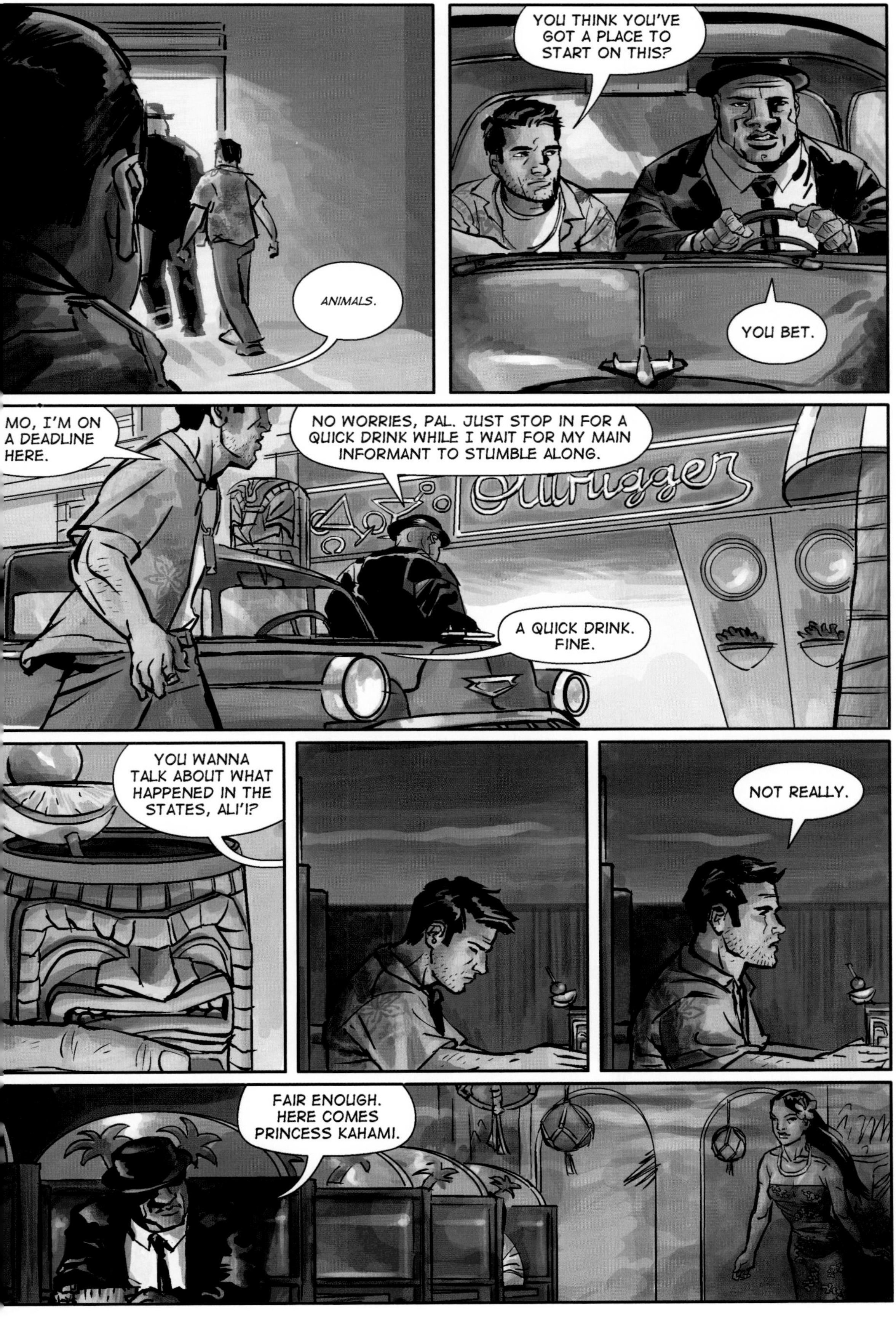
ANIMALS.
YOU THINK YOU'VE GOT A PLACE TO START ON THIS?
YOU BET.
MO, I'M ON A DEADLINE HERE.
NO WORRIES, PAL. JUST STOP IN FOR A QUICK DRINK WHILE I WAIT FOR MY MAIN INFORMANT TO STUMBLE ALONG.
A QUICK DRINK. FINE.
YOU WANNA TALK ABOUT WHAT HAPPENED IN THE STATES, ALI'I?
NOT REALLY.
FAIR ENOUGH. HERE COMES PRINCESS KAHAMI.

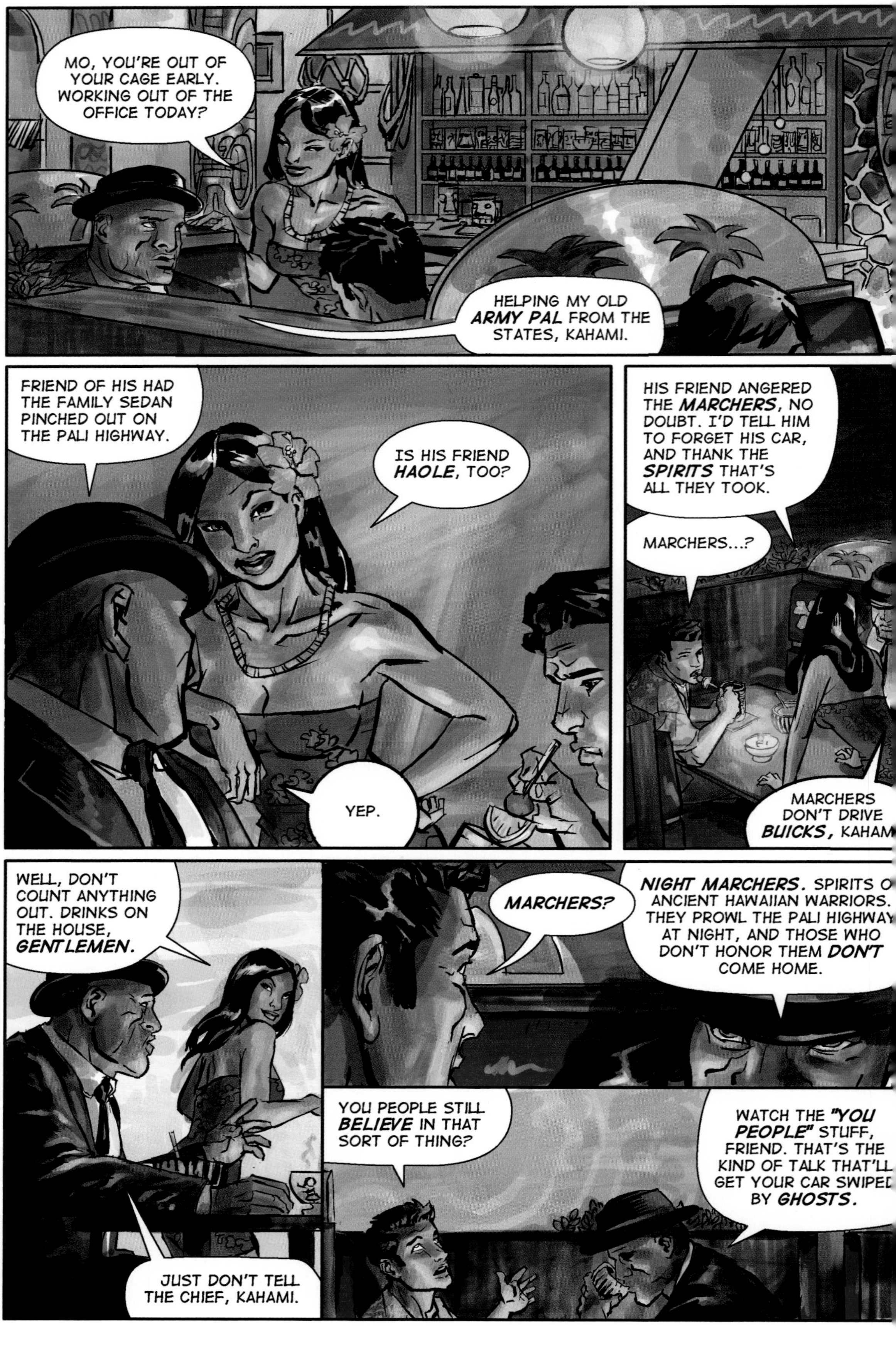
MO, YOU'RE OUT OF YOUR CAGE EARLY. WORKING OUT OF THE OFFICE TODAY?
HELPING MY OLD ARMY PAL FROM THE STATES, KAHAMI.
FRIEND OF HIS HAD THE FAMILY SEDAN PINCHED OUT ON THE PALI HIGHWAY.
IS HIS FRIEND HAOLE, TOO?
YEP.
HIS FRIEND ANGERED THE MARCHERS, NO DOUBT. I'D TELL HIM TO FORGET HIS CAR, AND THANK THE SPIRITS THAT'S ALL THEY TOOK.
MARCHERS...?
MARCHERS DON'T DRIVE BUICKS, KAHAM
WELL, DON'T COUNT ANYTHING OUT. DRINKS ON THE HOUSE, GENTLEMEN.
JUST DON'T TELL THE CHIEF, KAHAMI.
MARCHERS?
NIGHT MARCHERS. SPIRITS O ANCIENT HAWAIIAN WARRIORS. THEY PROWL THE PALI HIGHWAY AT NIGHT, AND THOSE WHO DON'T HONOR THEM DON'T COME HOME.
YOU PEOPLE STILL BELIEVE IN THAT SORT OF THING?
WATCH THE "YOU PEOPLE" STUFF, FRIEND. THAT'S THE KIND OF TALK THAT'LL GET YOUR CAR SWIPED BY GHOSTS.

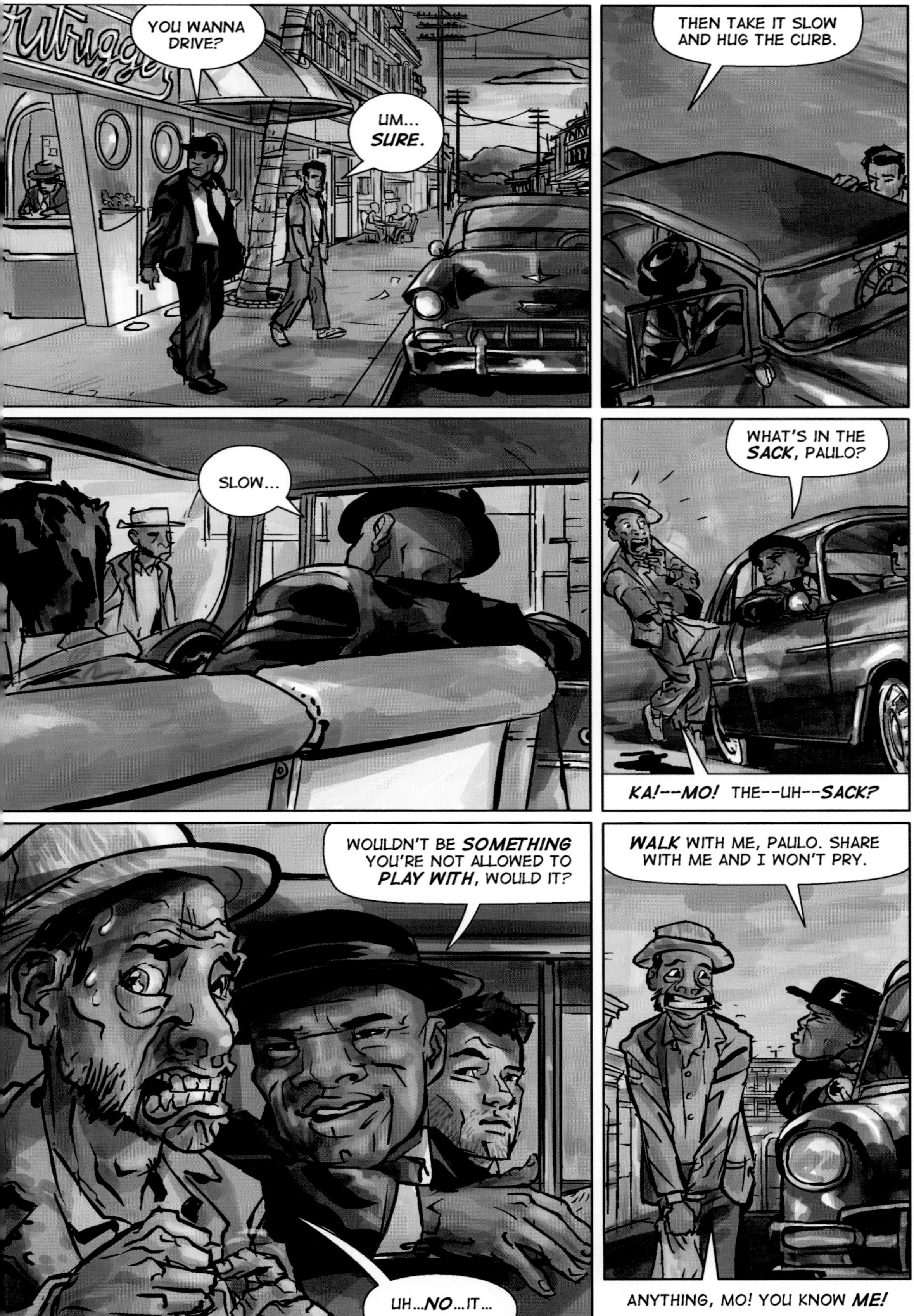
YOU WANNA DRIVE?
UM... SURE.
THEN TAKE IT SLOW AND HUG THE CURB.
SLOW...
WHAT'S IN THE SACK, PAULO?
KA!--MO! THE--UH--SACK?
WOULDN'T BE SOMETHING YOU'RE NOT ALLOWED TO PLAY WITH, WOULD IT?
UH...NO...IT...
WALK WITH ME, PAULO. SHARE WITH ME AND I WON'T PRY.
ANYTHING, MO! YOU KNOW ME!

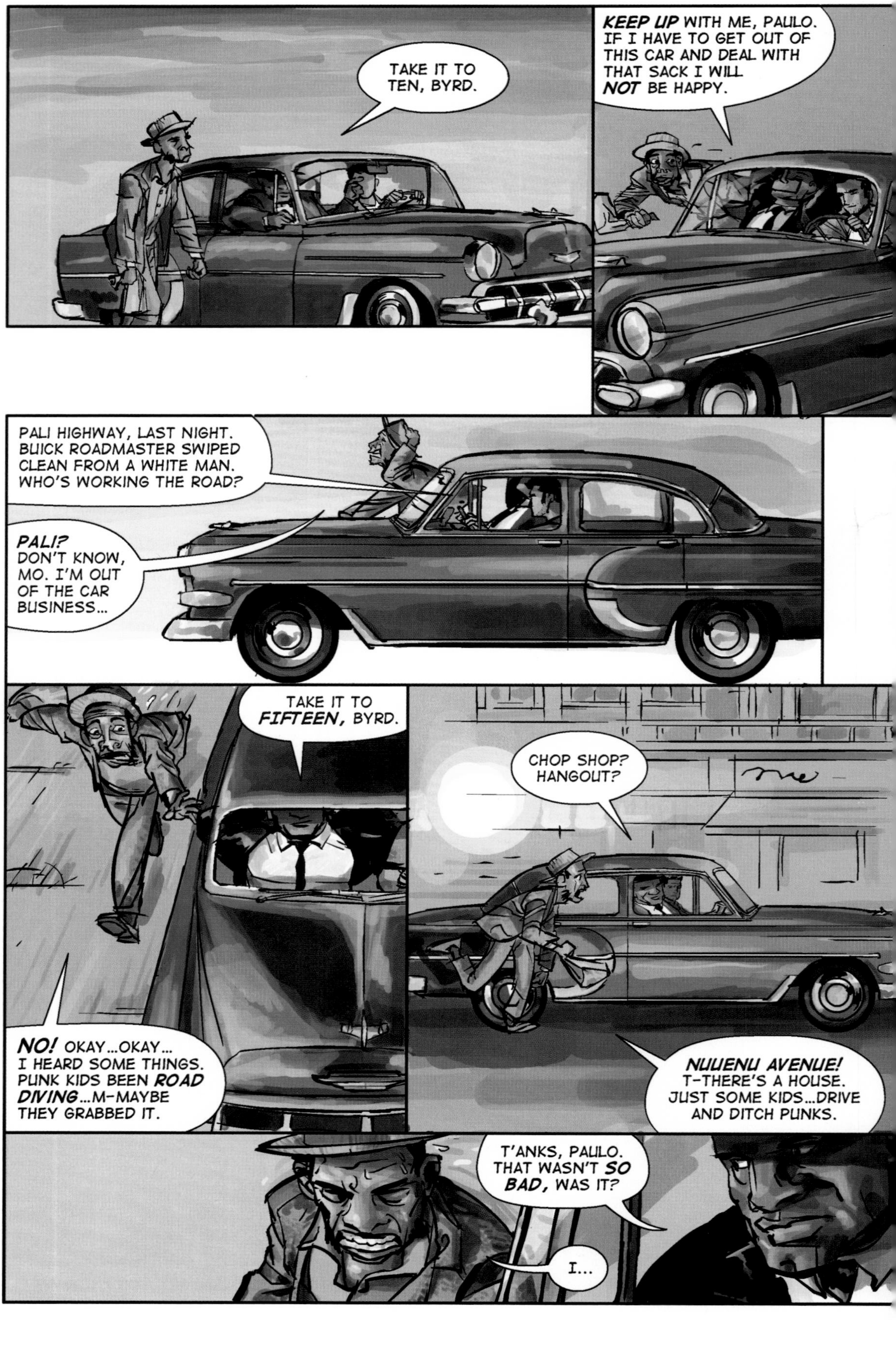
TAKE IT TO TEN, BYRD.
KEEP UP WITH ME, PAULO. IF I HAVE TO GET OUT OF THIS CAR AND DEAL WITH THAT SACK I WILL NOT BE HAPPY.
PALI HIGHWAY, LAST NIGHT. BUICK ROADMASTER SWIPED CLEAN FROM A WHITE MAN. WHO'S WORKING THE ROAD?
PALI? DON'T KNOW, MO. I'M OUT OF THE CAR BUSINESS...
TAKE IT TO FIFTEEN, BYRD.
NO! OKAY...OKAY... I HEARD SOME THINGS. PUNK KIDS BEEN ROAD DIVING...M-MAYBE THEY GRABBED IT.
CHOP SHOP? HANGOUT?
NUUENU AVENUE! T-THERE'S A HOUSE. JUST SOME KIDS...DRIVE AND DITCH PUNKS.
T'ANKS, PAULO. THAT WASN'T SO BAD, WAS IT?
I...

AND *I'M* THE ONE GETS KICKED OFF THE FORCE.

DIDN'T HURT HIM, PAL. MIGHT HAVE DENTED THAT MAILBOX, THOUGH.

YOU THINK THEY'VE ALREADY DITCHED THE CAR?

A *ROADMASTER?* DOUBT IT. EVEN IF THEY JUST THRILL RIDERS, THEY MAY TRY TO FENCE A RIDE LIKE THAT.

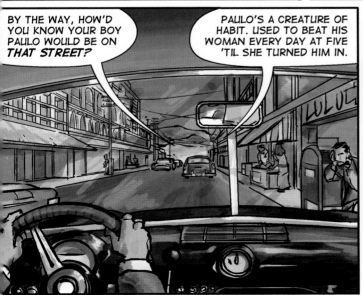

BY THE WAY, HOW'D YOU KNOW YOUR BOY PAULO WOULD BE ON *THAT STREET?*

PAULO'S A CREATURE OF HABIT. USED TO BEAT HIS WOMAN EVERY DAY AT FIVE 'TIL SHE TURNED HIM IN.

WHAT WAS IN THE *SACK?*

HELL IF I KNOW, PAL. BUT POSSESSION OF *ANYTHING* OTHER THAN *LOLLIPOPS* OR *CAPGUNS* SENDS HIM BACK TO THE JOINT.

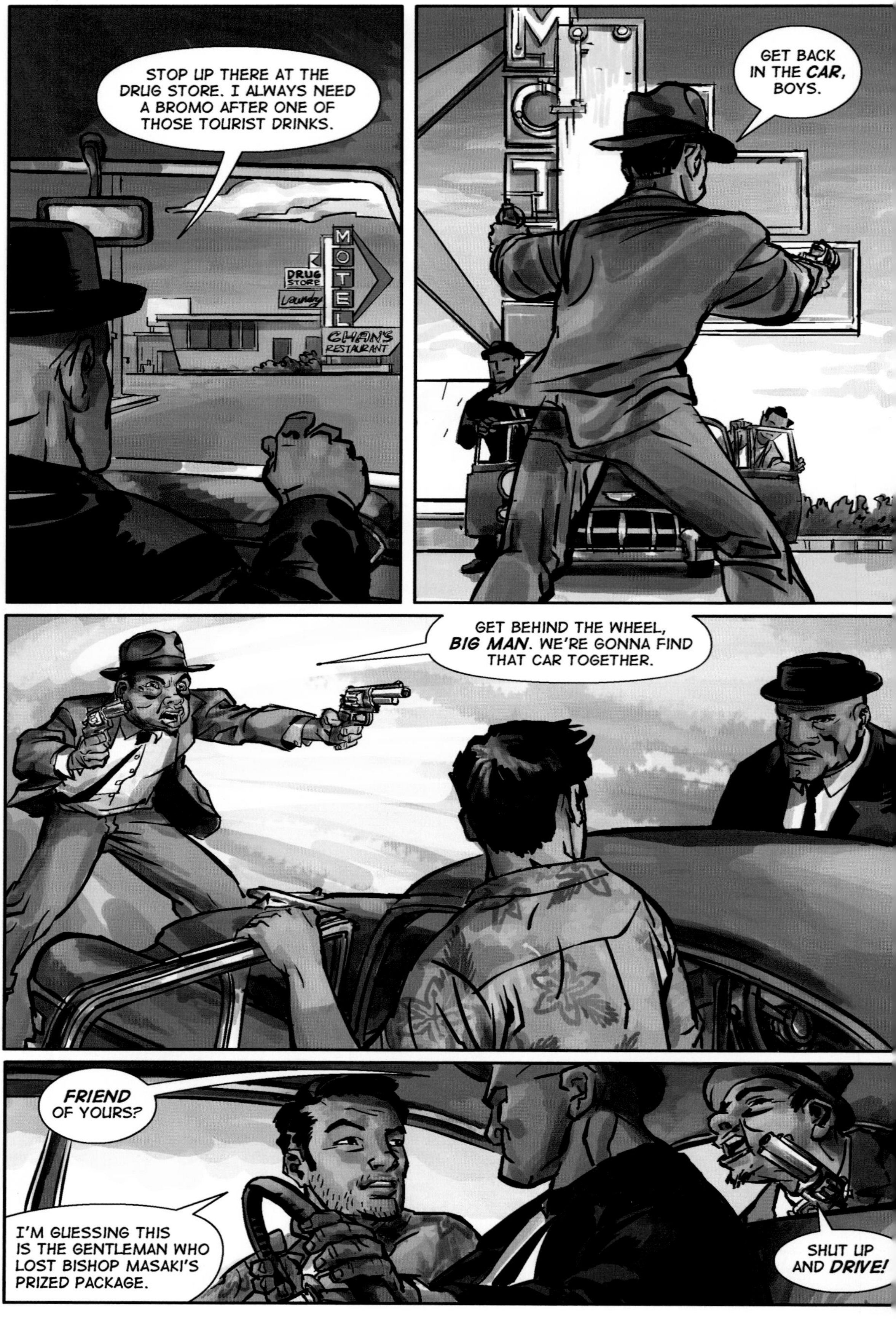
STOP UP THERE AT THE DRUG STORE. I ALWAYS NEED A BROMO AFTER ONE OF THOSE TOURIST DRINKS.
MOTEL
DRUG STORE
Laundry
CHAN'S RESTAURANT
GET BACK IN THE CAR, BOYS.
GET BEHIND THE WHEEL, BIG MAN. WE'RE GONNA FIND THAT CAR TOGETHER.
FRIEND OF YOURS?
I'M GUESSING THIS IS THE GENTLEMAN WHO LOST BISHOP MASAKI'S PRIZED PACKAGE.
SHUT UP AND DRIVE!

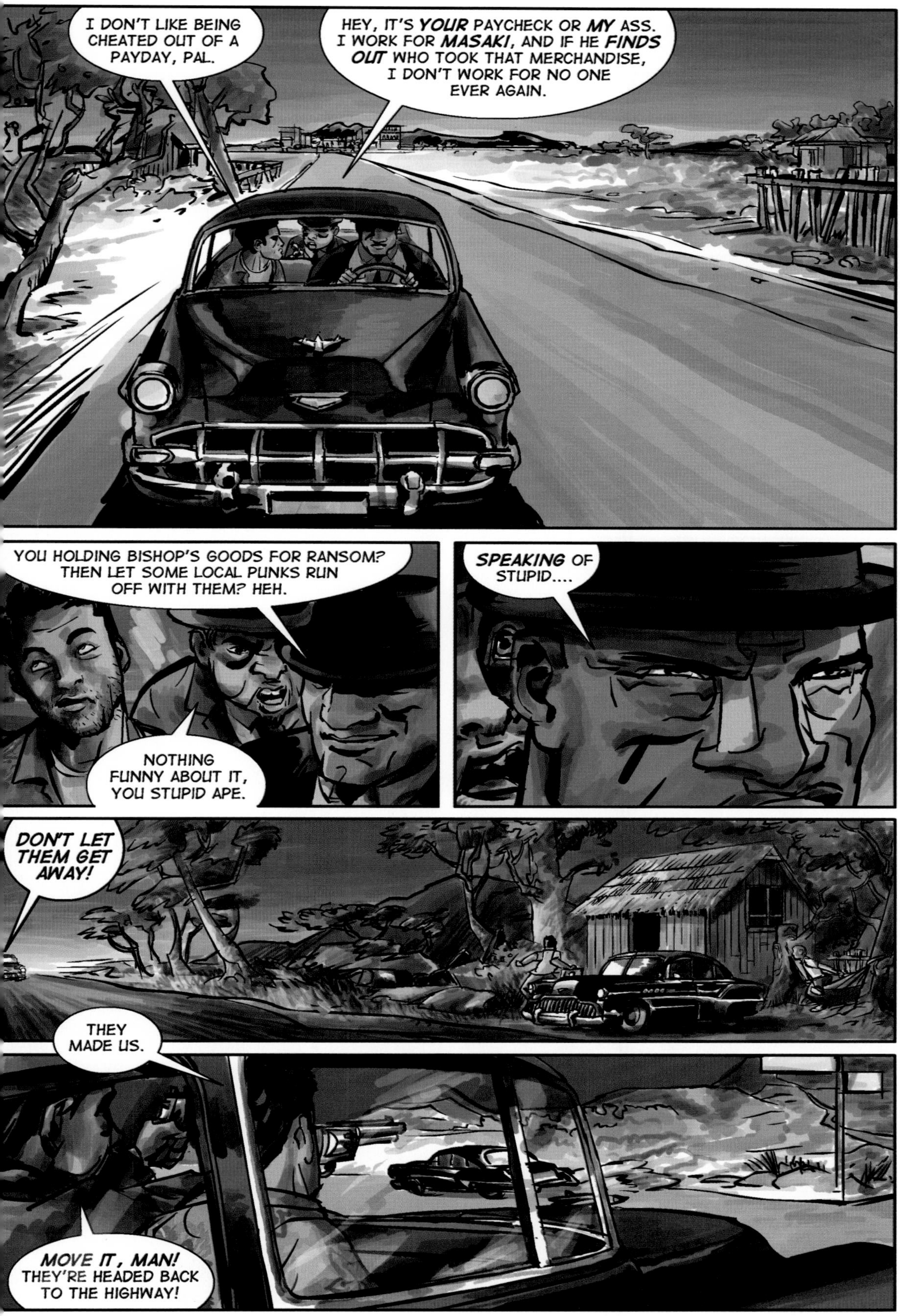

I DON'T LIKE BEING CHEATED OUT OF A PAYDAY, PAL.
HEY, IT'S *YOUR* PAYCHECK OR *MY* ASS. I WORK FOR *MASAKI*, AND IF HE *FINDS OUT* WHO TOOK THAT MERCHANDISE, I DON'T WORK FOR NO ONE EVER AGAIN.
YOU HOLDING BISHOP'S GOODS FOR RANSOM? THEN LET SOME LOCAL PUNKS RUN OFF WITH THEM? HEH.
NOTHING FUNNY ABOUT IT, YOU STUPID APE.
SPEAKING OF STUPID....
DON'T LET THEM GET AWAY!
THEY MADE US.
MOVE IT, MAN! THEY'RE HEADED BACK TO THE HIGHWAY!

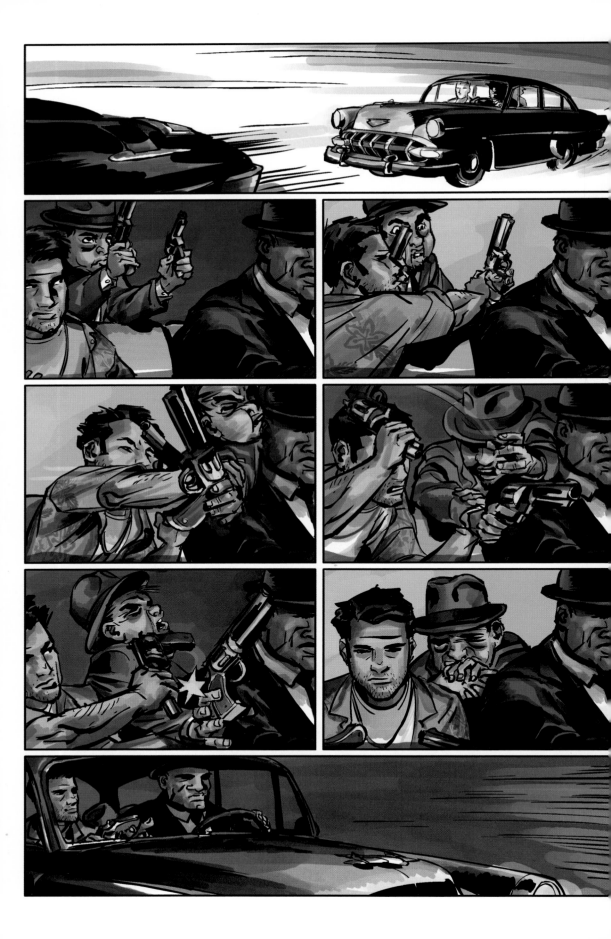

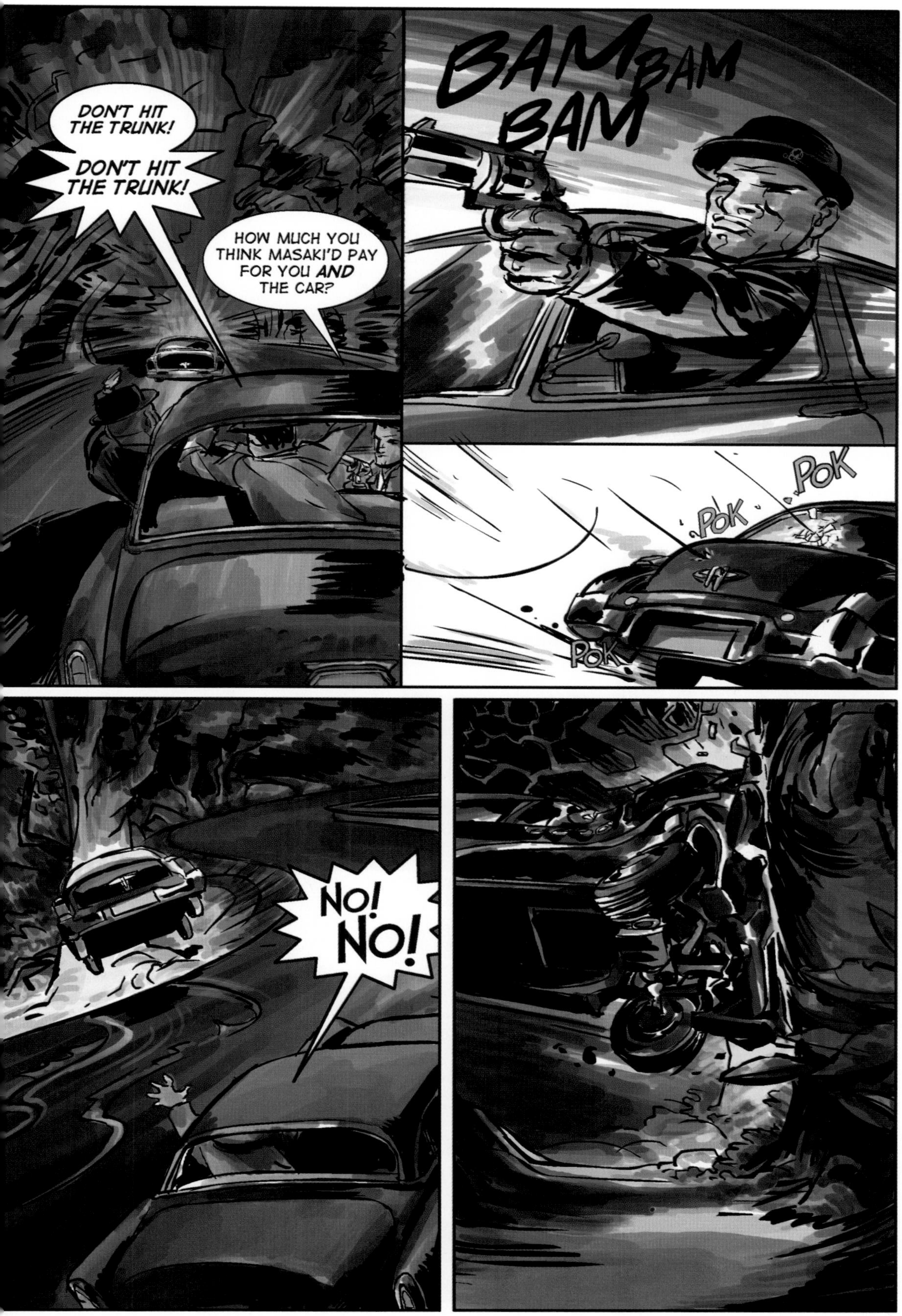
DON'T HIT THE TRUNK!
DON'T HIT THE TRUNK!
HOW MUCH YOU THINK MASAKI'D PAY FOR YOU AND THE CAR?
BAM BAM BAM
POK POK POK
NO! NO!

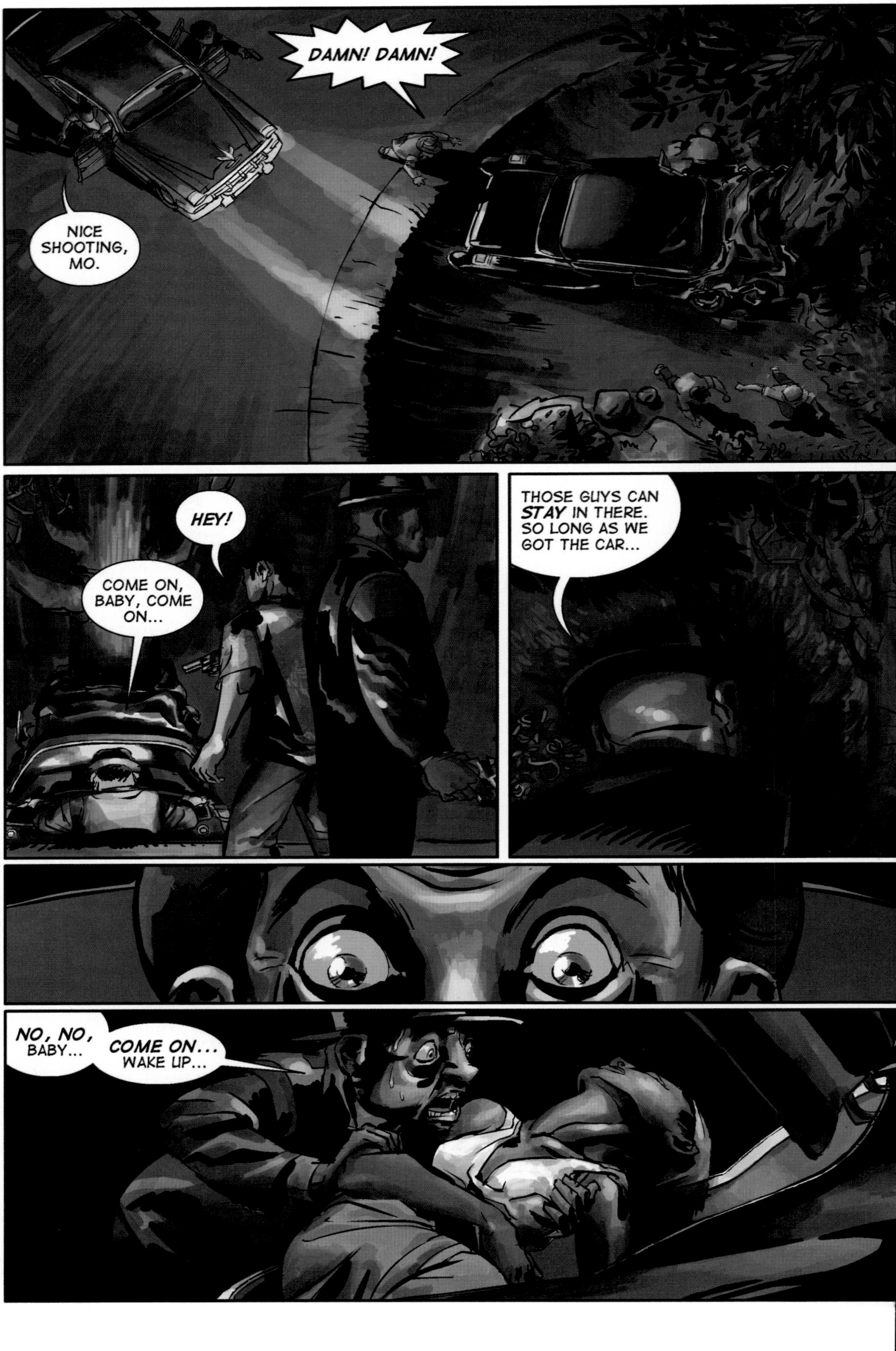
DAMN! DAMN!
NICE SHOOTING, MO.
HEY!
COME ON, BABY, COME ON...
THOSE GUYS CAN STAY IN THERE. SO LONG AS WE GOT THE CAR...
NO, NO, BABY...
COME ON... WAKE UP...

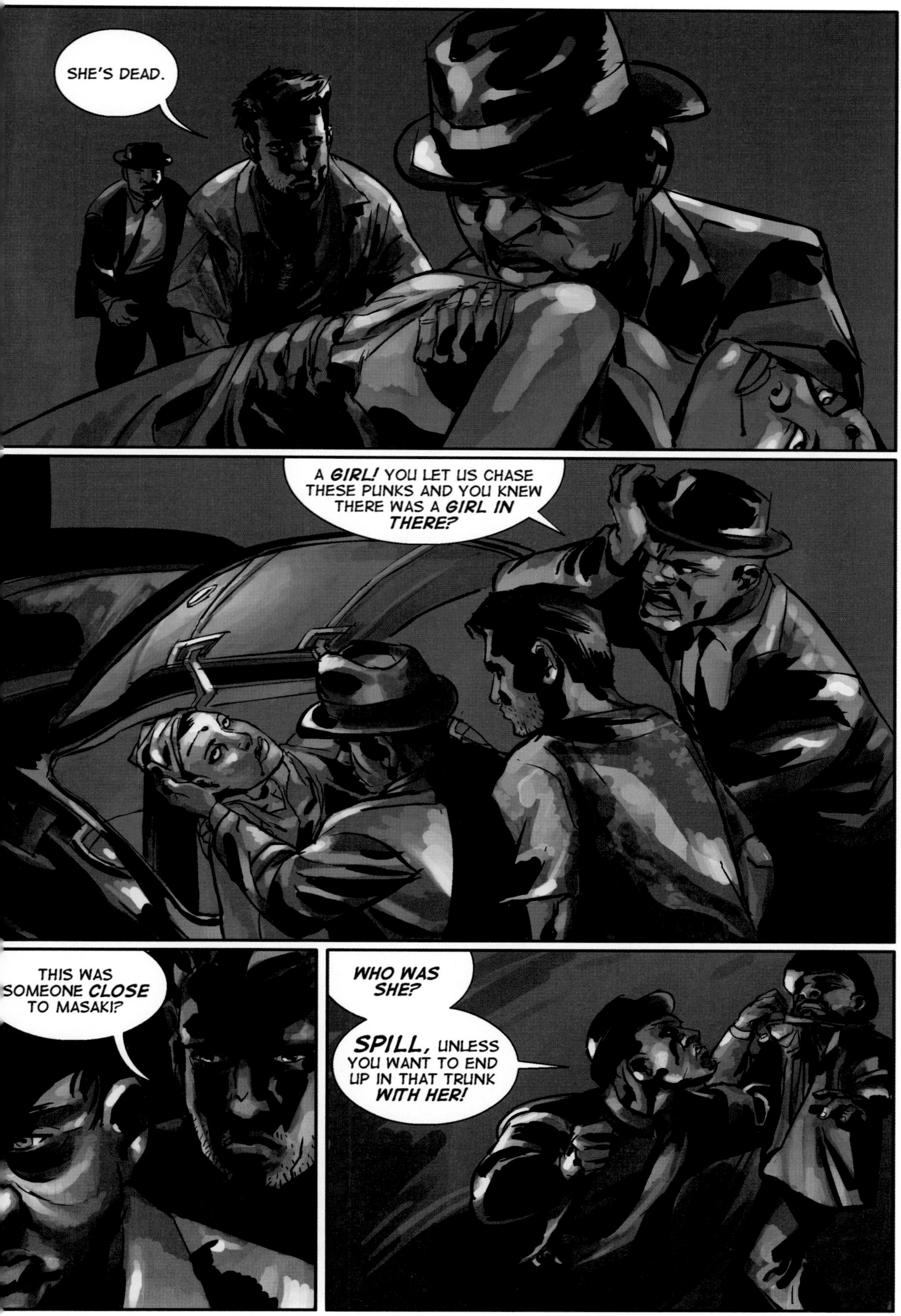
SHE'S DEAD.
A GIRL! YOU LET US CHASE THESE PUNKS AND YOU KNEW THERE WAS A GIRL IN THERE?
THIS WAS SOMEONE CLOSE TO MASAKI?
WHO WAS SHE?
SPILL, UNLESS YOU WANT TO END UP IN THAT TRUNK WITH HER!

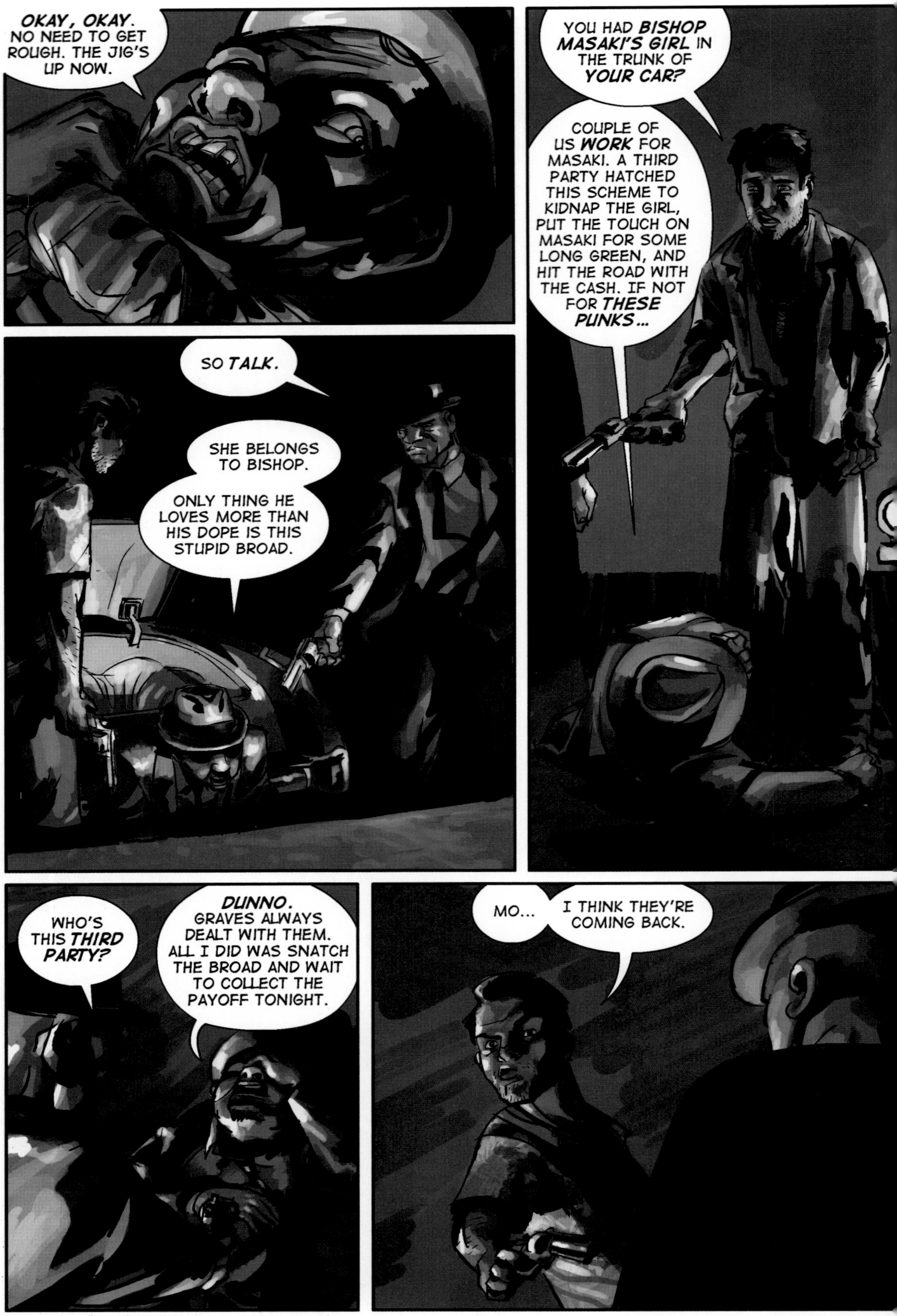
OKAY, OKAY. NO NEED TO GET ROUGH. THE JIG'S UP NOW.
SO TALK.
SHE BELONGS TO BISHOP.
ONLY THING HE LOVES MORE THAN HIS DOPE IS THIS STUPID BROAD.
YOU HAD BISHOP MASAKI'S GIRL IN THE TRUNK OF YOUR CAR?
COUPLE OF US WORK FOR MASAKI. A THIRD PARTY HATCHED THIS SCHEME TO KIDNAP THE GIRL, PUT THE TOUCH ON MASAKI FOR SOME LONG GREEN, AND HIT THE ROAD WITH THE CASH. IF NOT FOR THESE PUNKS...
WHO'S THIS THIRD PARTY?
DUNNO. GRAVES ALWAYS DEALT WITH THEM. ALL I DID WAS SNATCH THE BROAD AND WAIT TO COLLECT THE PAYOFF TONIGHT.
MO...
I THINK THEY'RE COMING BACK.

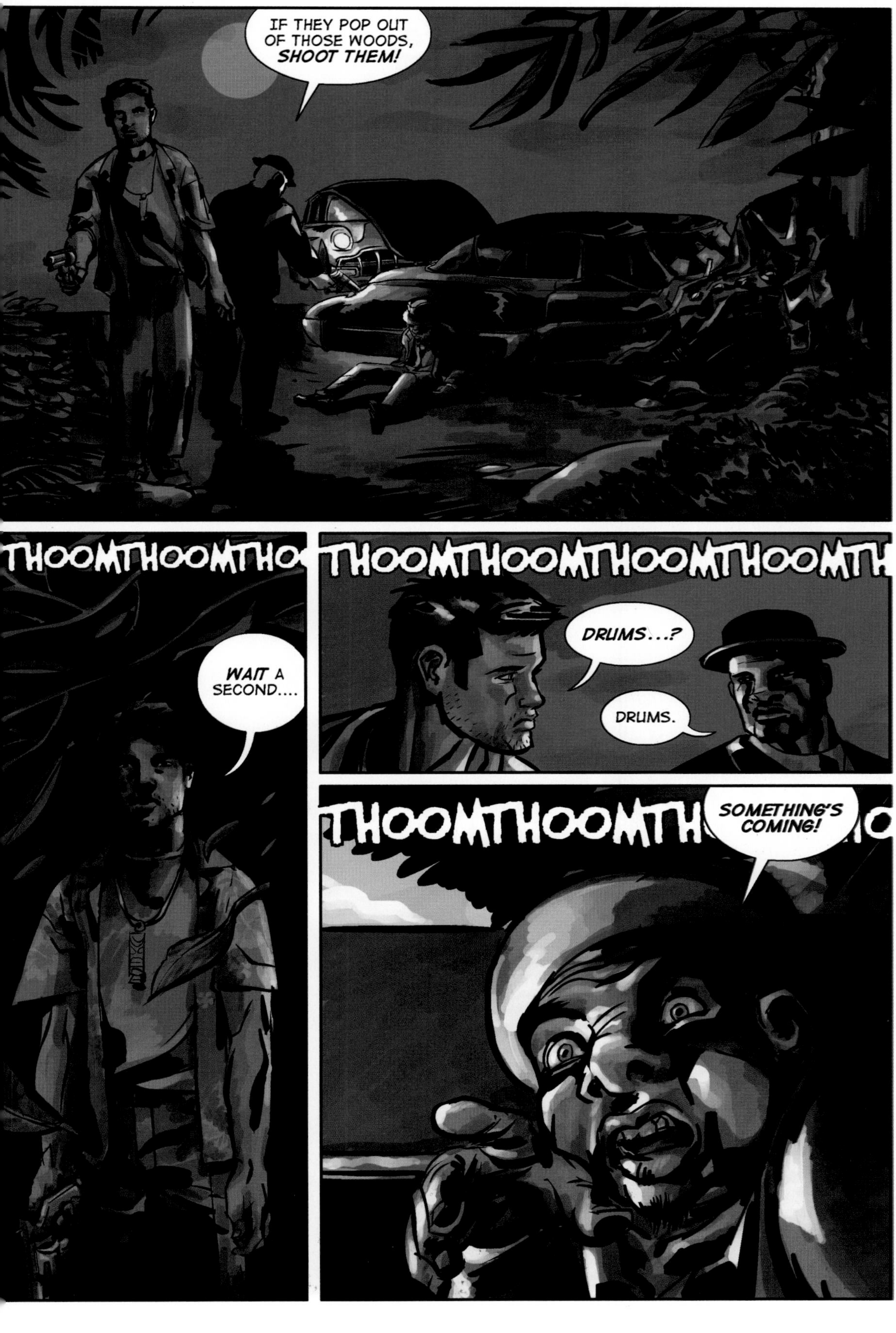
IF THEY POP OUT OF THOSE WOODS, *SHOOT THEM!*
THOOMTHOOMTHO
THOOMTHOOMTHOOMTHOOMTH
WAIT A SECOND....
DRUMS...?
DRUMS.
THOOMTHOOMTH
SOMETHING'S COMING!

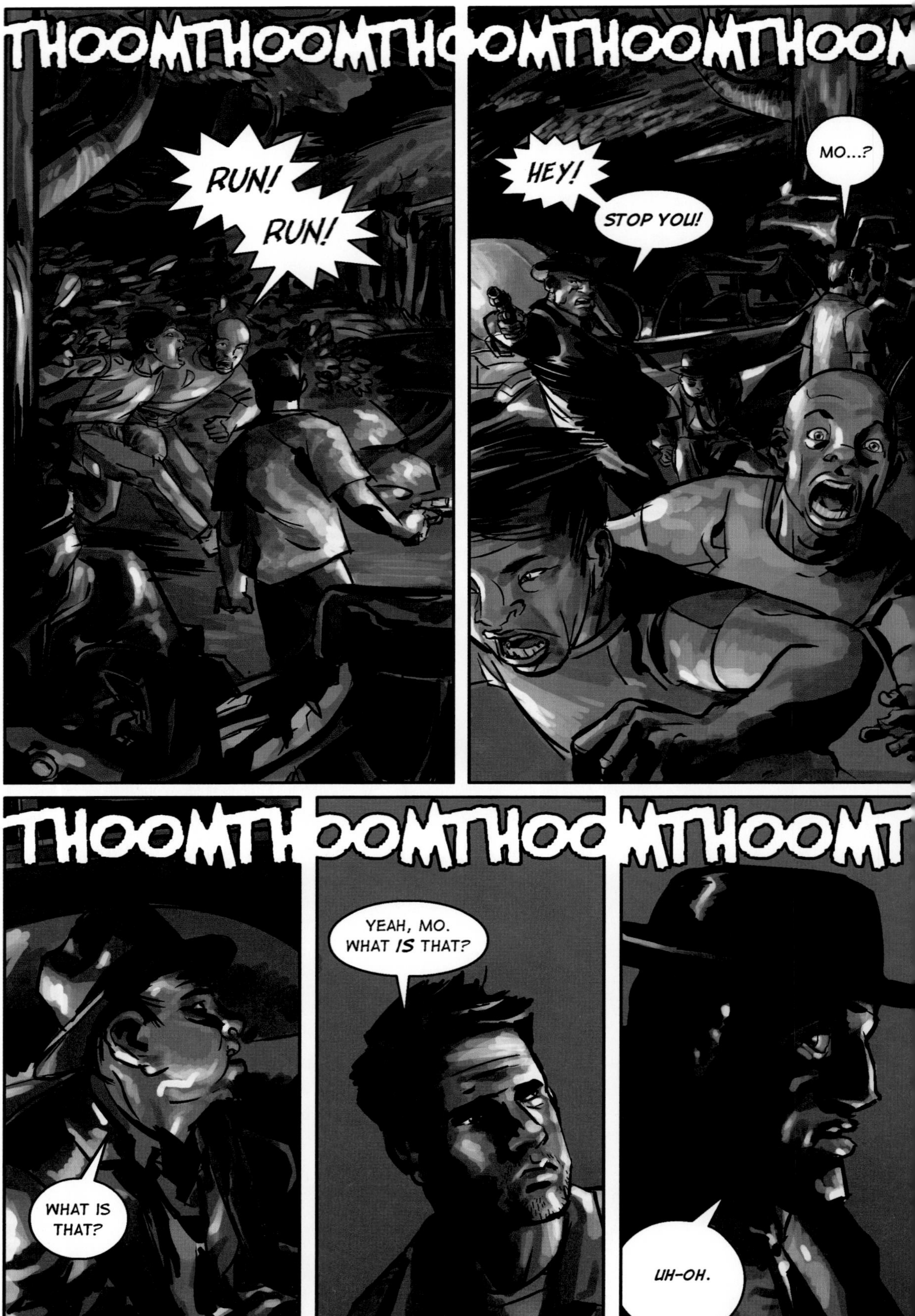

THOOMTHOOMTHOOMTHOOMTHOOM
RUN!
RUN!
HEY!
STOP YOU!
MO...?
THOOMTHOOMTHOOMTHOOMT
WHAT IS THAT?
YEAH, MO. WHAT IS THAT?
UH-OH.

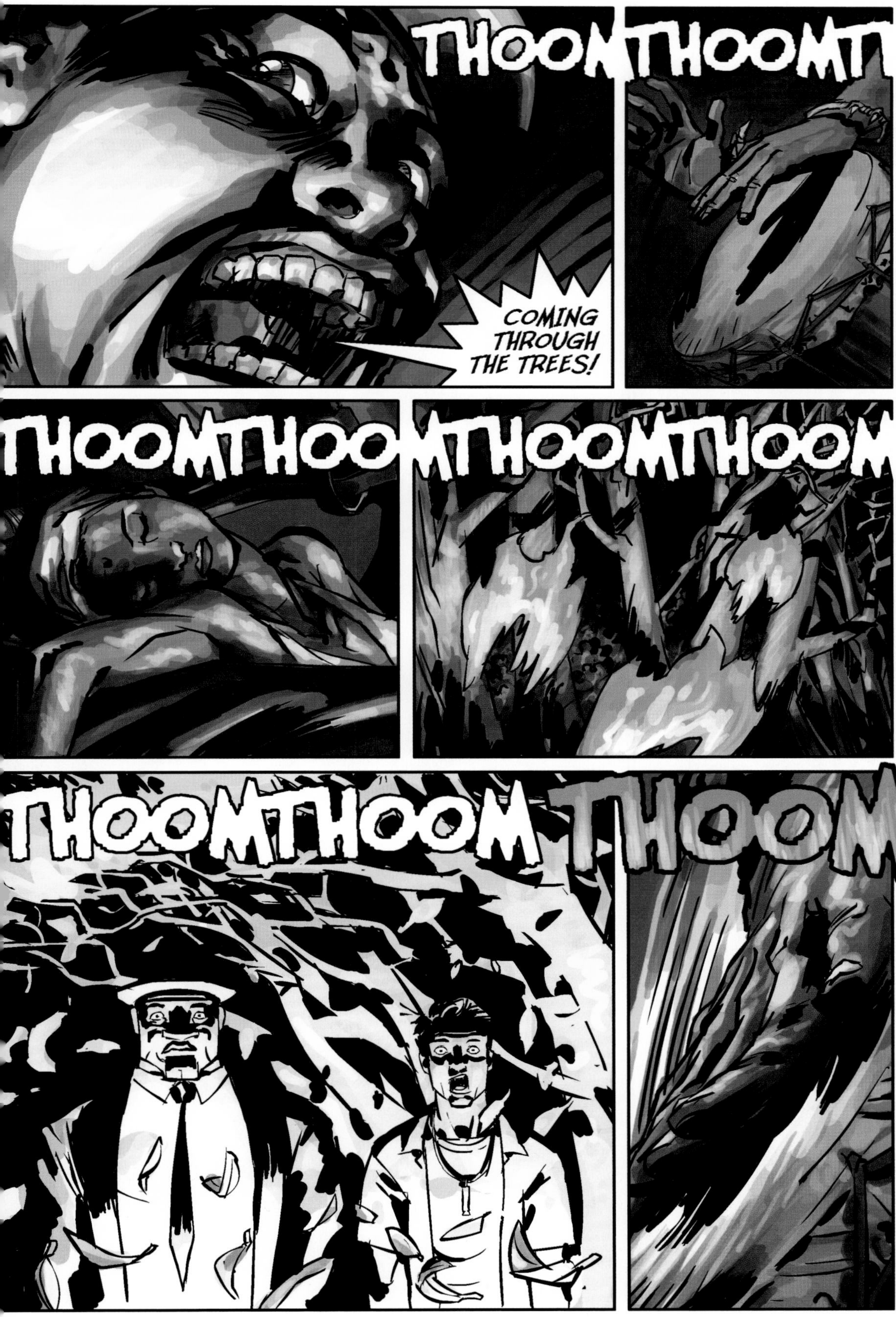
THOOMTHOOMT
COMING THROUGH THE TREES!
THOOMTHOOMTHOOMTHOOM
THOOMTHOOM THOOM

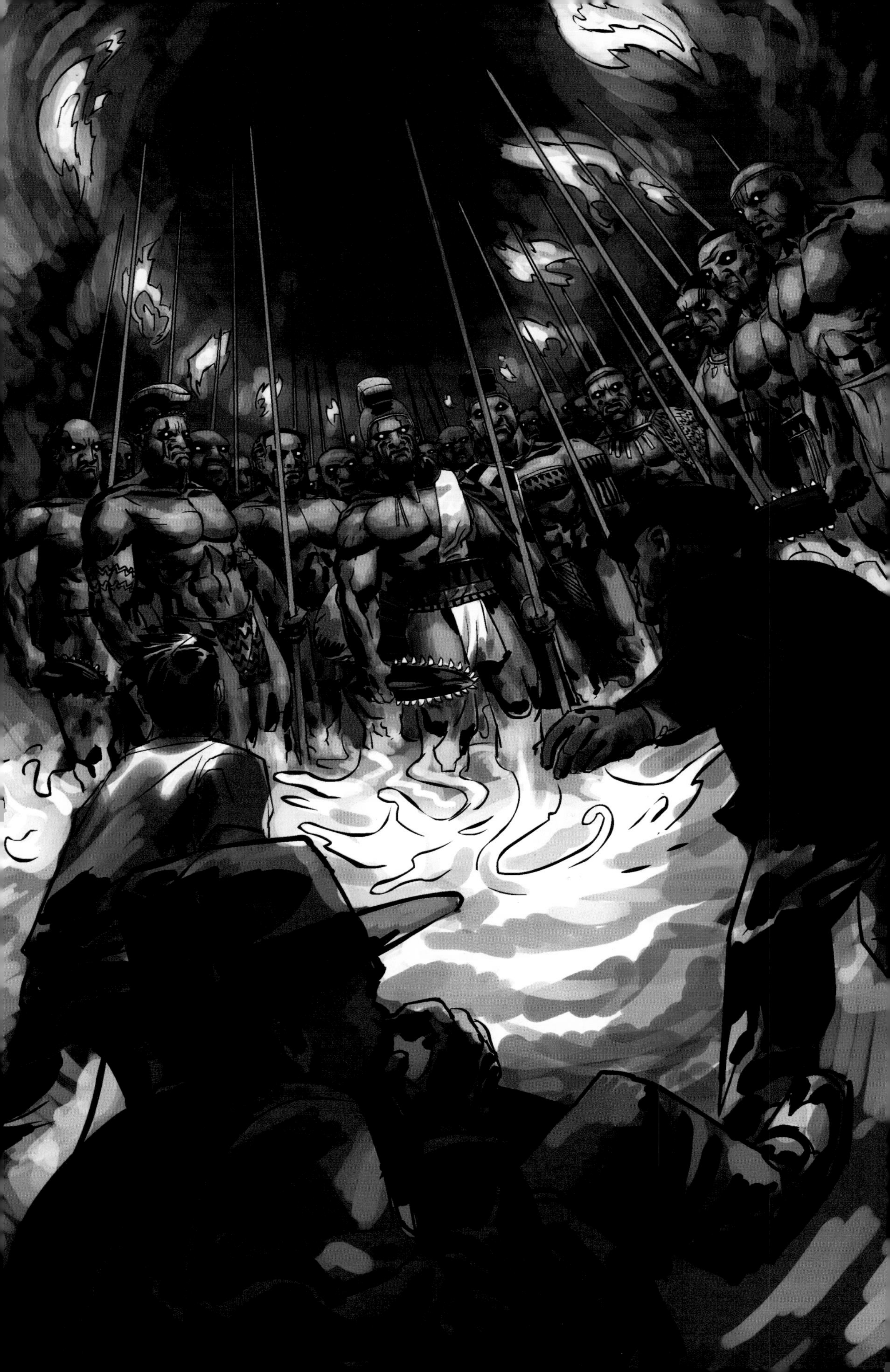

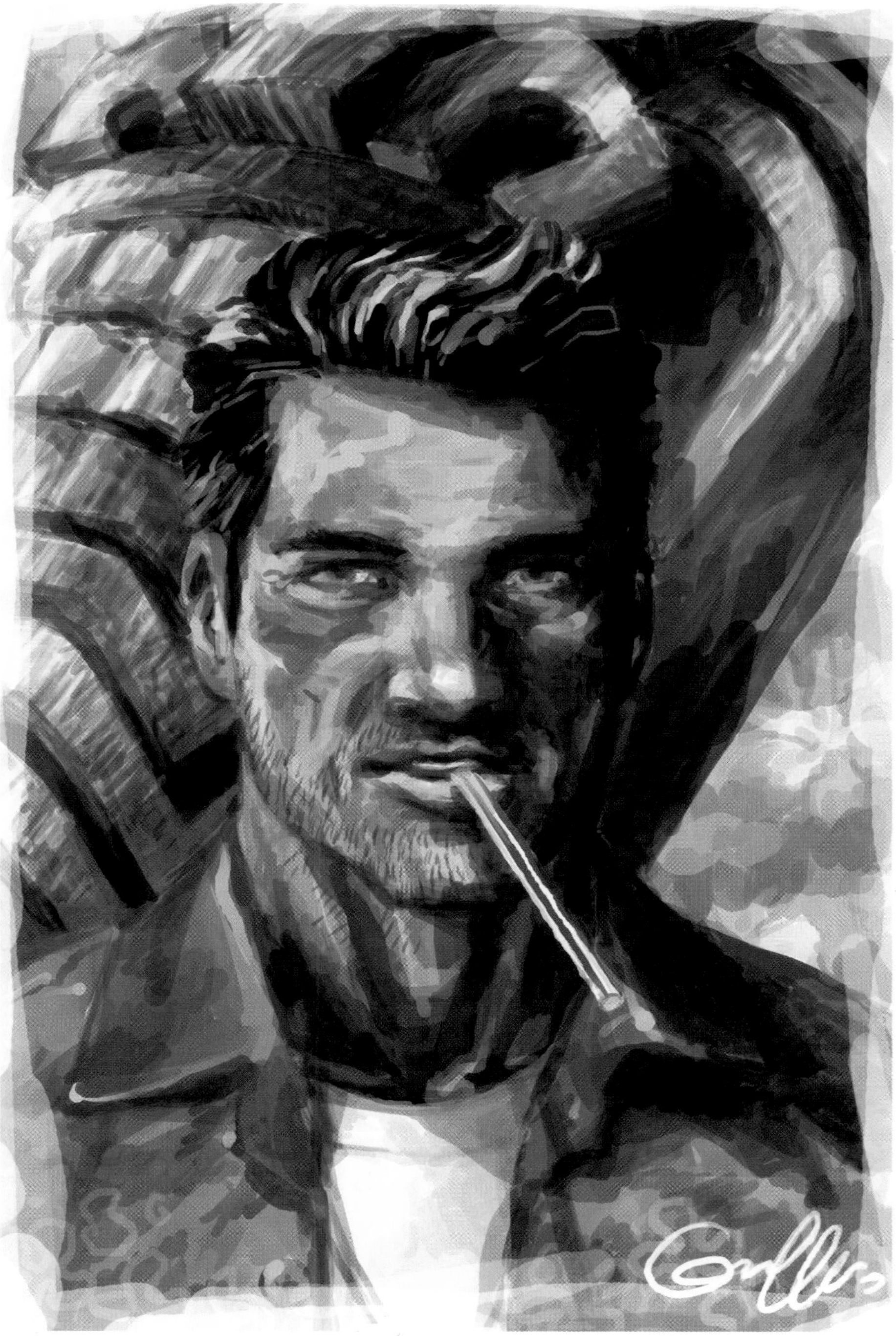

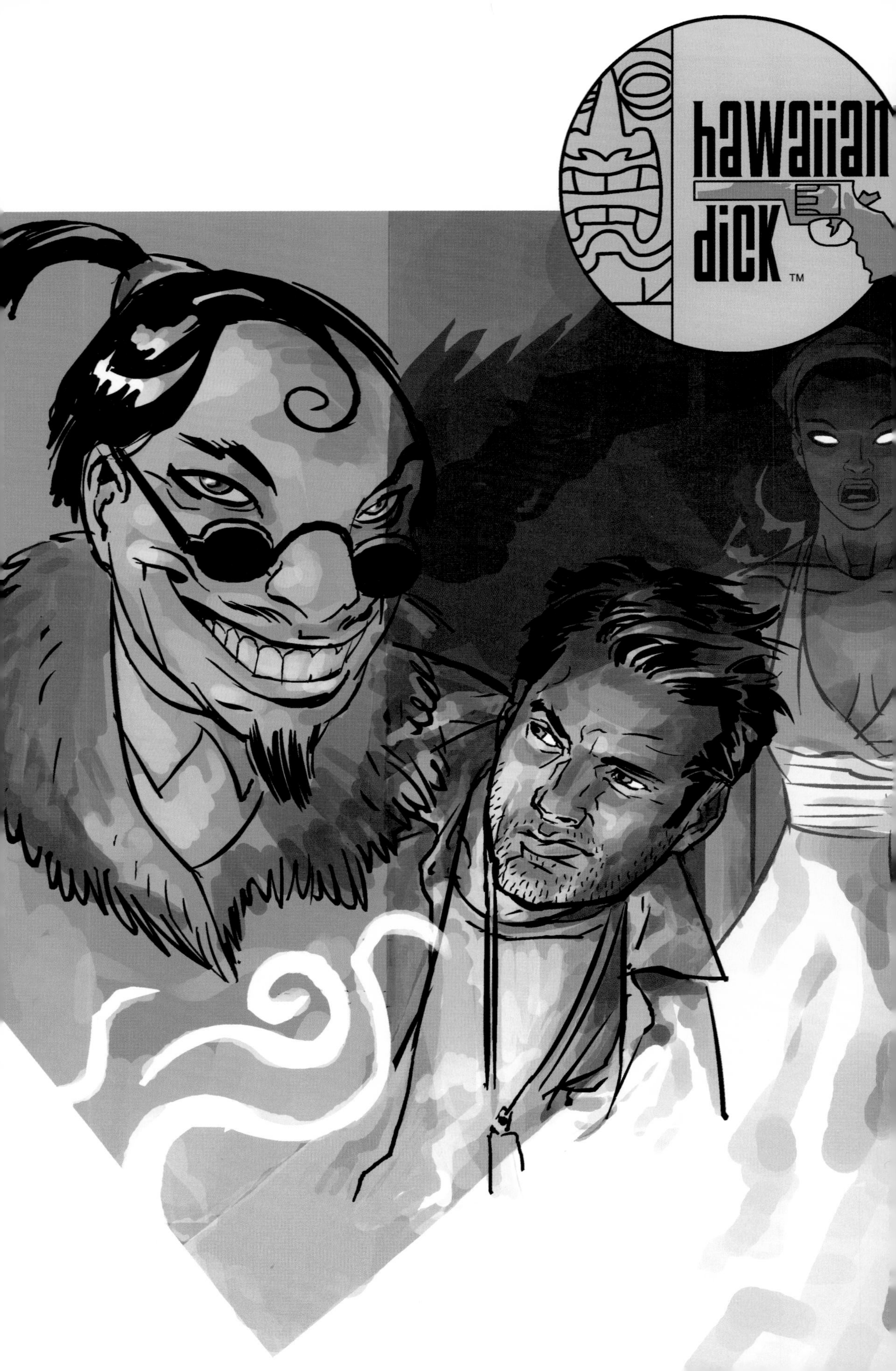
hawaiian dick ™

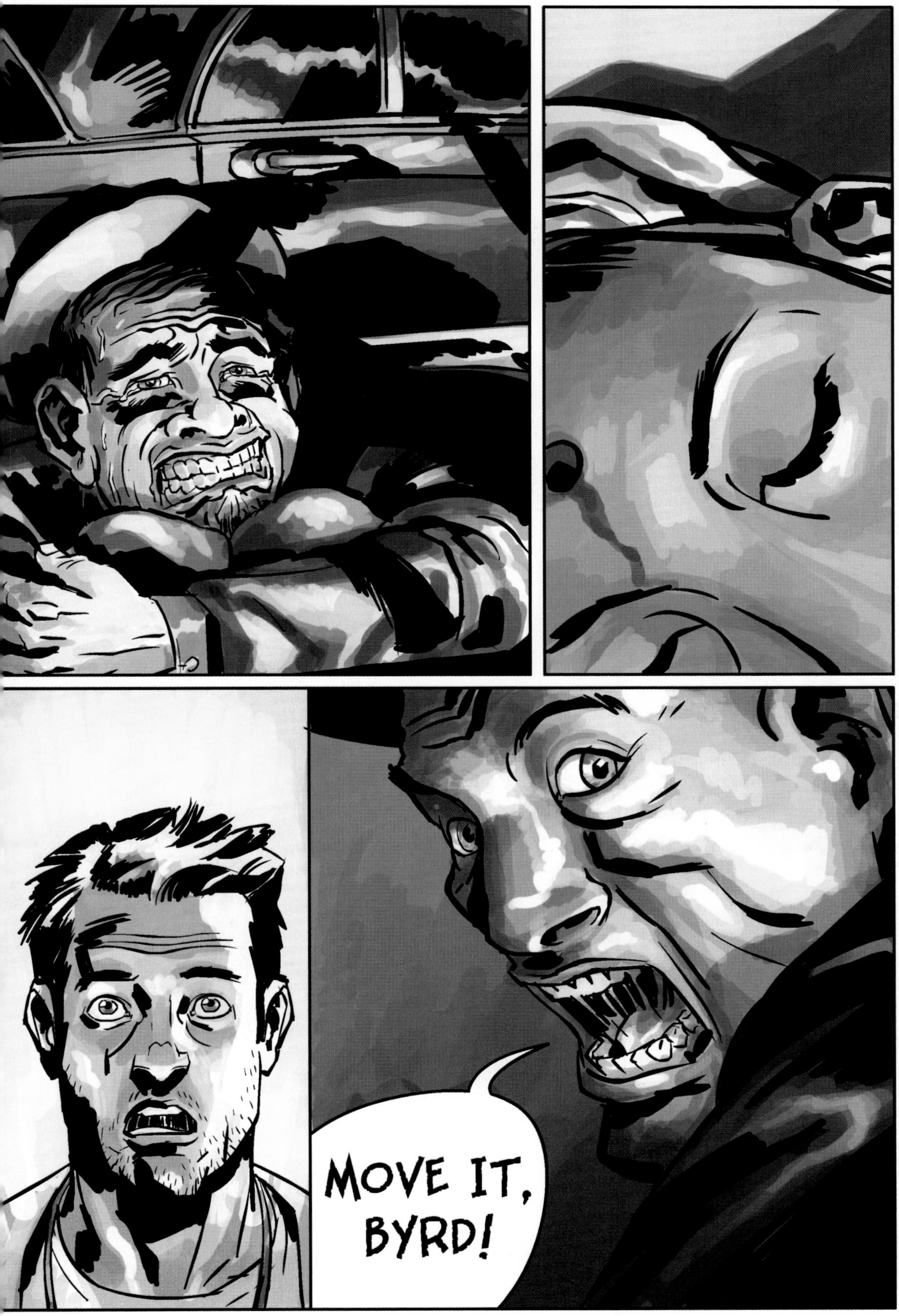
MOVE IT, BYRD!

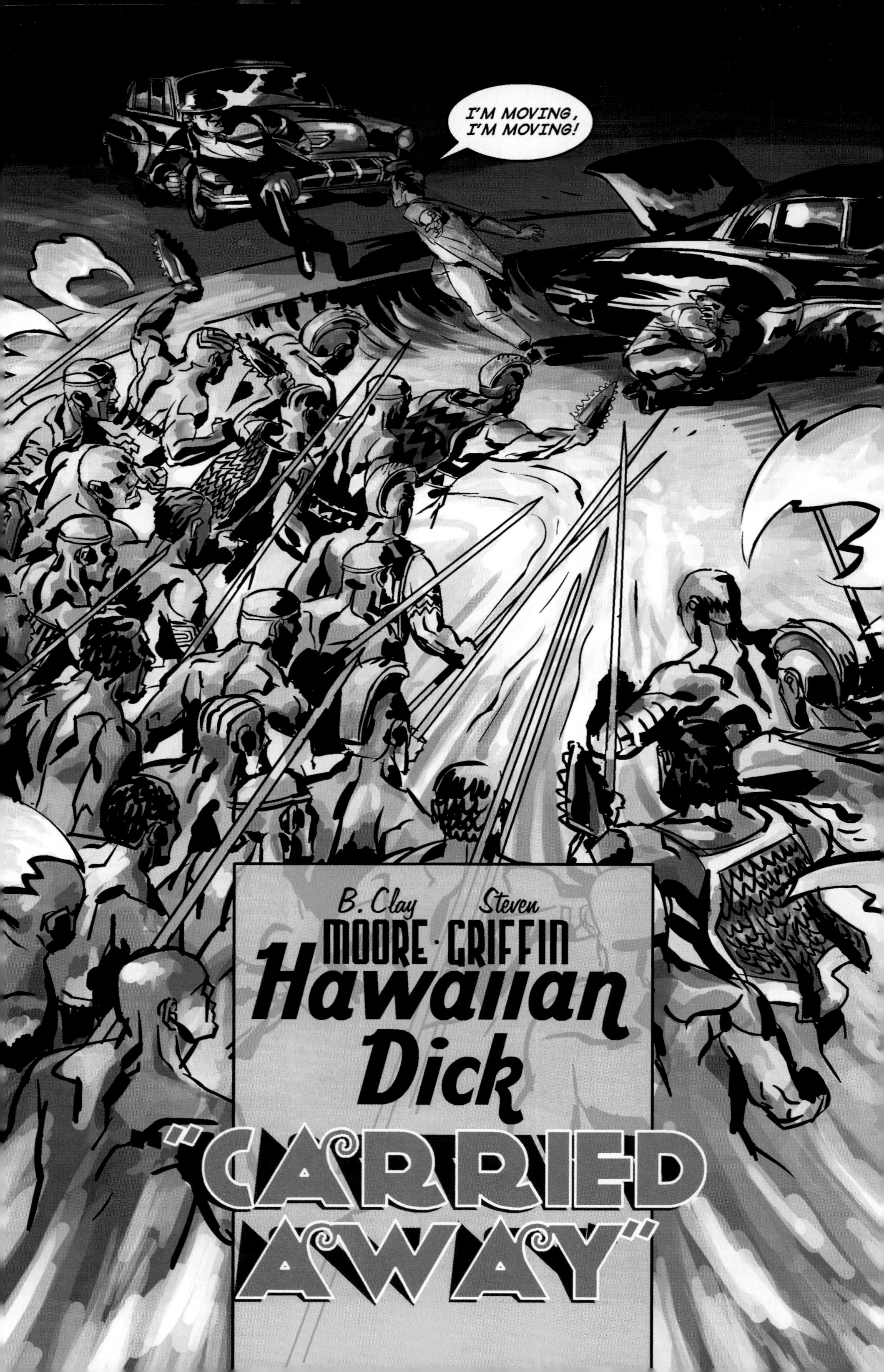
I'M MOVING, I'M MOVING!
B. Clay MOORE · Steven GRIFFIN
Hawaiian Dick
"CARRIED AWAY"

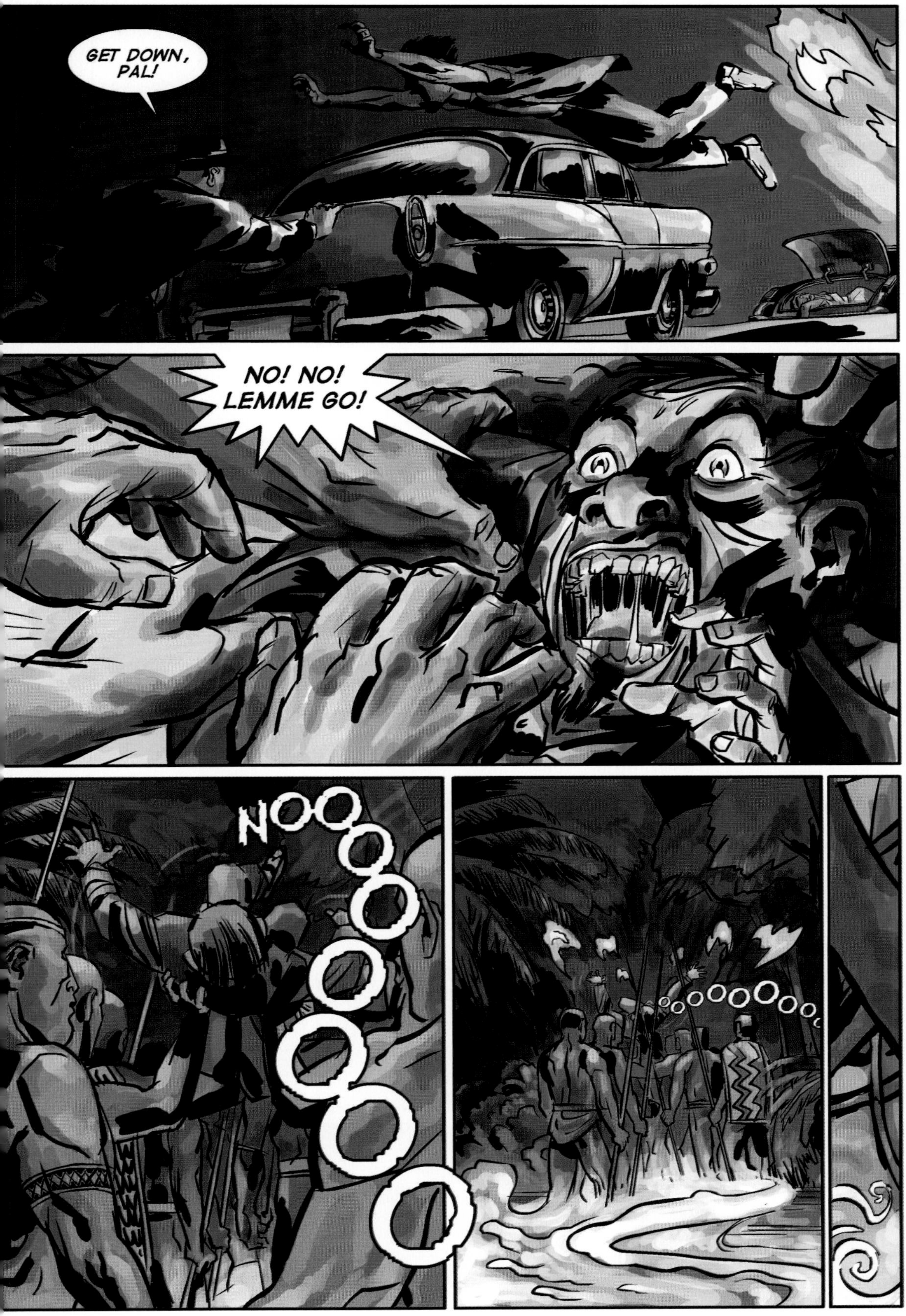
GET DOWN, PAL!
NO! NO! LEMME GO!
NOOOOOOOOO
oOOOOOOOo

MO...

I KNOW, I KNOW. COME ON, LET'S GET THE GIRL.

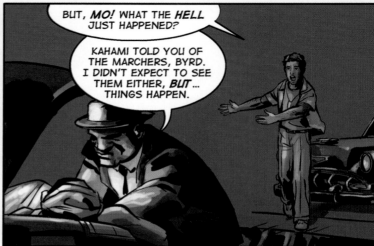

BUT, *MO!* WHAT THE *HELL* JUST HAPPENED?

KAHAMI TOLD YOU OF THE MARCHERS, BYRD. I DIDN'T EXPECT TO SEE THEM EITHER, *BUT*... THINGS HAPPEN.

THINGS *HAPPEN?*

THE *GIRL*, BYRD! LET'S GET OUT OF HERE BEFORE ANYTHING ELSE SHOWS UP!

'THINGS HAPPEN,' HE SAYS...

I'LL DRIVE.

LET'S GO BACK TO YOUR PLACE. FIGURE OUT WHAT TO DO FROM THERE.

WE HAVE TO DO SOMETHING WITH THE GIRL, MO.

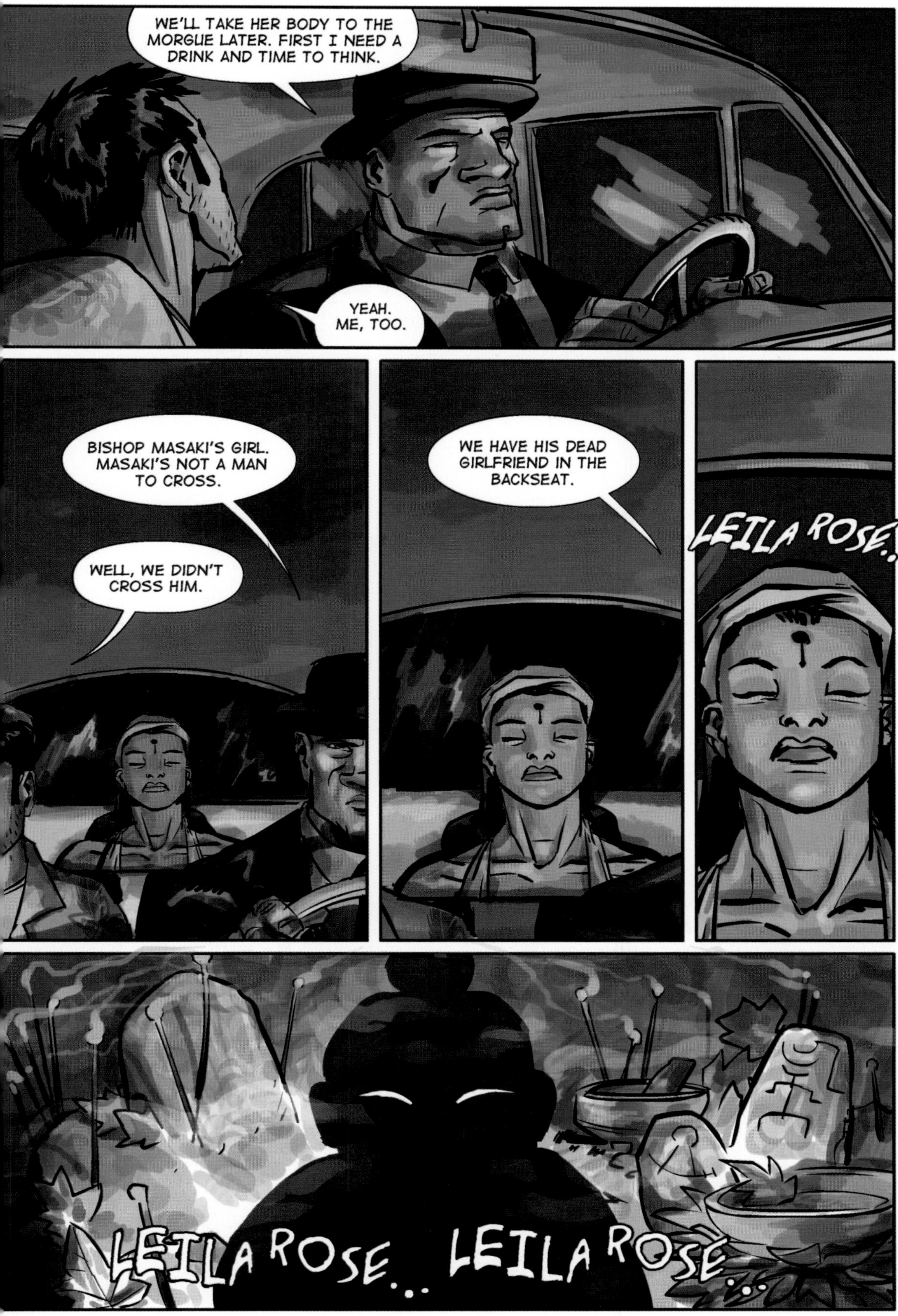
WE'LL TAKE HER BODY TO THE MORGUE LATER. FIRST I NEED A DRINK AND TIME TO THINK.
YEAH. ME, TOO.
BISHOP MASAKI'S GIRL. MASAKI'S NOT A MAN TO CROSS.
WELL, WE DIDN'T CROSS HIM.
WE HAVE HIS DEAD GIRLFRIEND IN THE BACKSEAT.
LEILA ROSE...
LEILA ROSE... LEILA ROSE...

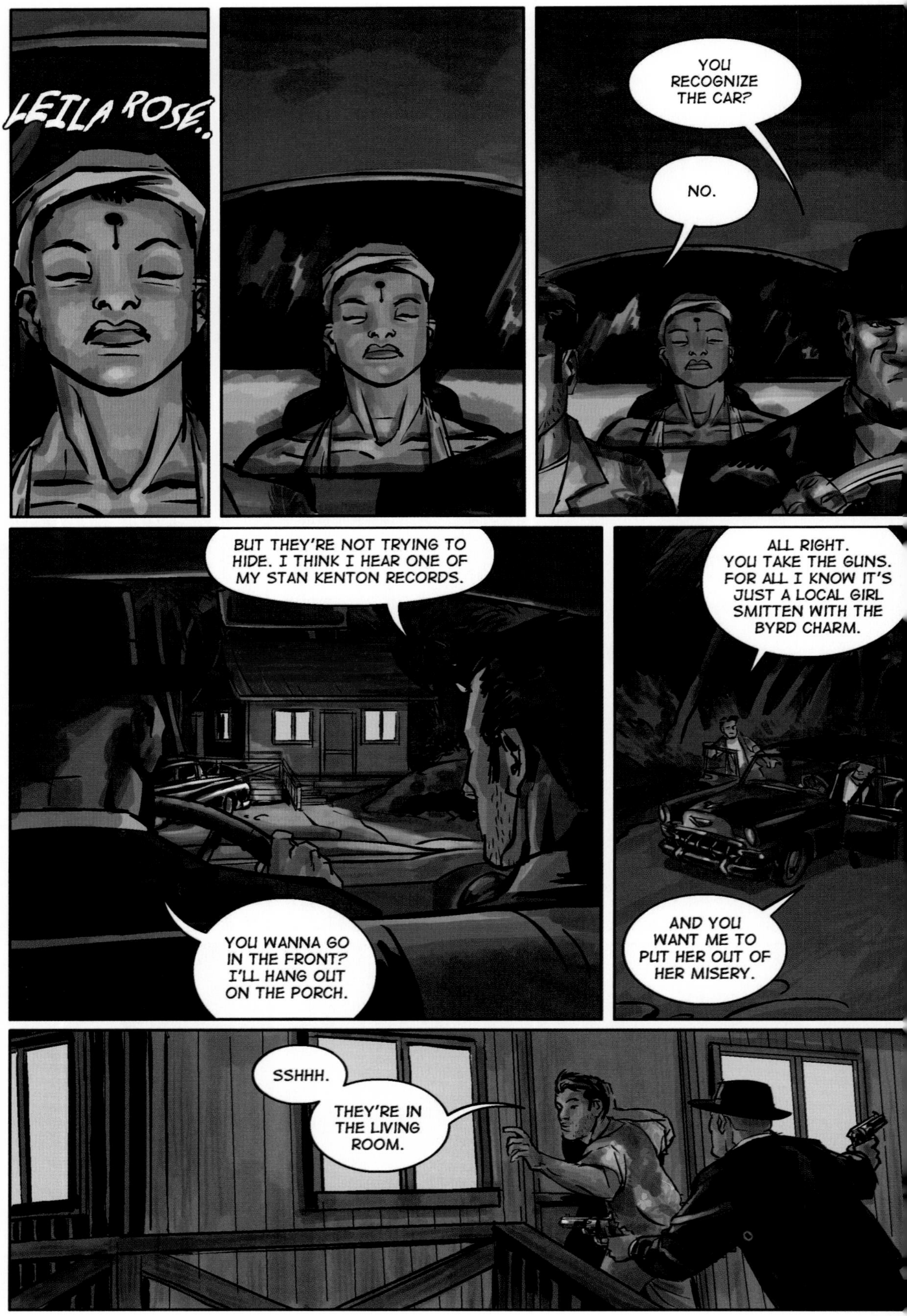
LEILA ROSE..
YOU RECOGNIZE THE CAR?
NO.
BUT THEY'RE NOT TRYING TO HIDE. I THINK I HEAR ONE OF MY STAN KENTON RECORDS.
YOU WANNA GO IN THE FRONT? I'LL HANG OUT ON THE PORCH.
ALL RIGHT. YOU TAKE THE GUNS. FOR ALL I KNOW IT'S JUST A LOCAL GIRL SMITTEN WITH THE BYRD CHARM.
AND YOU WANT ME TO PUT HER OUT OF HER MISERY.
SSHHH.
THEY'RE IN THE LIVING ROOM.

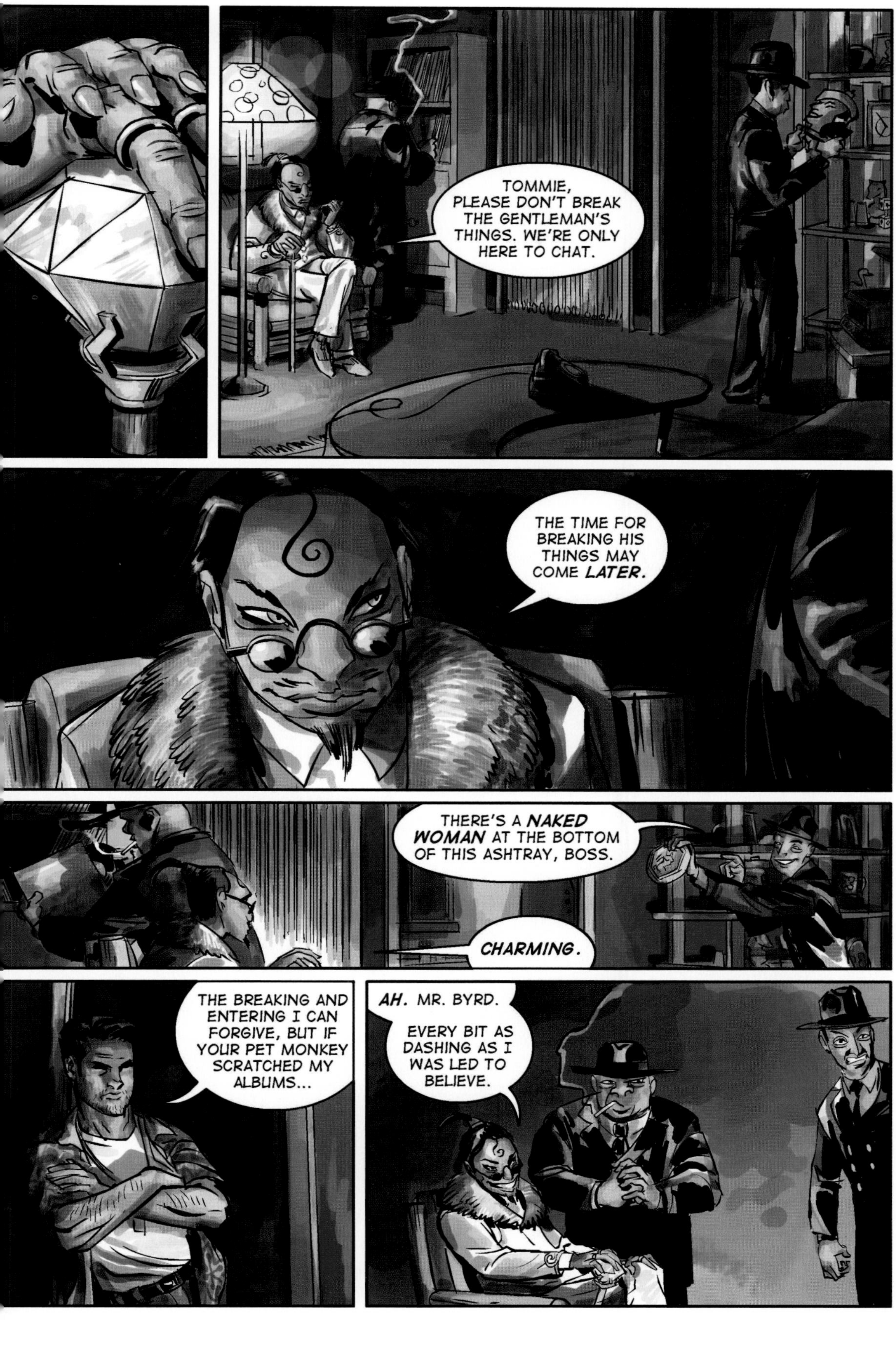
TOMMIE, PLEASE DON'T BREAK THE GENTLEMAN'S THINGS. WE'RE ONLY HERE TO CHAT.
THE TIME FOR BREAKING HIS THINGS MAY COME *LATER.*
THERE'S A ***NAKED WOMAN*** AT THE BOTTOM OF THIS ASHTRAY, BOSS.
CHARMING.
THE BREAKING AND ENTERING I CAN FORGIVE, BUT IF YOUR PET MONKEY SCRATCHED MY ALBUMS...
AH. MR. BYRD.
EVERY BIT AS DASHING AS I WAS LED TO BELIEVE.

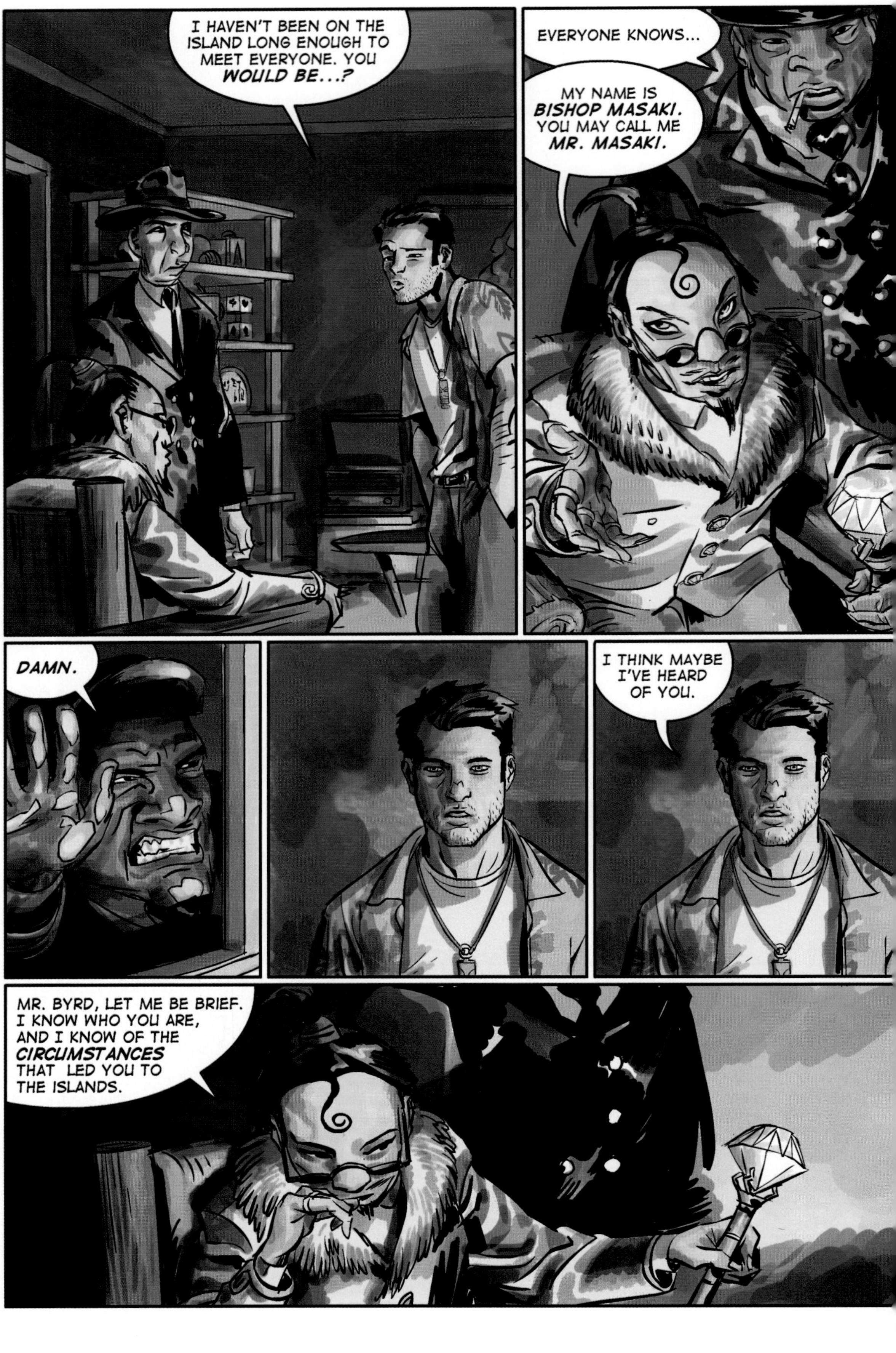
I HAVEN'T BEEN ON THE ISLAND LONG ENOUGH TO MEET EVERYONE. YOU *WOULD BE...?*
EVERYONE KNOWS...
MY NAME IS *BISHOP MASAKI.* YOU MAY CALL ME *MR. MASAKI.*
DAMN.
I THINK MAYBE I'VE HEARD OF YOU.
MR. BYRD, LET ME BE BRIEF. I KNOW WHO YOU ARE, AND I KNOW OF THE *CIRCUMSTANCES* THAT LED YOU TO THE ISLANDS.

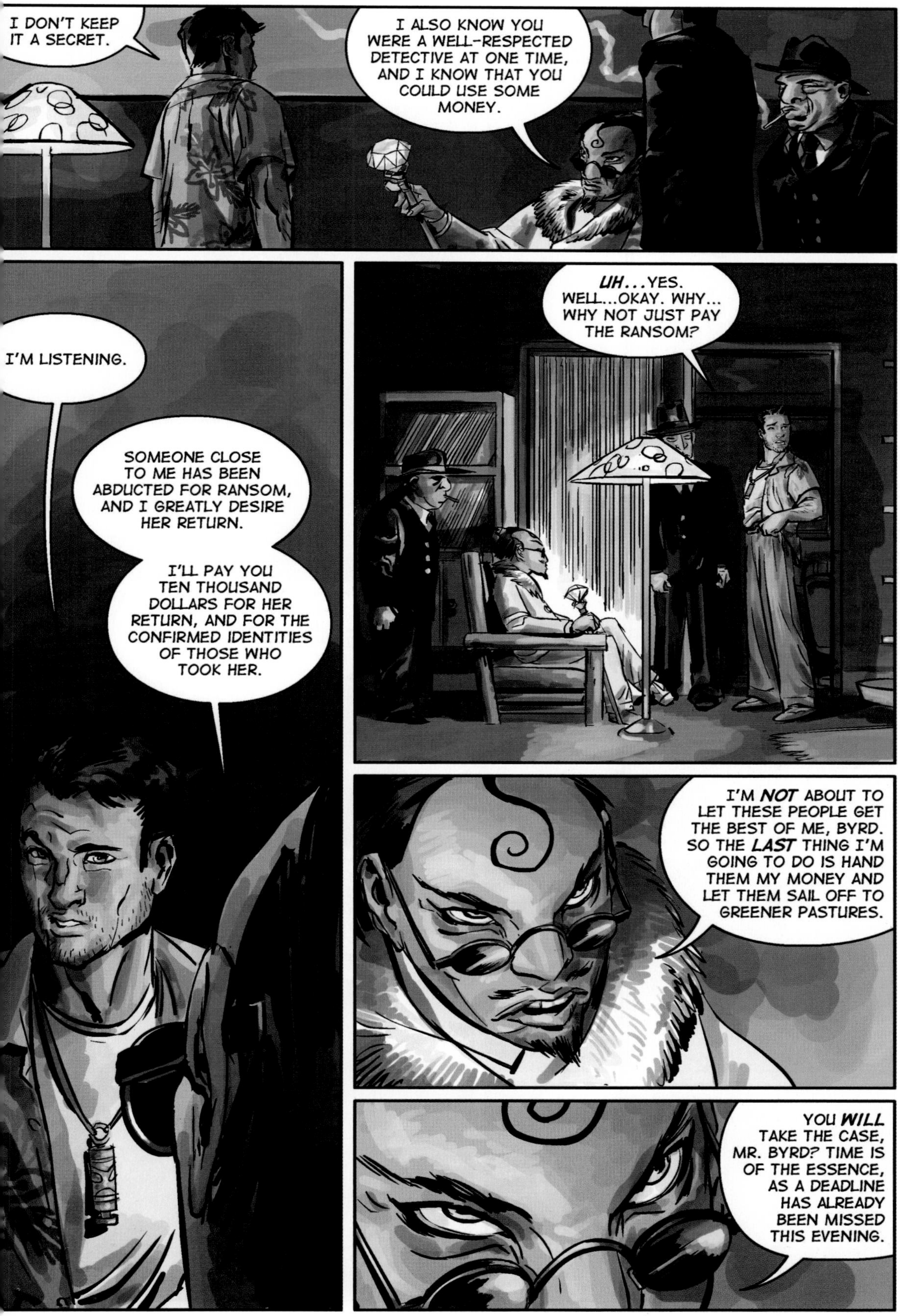
I DON'T KEEP IT A SECRET.
I ALSO KNOW YOU WERE A WELL-RESPECTED DETECTIVE AT ONE TIME, AND I KNOW THAT YOU COULD USE SOME MONEY.
I'M LISTENING.
SOMEONE CLOSE TO ME HAS BEEN ABDUCTED FOR RANSOM, AND I GREATLY DESIRE HER RETURN.
I'LL PAY YOU TEN THOUSAND DOLLARS FOR HER RETURN, AND FOR THE CONFIRMED IDENTITIES OF THOSE WHO TOOK HER.
UH...YES. WELL...OKAY. WHY... WHY NOT JUST PAY THE RANSOM?
I'M ***NOT*** ABOUT TO LET THESE PEOPLE GET THE BEST OF ME, BYRD. SO THE ***LAST*** THING I'M GOING TO DO IS HAND THEM MY MONEY AND LET THEM SAIL OFF TO GREENER PASTURES.
YOU ***WILL*** TAKE THE CASE, MR. BYRD? TIME IS OF THE ESSENCE, AS A DEADLINE HAS ALREADY BEEN MISSED THIS EVENING.

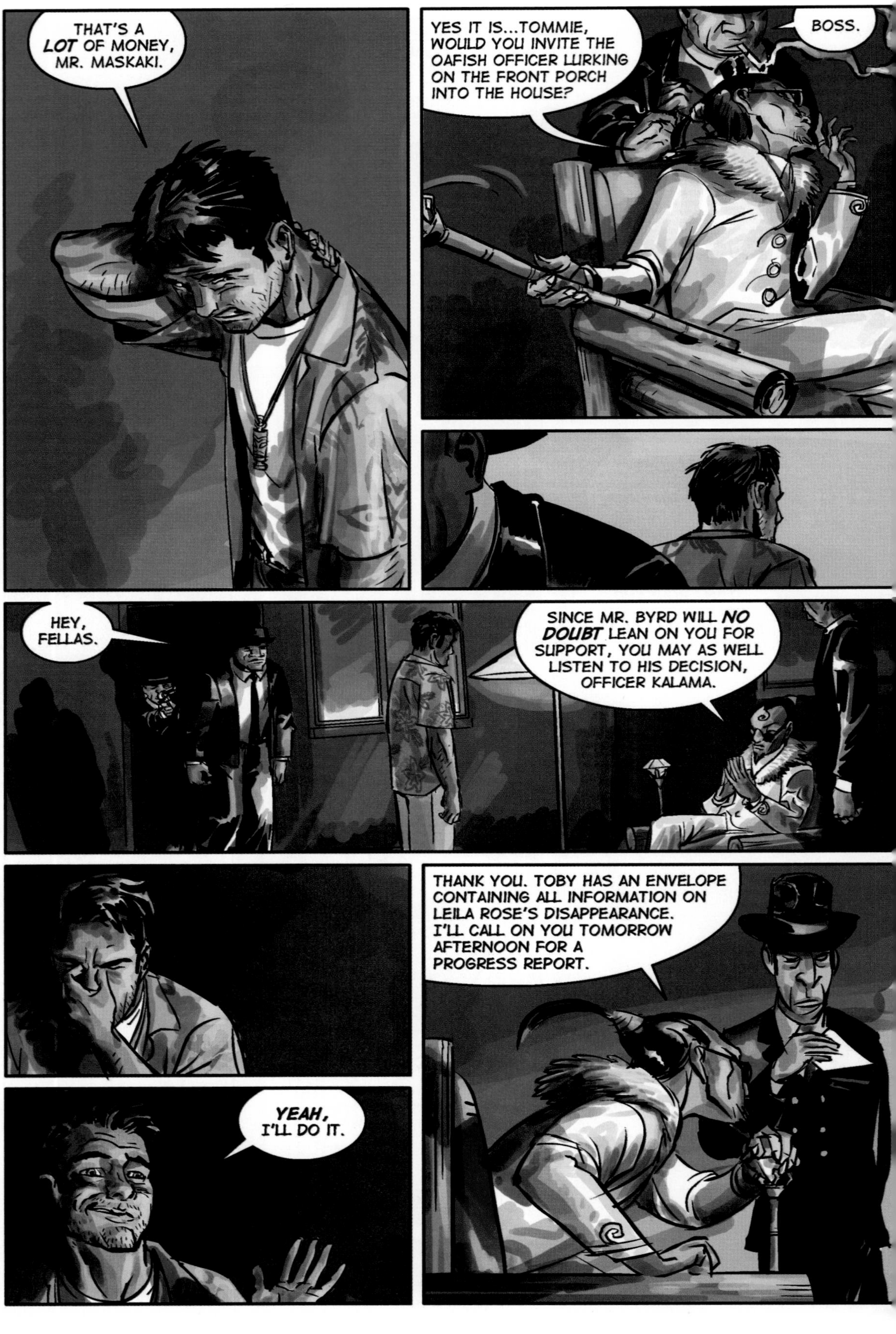
THAT'S A LOT OF MONEY, MR. MASKAKI.
YES IT IS...TOMMIE, WOULD YOU INVITE THE OAFISH OFFICER LURKING ON THE FRONT PORCH INTO THE HOUSE?
BOSS.
HEY, FELLAS.
SINCE MR. BYRD WILL NO DOUBT LEAN ON YOU FOR SUPPORT, YOU MAY AS WELL LISTEN TO HIS DECISION, OFFICER KALAMA.
YEAH, I'LL DO IT.
THANK YOU. TOBY HAS AN ENVELOPE CONTAINING ALL INFORMATION ON LEILA ROSE'S DISAPPEARANCE. I'LL CALL ON YOU TOMORROW AFTERNOON FOR A PROGRESS REPORT.

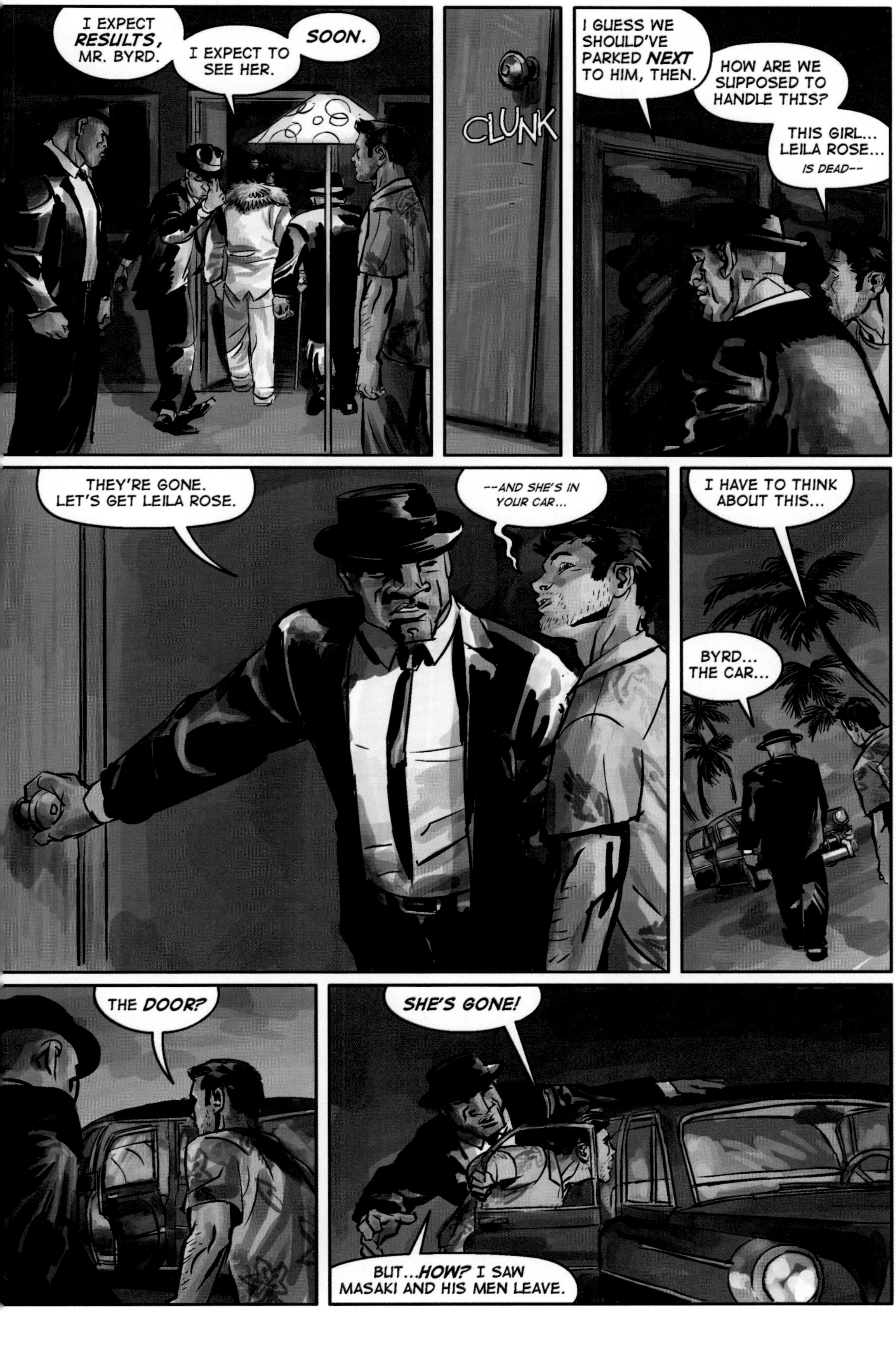
I EXPECT RESULTS, MR. BYRD.
I EXPECT TO SEE HER.
SOON.
CLUNK
I GUESS WE SHOULD'VE PARKED NEXT TO HIM, THEN.
HOW ARE WE SUPPOSED TO HANDLE THIS?
THIS GIRL... LEILA ROSE... IS DEAD--
THEY'RE GONE. LET'S GET LEILA ROSE.
--AND SHE'S IN YOUR CAR...
I HAVE TO THINK ABOUT THIS...
BYRD... THE CAR...
THE DOOR?
SHE'S GONE!
BUT...HOW? I SAW MASAKI AND HIS MEN LEAVE.

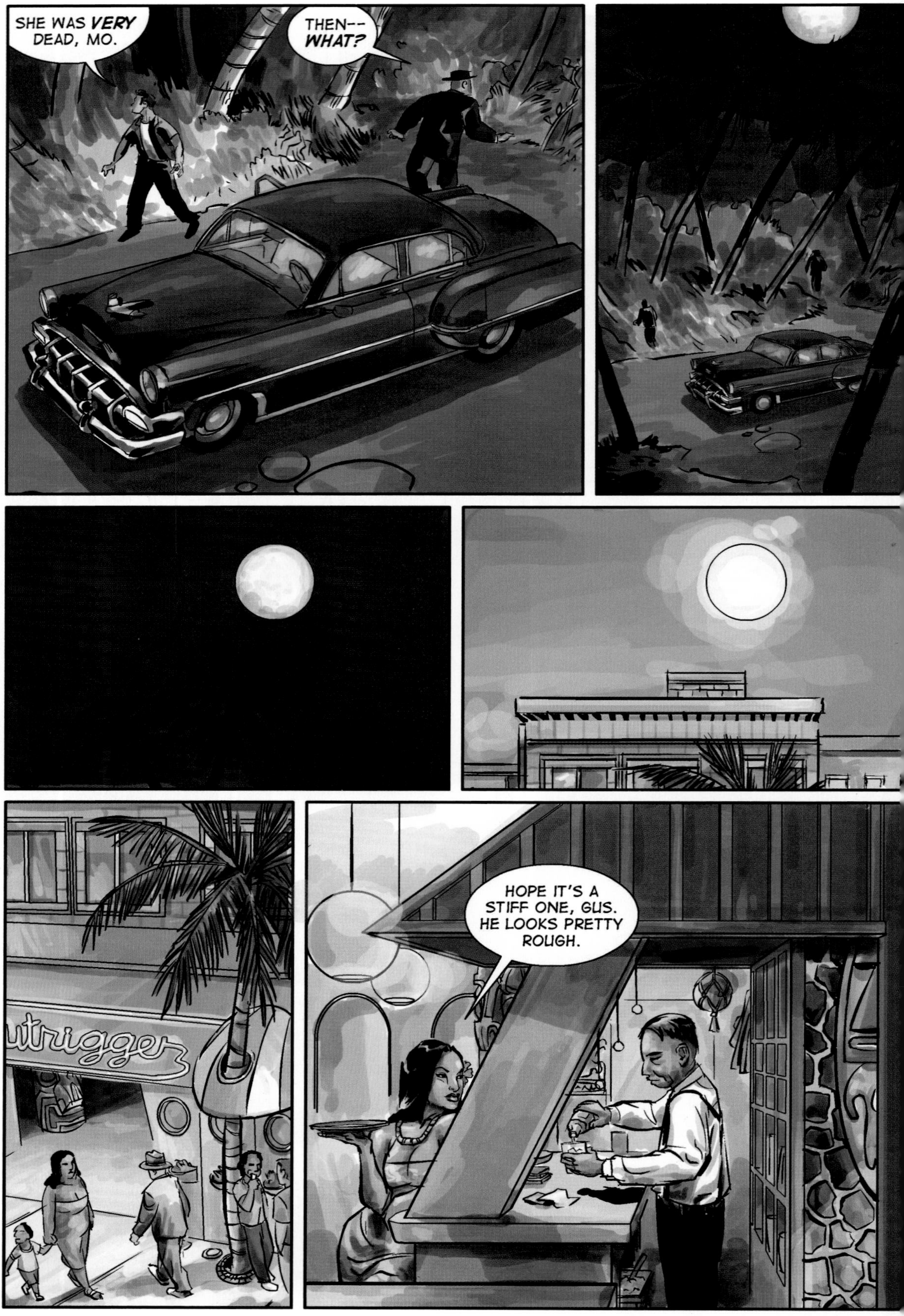
SHE WAS *VERY* DEAD, MO.
THEN-- *WHAT?*
HOPE IT'S A STIFF ONE, GUS. HE LOOKS PRETTY ROUGH.

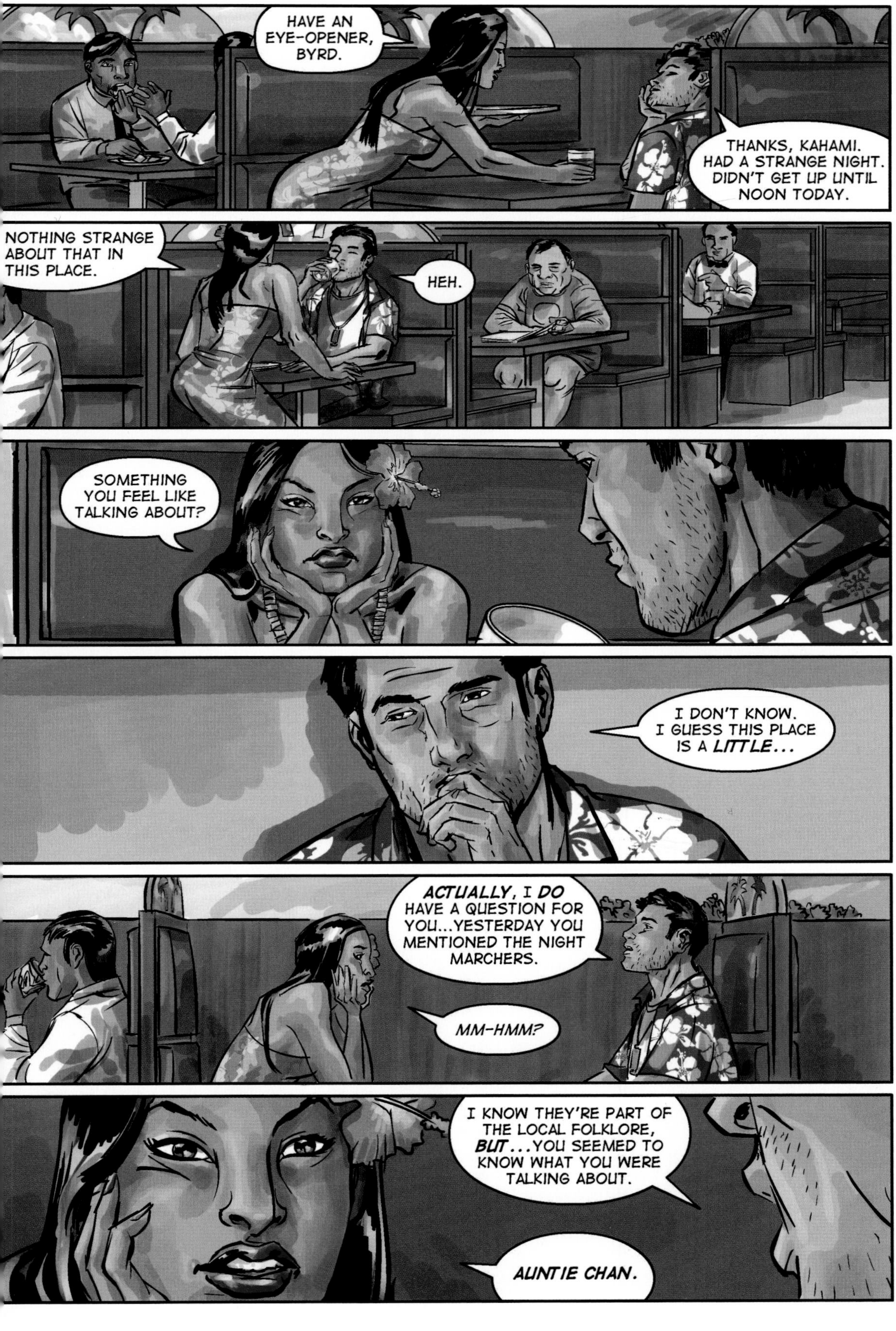
HAVE AN EYE-OPENER, BYRD.
THANKS, KAHAMI. HAD A STRANGE NIGHT. DIDN'T GET UP UNTIL NOON TODAY.
NOTHING STRANGE ABOUT THAT IN THIS PLACE.
HEH.
SOMETHING YOU FEEL LIKE TALKING ABOUT?
I DON'T KNOW. I GUESS THIS PLACE IS A *LITTLE*...
ACTUALLY, I *DO* HAVE A QUESTION FOR YOU...YESTERDAY YOU MENTIONED THE NIGHT MARCHERS.
MM-HMM?
I KNOW THEY'RE PART OF THE LOCAL FOLKLORE, *BUT*...YOU SEEMED TO KNOW WHAT YOU WERE TALKING ABOUT.
AUNTIE CHAN.

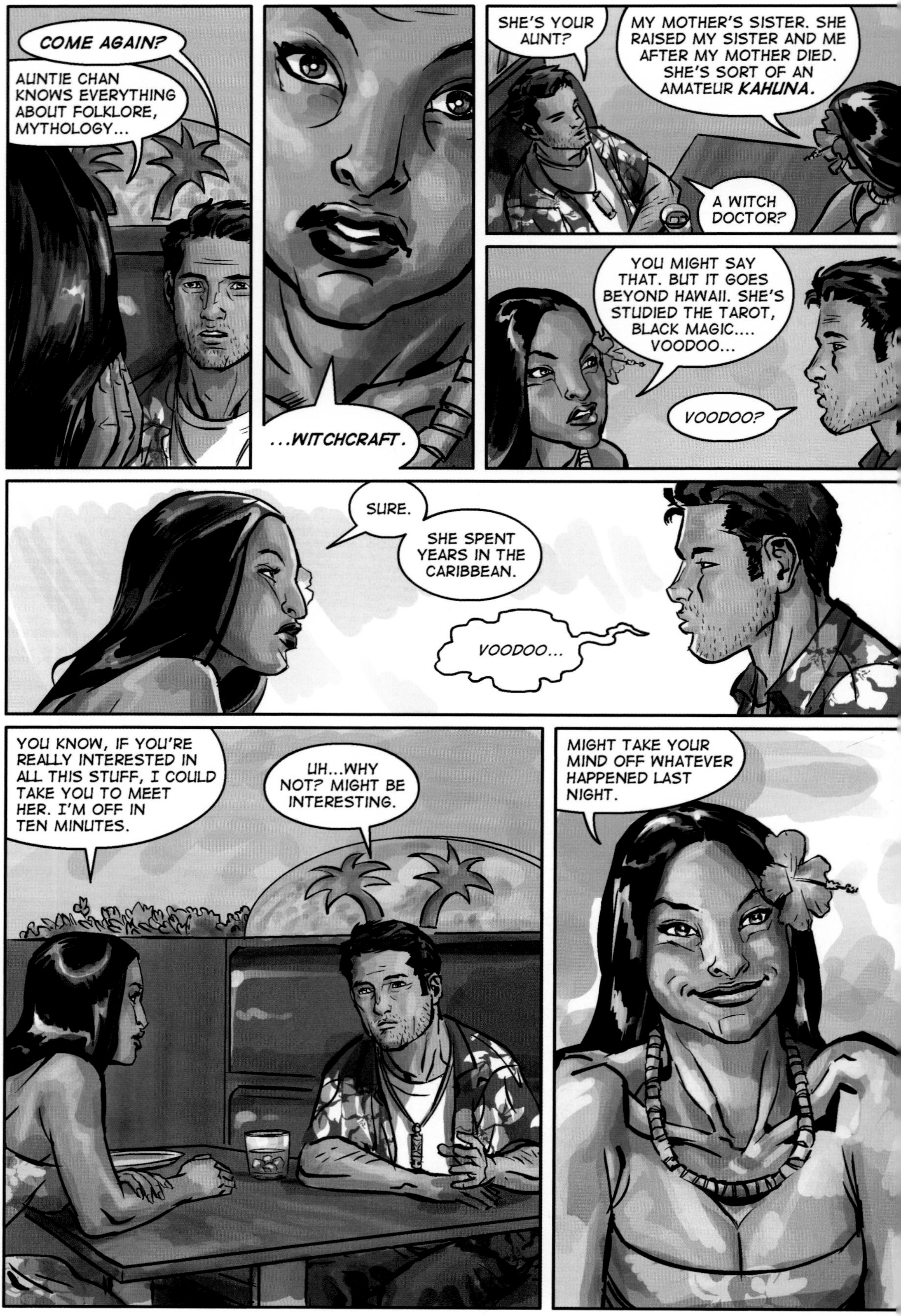
COME AGAIN?
AUNTIE CHAN KNOWS EVERYTHING ABOUT FOLKLORE, MYTHOLOGY...
...WITCHCRAFT.
SHE'S YOUR AUNT?
MY MOTHER'S SISTER. SHE RAISED MY SISTER AND ME AFTER MY MOTHER DIED. SHE'S SORT OF AN AMATEUR KAHUNA.
A WITCH DOCTOR?
YOU MIGHT SAY THAT. BUT IT GOES BEYOND HAWAII. SHE'S STUDIED THE TAROT, BLACK MAGIC.... VOODOO...
VOODOO?
SURE.
SHE SPENT YEARS IN THE CARIBBEAN.
VOODOO...
YOU KNOW, IF YOU'RE REALLY INTERESTED IN ALL THIS STUFF, I COULD TAKE YOU TO MEET HER. I'M OFF IN TEN MINUTES.
UH...WHY NOT? MIGHT BE INTERESTING.
MIGHT TAKE YOUR MIND OFF WHATEVER HAPPENED LAST NIGHT.

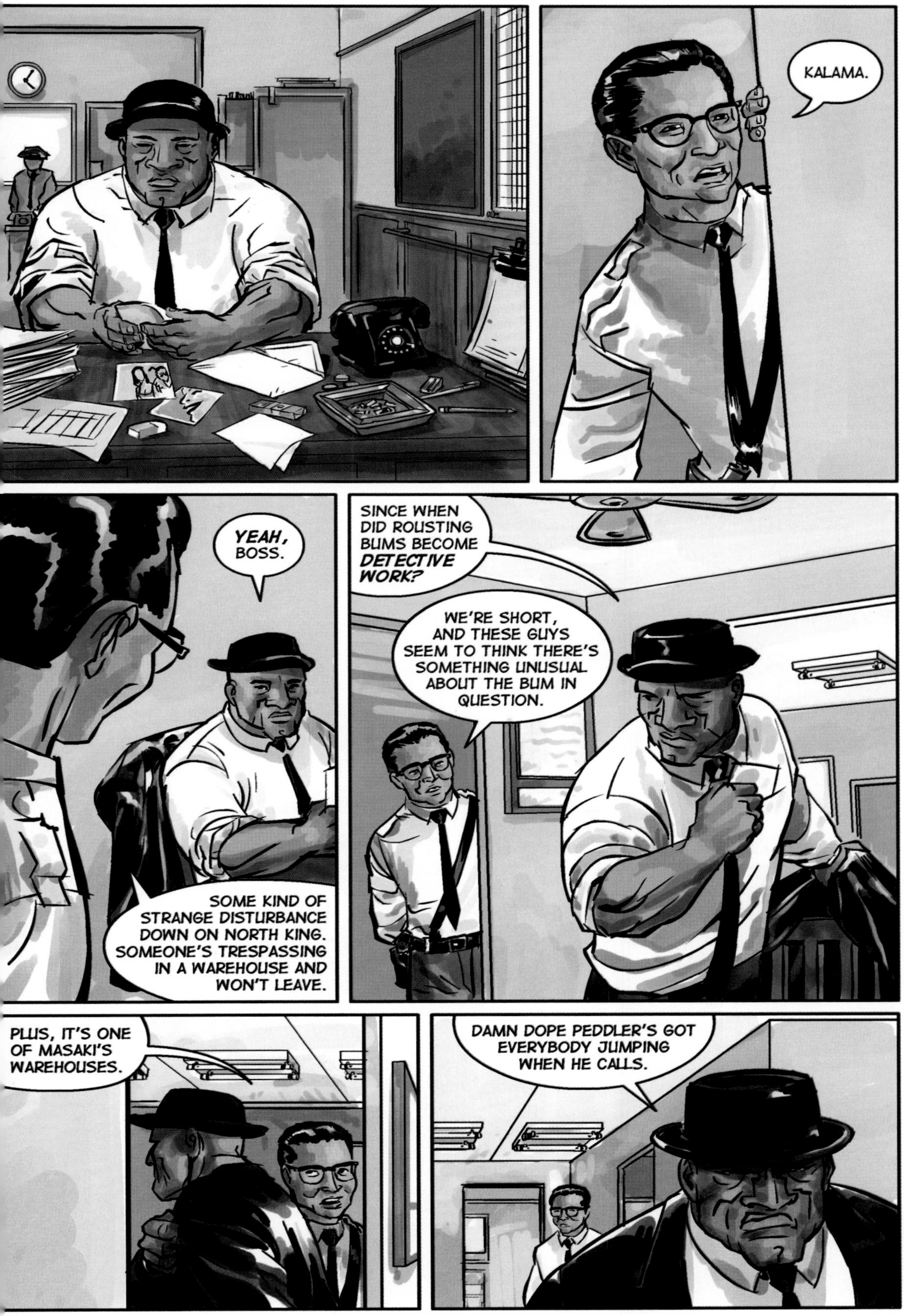
KALAMA.
YEAH, BOSS.
SOME KIND OF STRANGE DISTURBANCE DOWN ON NORTH KING. SOMEONE'S TRESPASSING IN A WAREHOUSE AND WON'T LEAVE.
SINCE WHEN DID ROUSTING BUMS BECOME DETECTIVE WORK?
WE'RE SHORT, AND THESE GUYS SEEM TO THINK THERE'S SOMETHING UNUSUAL ABOUT THE BUM IN QUESTION.
PLUS, IT'S ONE OF MASAKI'S WAREHOUSES.
DAMN DOPE PEDDLER'S GOT EVERYBODY JUMPING WHEN HE CALLS.

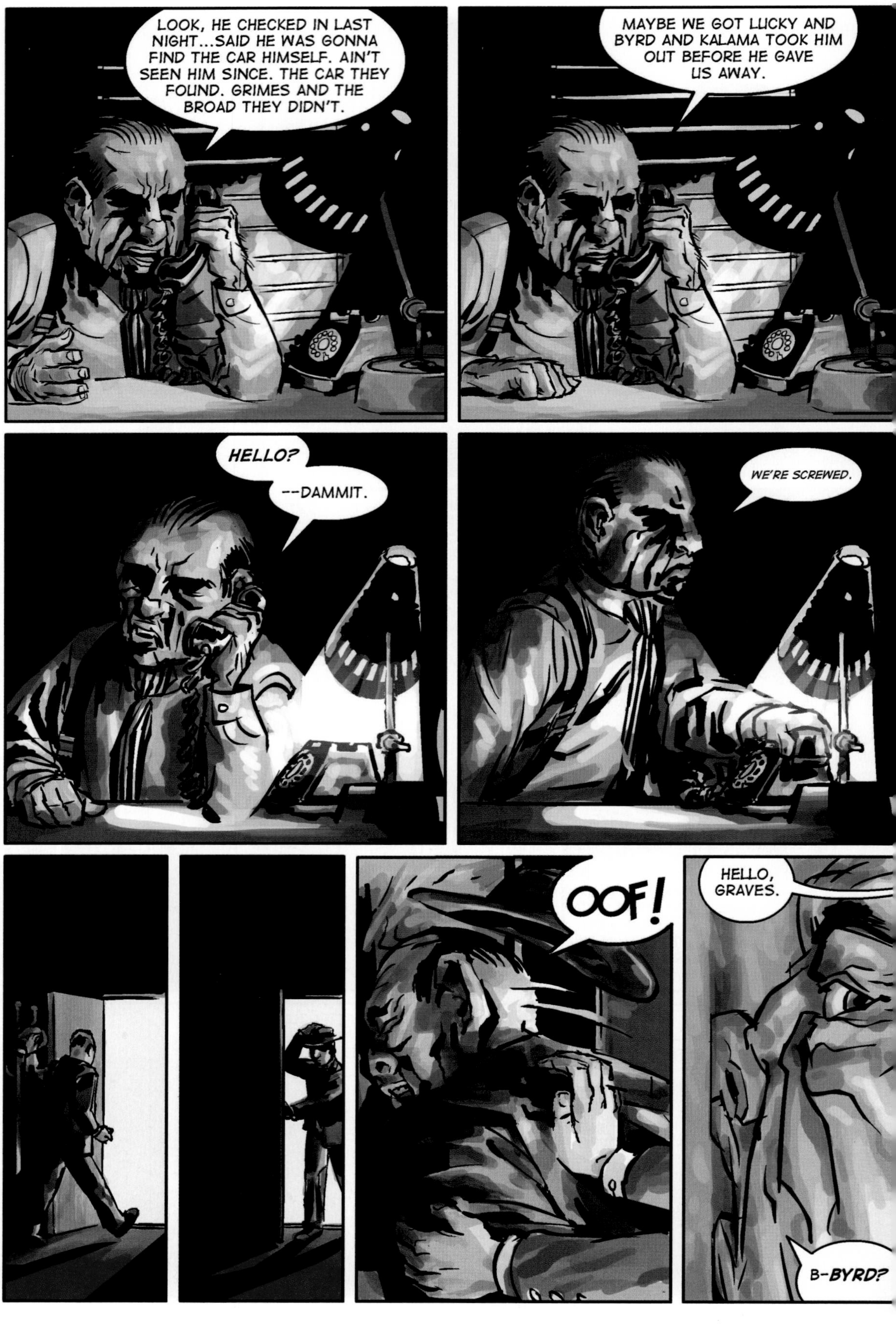
LOOK, HE CHECKED IN LAST NIGHT...SAID HE WAS GONNA FIND THE CAR HIMSELF. AIN'T SEEN HIM SINCE. THE CAR THEY FOUND. GRIMES AND THE BROAD THEY DIDN'T.
MAYBE WE GOT LUCKY AND BYRD AND KALAMA TOOK HIM OUT BEFORE HE GAVE US AWAY.
HELLO?
--DAMMIT.
WE'RE SCREWED.
OOF!
HELLO, GRAVES.
B-BYRD?

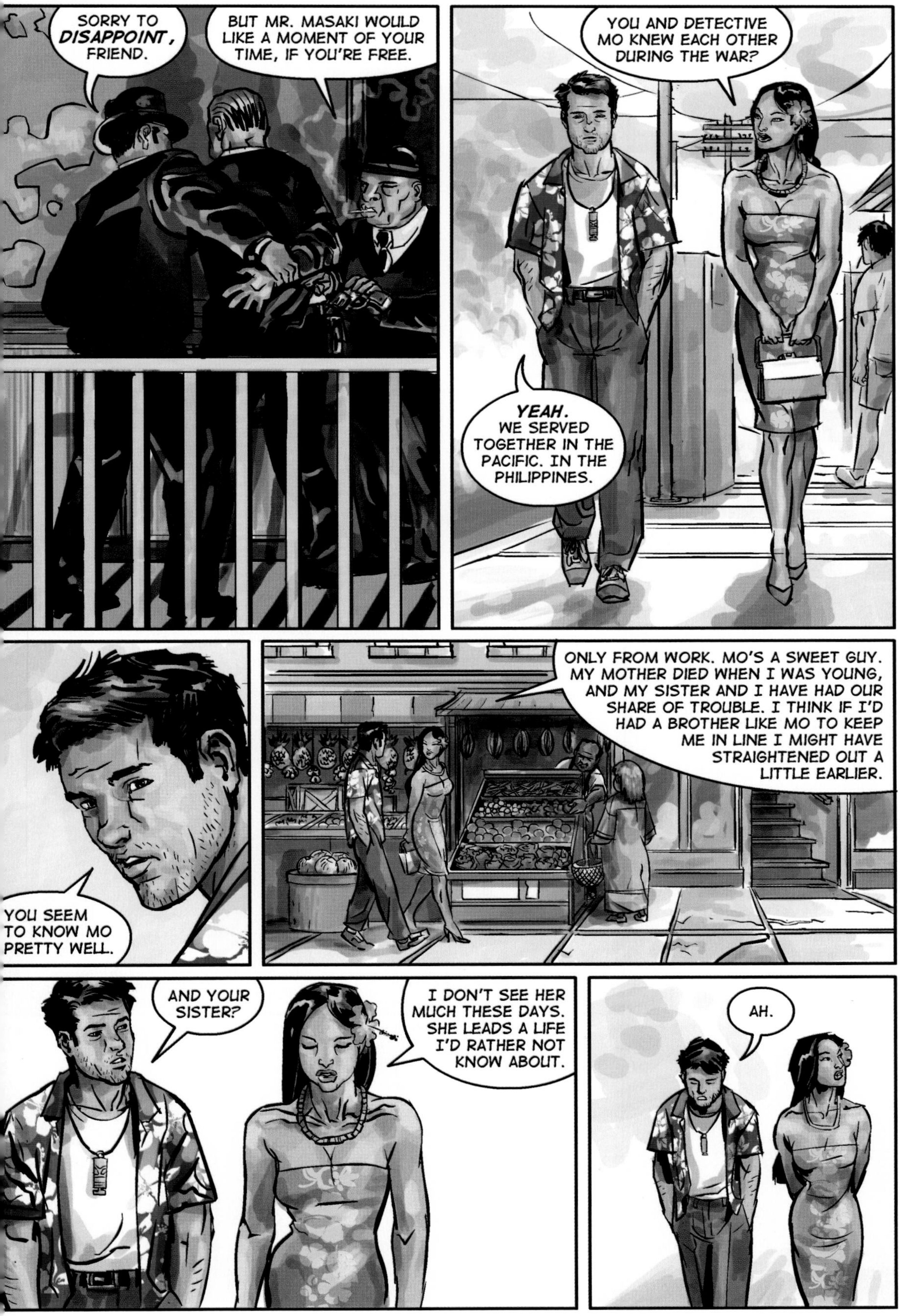
SORRY TO *DISAPPOINT*, FRIEND.
BUT MR. MASAKI WOULD LIKE A MOMENT OF YOUR TIME, IF YOU'RE FREE.
YOU AND DETECTIVE MO KNEW EACH OTHER DURING THE WAR?
YEAH. WE SERVED TOGETHER IN THE PACIFIC. IN THE PHILIPPINES.
YOU SEEM TO KNOW MO PRETTY WELL.
ONLY FROM WORK. MO'S A SWEET GUY. MY MOTHER DIED WHEN I WAS YOUNG, AND MY SISTER AND I HAVE HAD OUR SHARE OF TROUBLE. I THINK IF I'D HAD A BROTHER LIKE MO TO KEEP ME IN LINE I MIGHT HAVE STRAIGHTENED OUT A LITTLE EARLIER.
AND YOUR SISTER?
I DON'T SEE HER MUCH THESE DAYS. SHE LEADS A LIFE I'D RATHER NOT KNOW ABOUT.
AH.

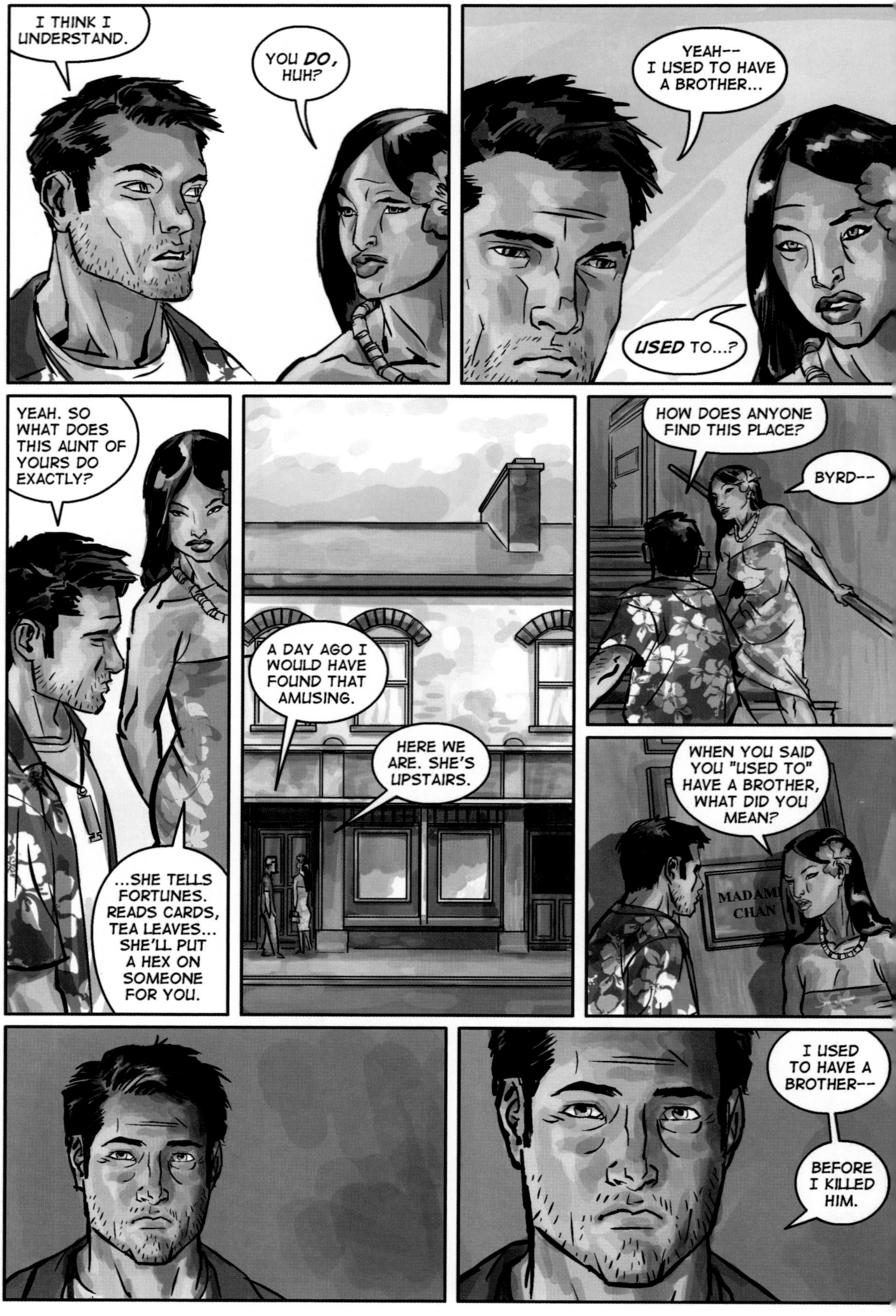
I THINK I UNDERSTAND.
YOU DO, HUH?
YEAH-- I USED TO HAVE A BROTHER...
USED TO...?
YEAH. SO WHAT DOES THIS AUNT OF YOURS DO EXACTLY?
...SHE TELLS FORTUNES. READS CARDS, TEA LEAVES... SHE'LL PUT A HEX ON SOMEONE FOR YOU.
A DAY AGO I WOULD HAVE FOUND THAT AMUSING.
HERE WE ARE. SHE'S UPSTAIRS.
HOW DOES ANYONE FIND THIS PLACE?
BYRD--
WHEN YOU SAID YOU "USED TO" HAVE A BROTHER, WHAT DID YOU MEAN?
MADAME CHAN
I USED TO HAVE A BROTHER--
BEFORE I KILLED HIM.

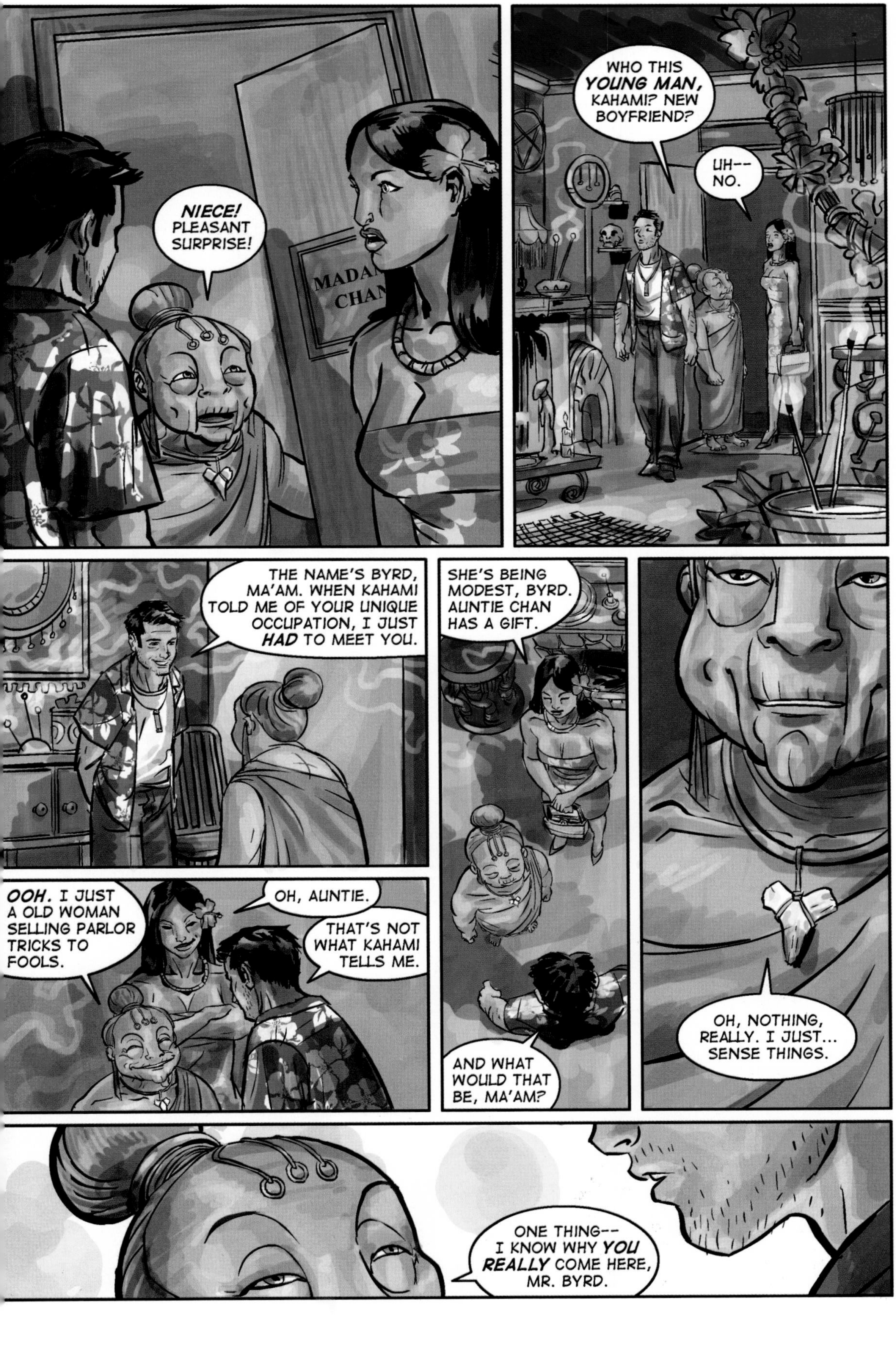
NIECE! PLEASANT SURPRISE!
MADAM CHAN
WHO THIS YOUNG MAN, KAHAMI? NEW BOYFRIEND?
UH-- NO.
THE NAME'S BYRD, MA'AM. WHEN KAHAMI TOLD ME OF YOUR UNIQUE OCCUPATION, I JUST HAD TO MEET YOU.
OOH. I JUST A OLD WOMAN SELLING PARLOR TRICKS TO FOOLS.
OH, AUNTIE.
THAT'S NOT WHAT KAHAMI TELLS ME.
SHE'S BEING MODEST, BYRD. AUNTIE CHAN HAS A GIFT.
AND WHAT WOULD THAT BE, MA'AM?
OH, NOTHING, REALLY. I JUST... SENSE THINGS.
ONE THING-- I KNOW WHY YOU REALLY COME HERE, MR. BYRD.

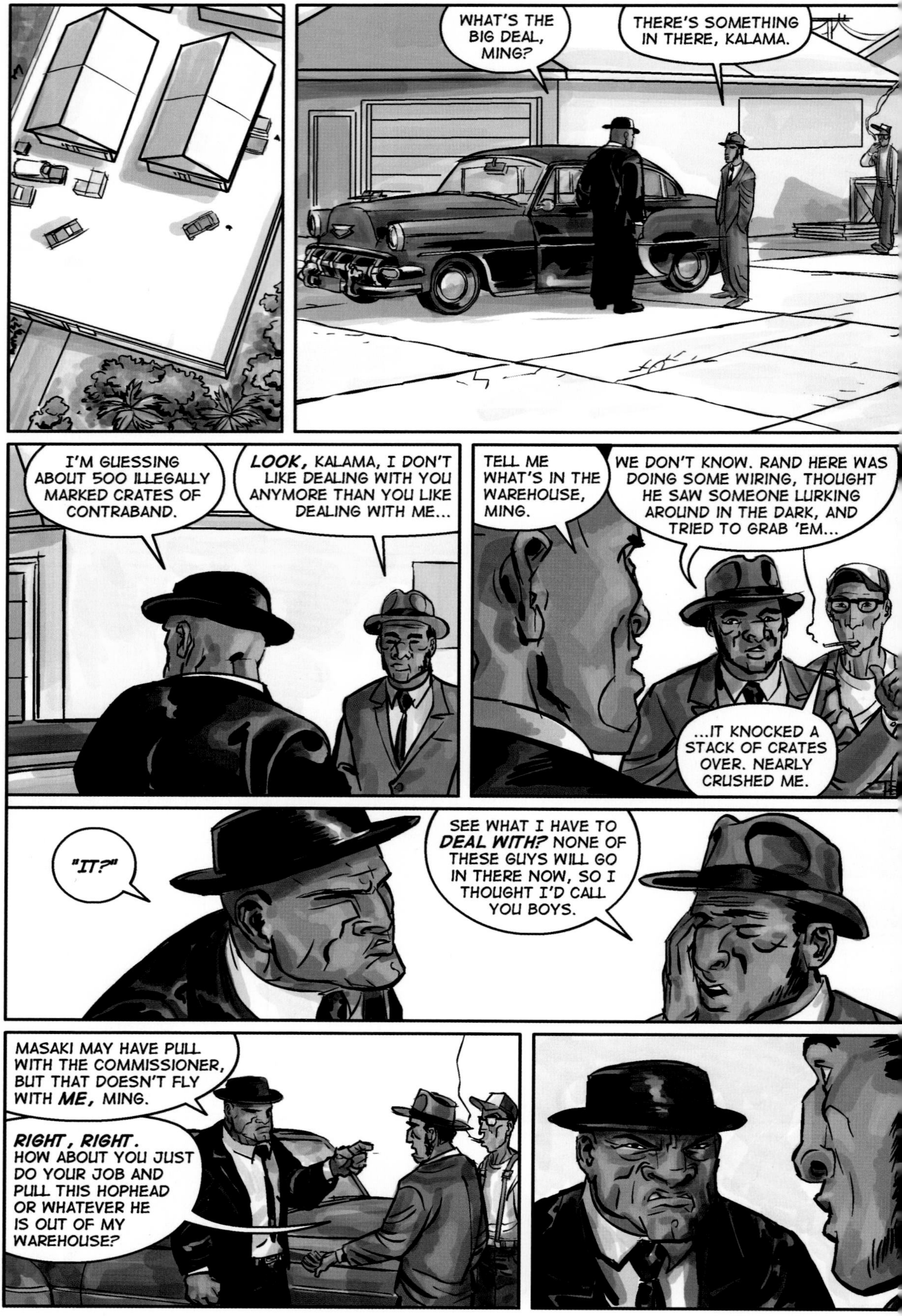
WHAT'S THE BIG DEAL, MING?
THERE'S SOMETHING IN THERE, KALAMA.
I'M GUESSING ABOUT 500 ILLEGALLY MARKED CRATES OF CONTRABAND.
LOOK, KALAMA, I DON'T LIKE DEALING WITH YOU ANYMORE THAN YOU LIKE DEALING WITH ME...
TELL ME WHAT'S IN THE WAREHOUSE, MING.
WE DON'T KNOW. RAND HERE WAS DOING SOME WIRING, THOUGHT HE SAW SOMEONE LURKING AROUND IN THE DARK, AND TRIED TO GRAB 'EM...
...IT KNOCKED A STACK OF CRATES OVER. NEARLY CRUSHED ME.
"IT?"
SEE WHAT I HAVE TO DEAL WITH? NONE OF THESE GUYS WILL GO IN THERE NOW, SO I THOUGHT I'D CALL YOU BOYS.
MASAKI MAY HAVE PULL WITH THE COMMISSIONER, BUT THAT DOESN'T FLY WITH ME, MING.
RIGHT, RIGHT. HOW ABOUT YOU JUST DO YOUR JOB AND PULL THIS HOPHEAD OR WHATEVER HE IS OUT OF MY WAREHOUSE?

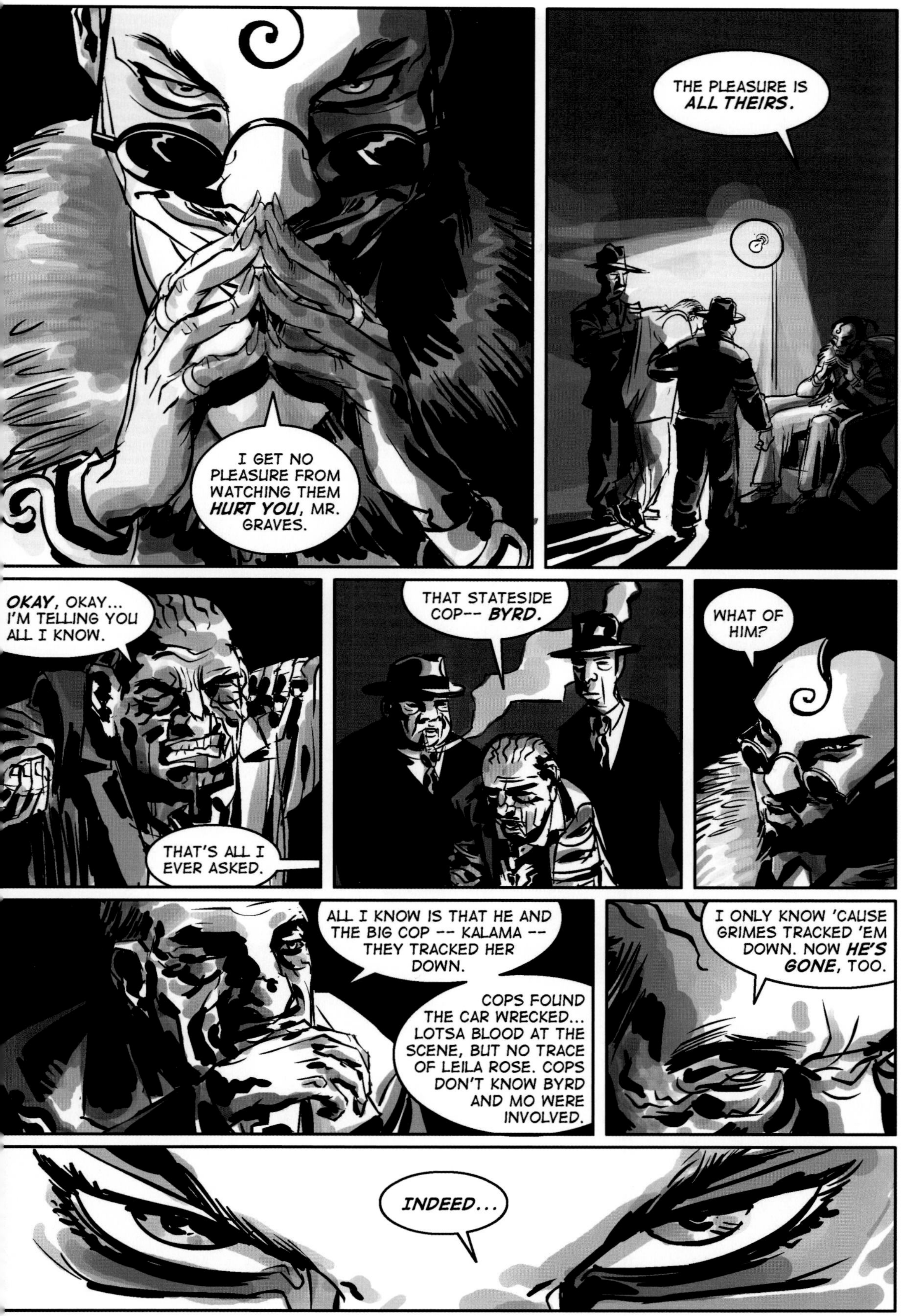

I GET NO PLEASURE FROM WATCHING THEM *HURT YOU*, MR. GRAVES.
THE PLEASURE IS *ALL THEIRS.*
OKAY, OKAY... I'M TELLING YOU ALL I KNOW.
THAT'S ALL I EVER ASKED.
THAT STATESIDE COP-- *BYRD.*
WHAT OF HIM?
ALL I KNOW IS THAT HE AND THE BIG COP -- KALAMA -- THEY TRACKED HER DOWN.
COPS FOUND THE CAR WRECKED... LOTSA BLOOD AT THE SCENE, BUT NO TRACE OF LEILA ROSE. COPS DON'T KNOW BYRD AND MO WERE INVOLVED.
I ONLY KNOW 'CAUSE GRIMES TRACKED 'EM DOWN. NOW *HE'S GONE*, TOO.
INDEED...

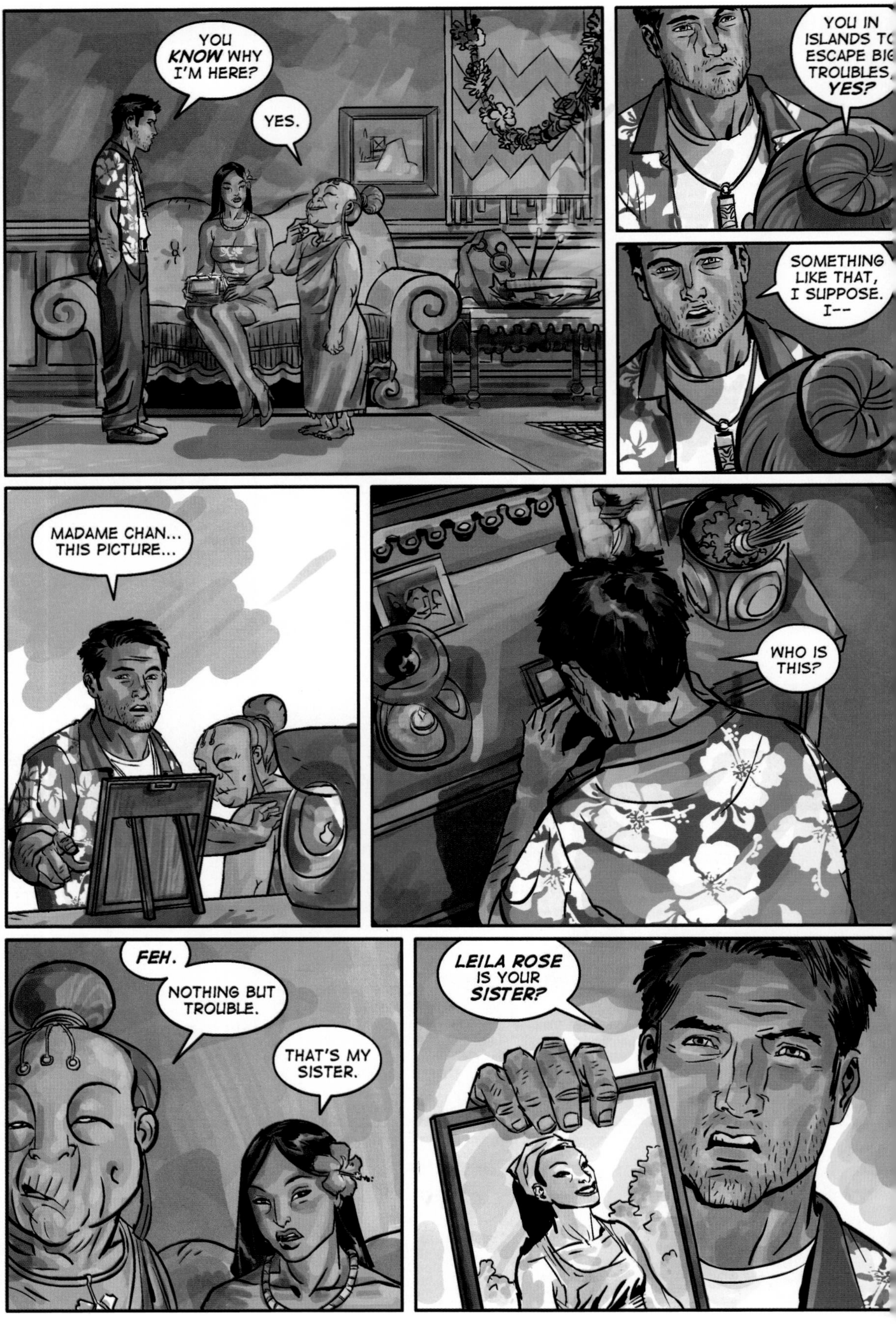
YOU KNOW WHY I'M HERE?
YES.
YOU IN ISLANDS TO ESCAPE BIG TROUBLES, YES?
SOMETHING LIKE THAT, I SUPPOSE. I--
MADAME CHAN... THIS PICTURE...
WHO IS THIS?
FEH.
NOTHING BUT TROUBLE.
THAT'S MY SISTER.
LEILA ROSE IS YOUR SISTER?

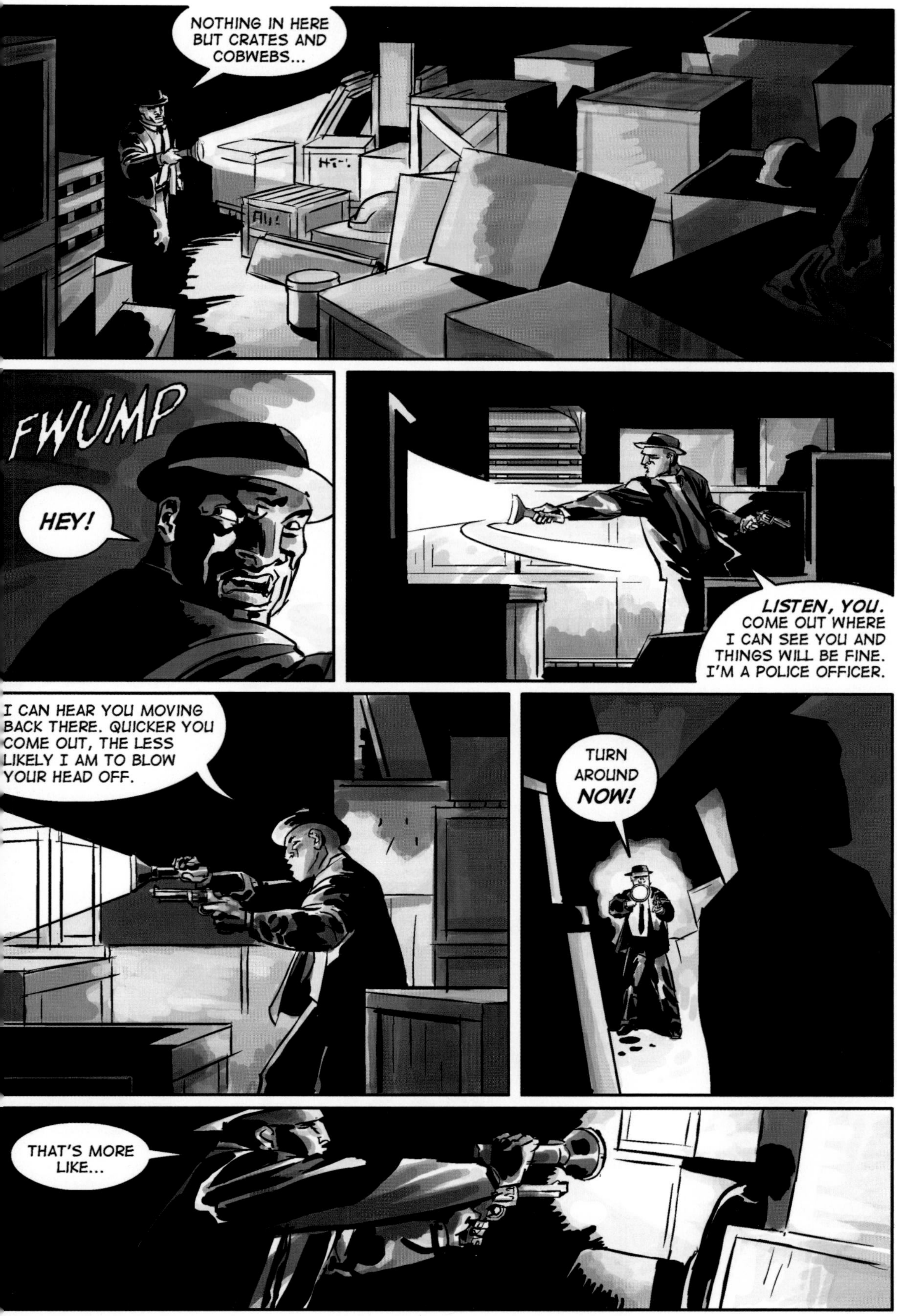
NOTHING IN HERE BUT CRATES AND COBWEBS...
FWUMP
HEY!
LISTEN, YOU. COME OUT WHERE I CAN SEE YOU AND THINGS WILL BE FINE. I'M A POLICE OFFICER.
I CAN HEAR YOU MOVING BACK THERE. QUICKER YOU COME OUT, THE LESS LIKELY I AM TO BLOW YOUR HEAD OFF.
TURN AROUND NOW!
THAT'S MORE LIKE...

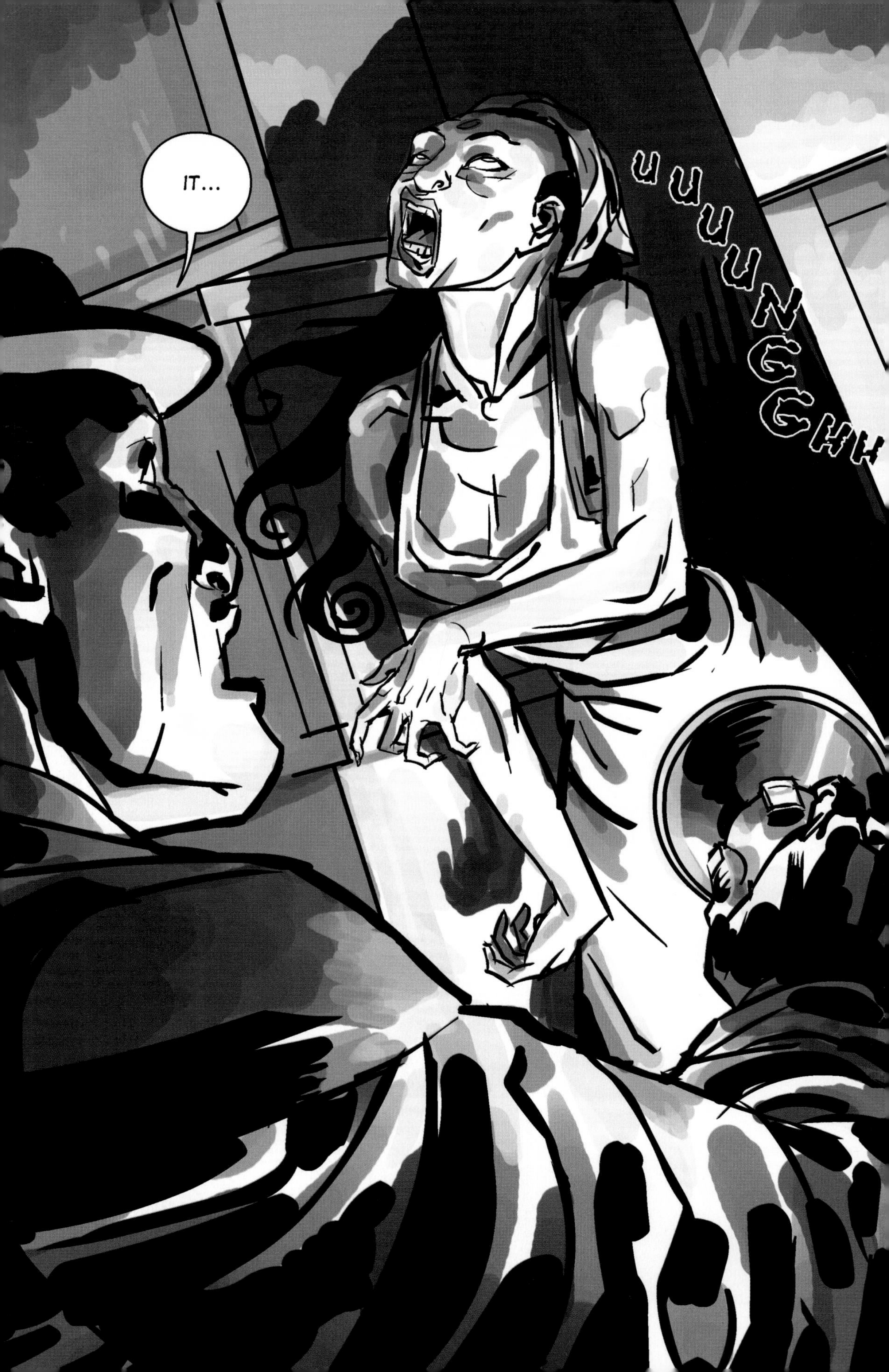
IT...
UUUUUNGGHH

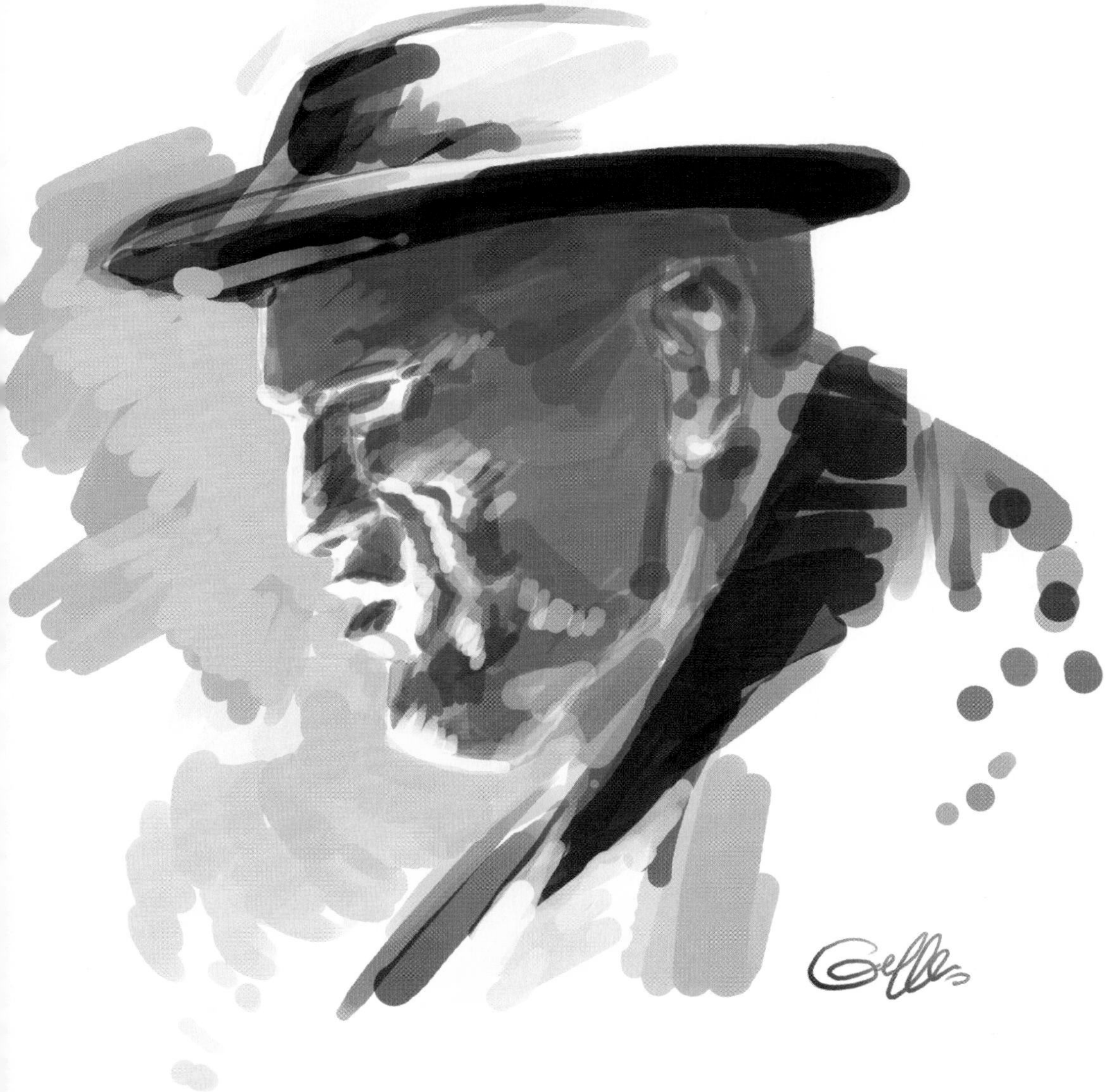

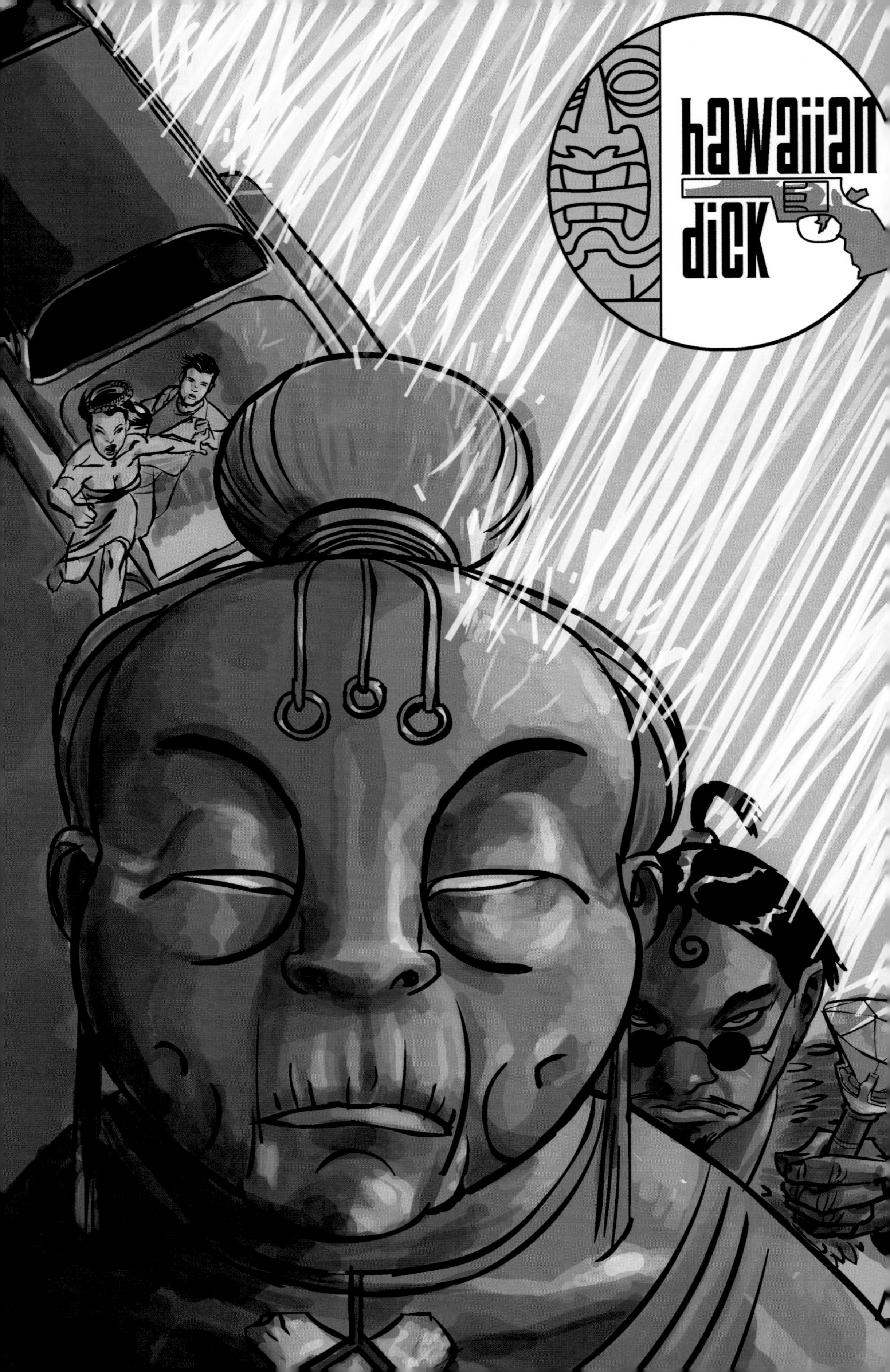
hawaiian
dick

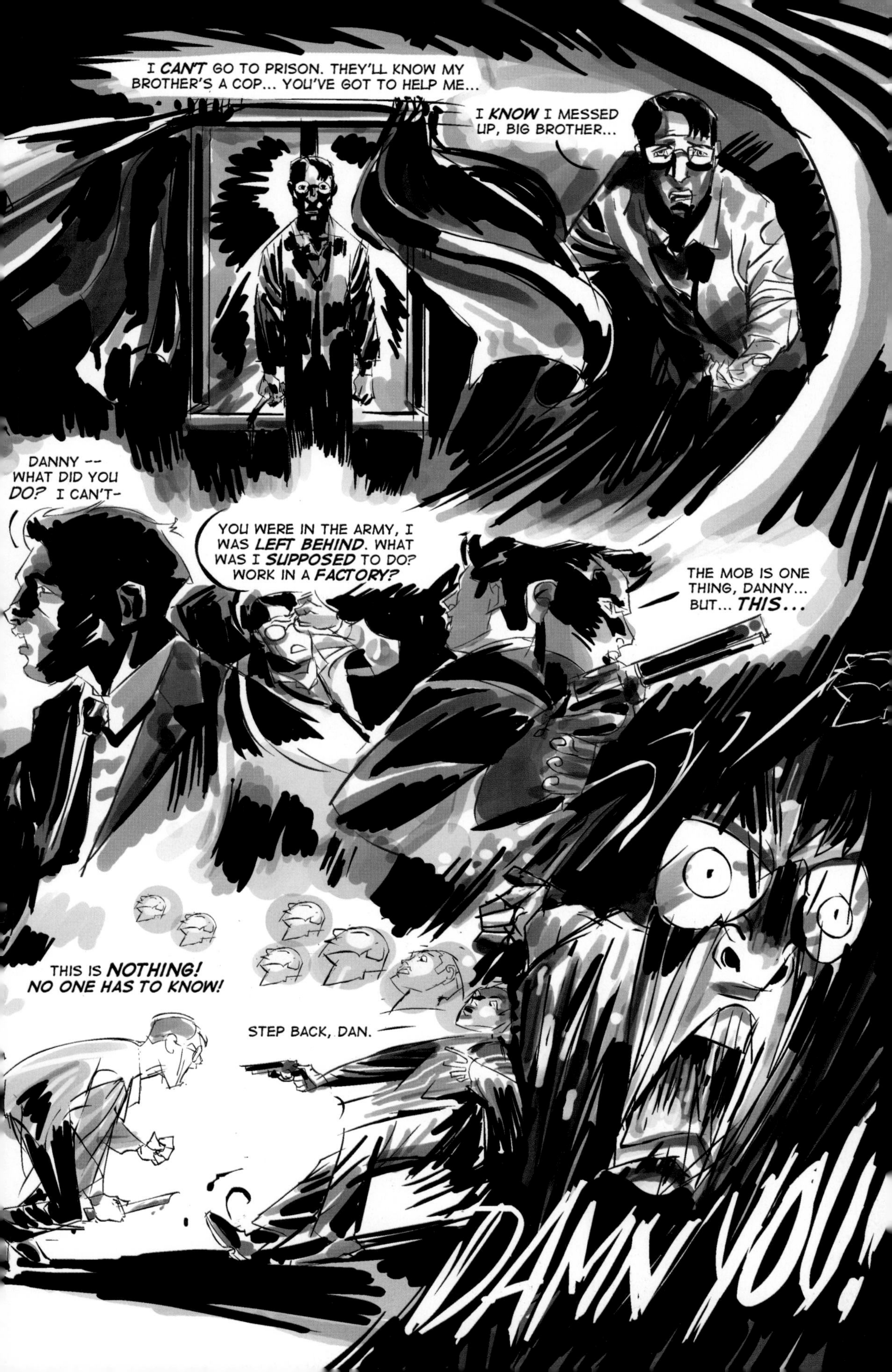
I CAN'T GO TO PRISON. THEY'LL KNOW MY BROTHER'S A COP... YOU'VE GOT TO HELP ME...
I KNOW I MESSED UP, BIG BROTHER...
DANNY -- WHAT DID YOU DO? I CAN'T-
YOU WERE IN THE ARMY, I WAS LEFT BEHIND. WHAT WAS I SUPPOSED TO DO? WORK IN A FACTORY?
THE MOB IS ONE THING, DANNY... BUT... THIS...
THIS IS NOTHING! NO ONE HAS TO KNOW!
STEP BACK, DAN.
DAMN YOU!

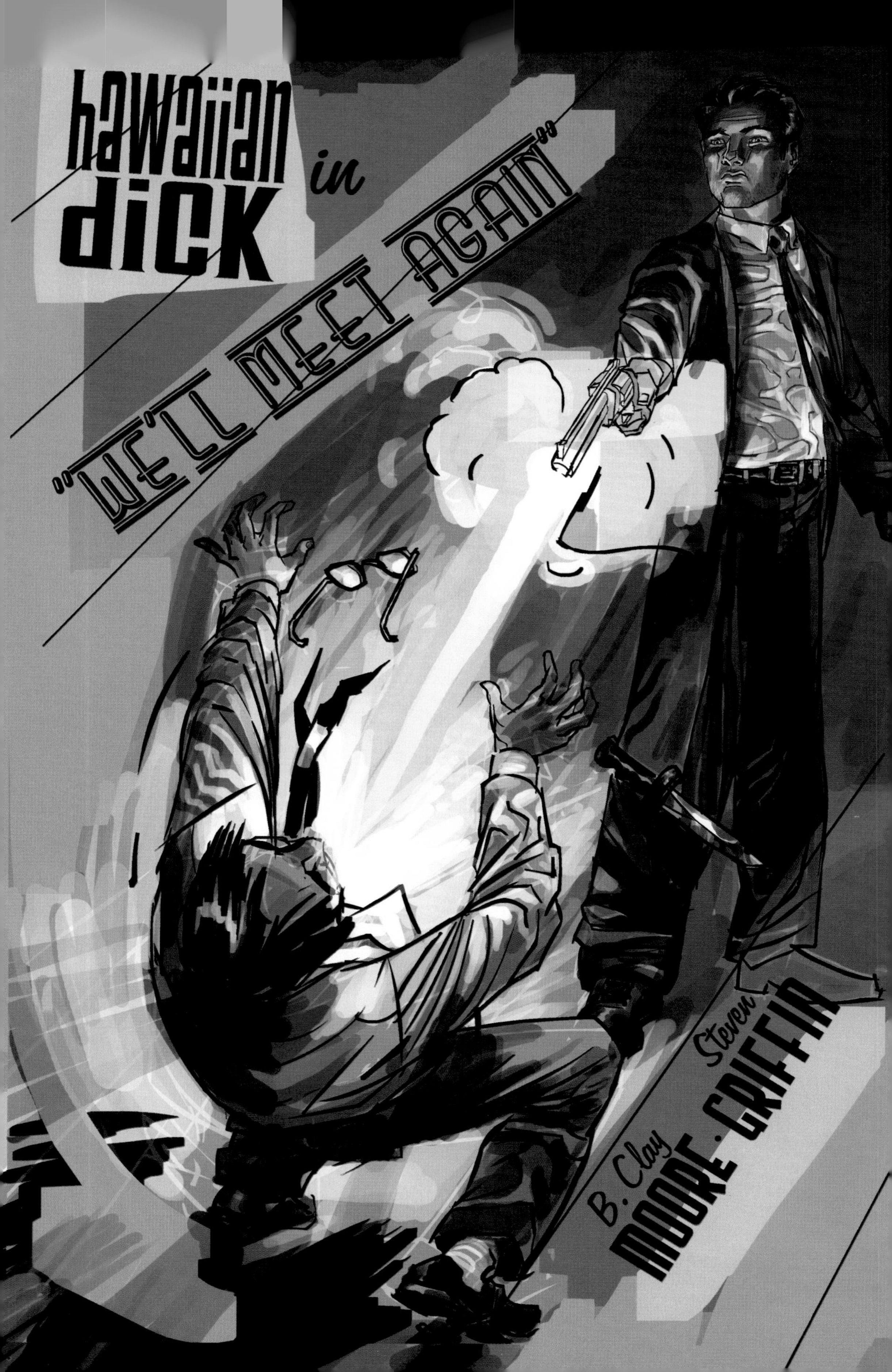
hawaiian dick
in
"WE'LL MEET AGAIN"
B. Clay MOORE
Steven GRIFFIN

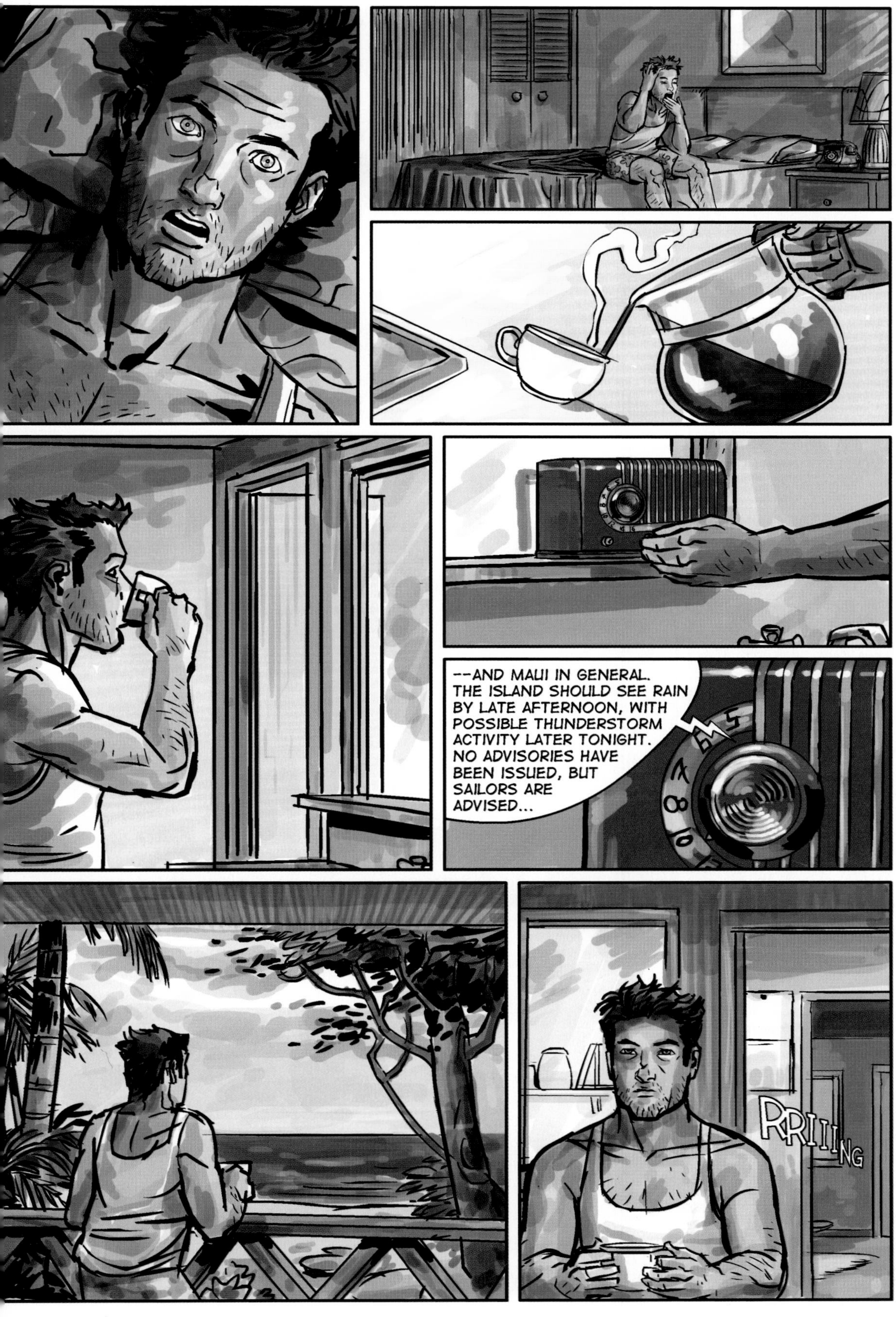
--AND MAUI IN GENERAL. THE ISLAND SHOULD SEE RAIN BY LATE AFTERNOON, WITH POSSIBLE THUNDERSTORM ACTIVITY LATER TONIGHT. NO ADVISORIES HAVE BEEN ISSUED, BUT SAILORS ARE ADVISED...
RRIIIING

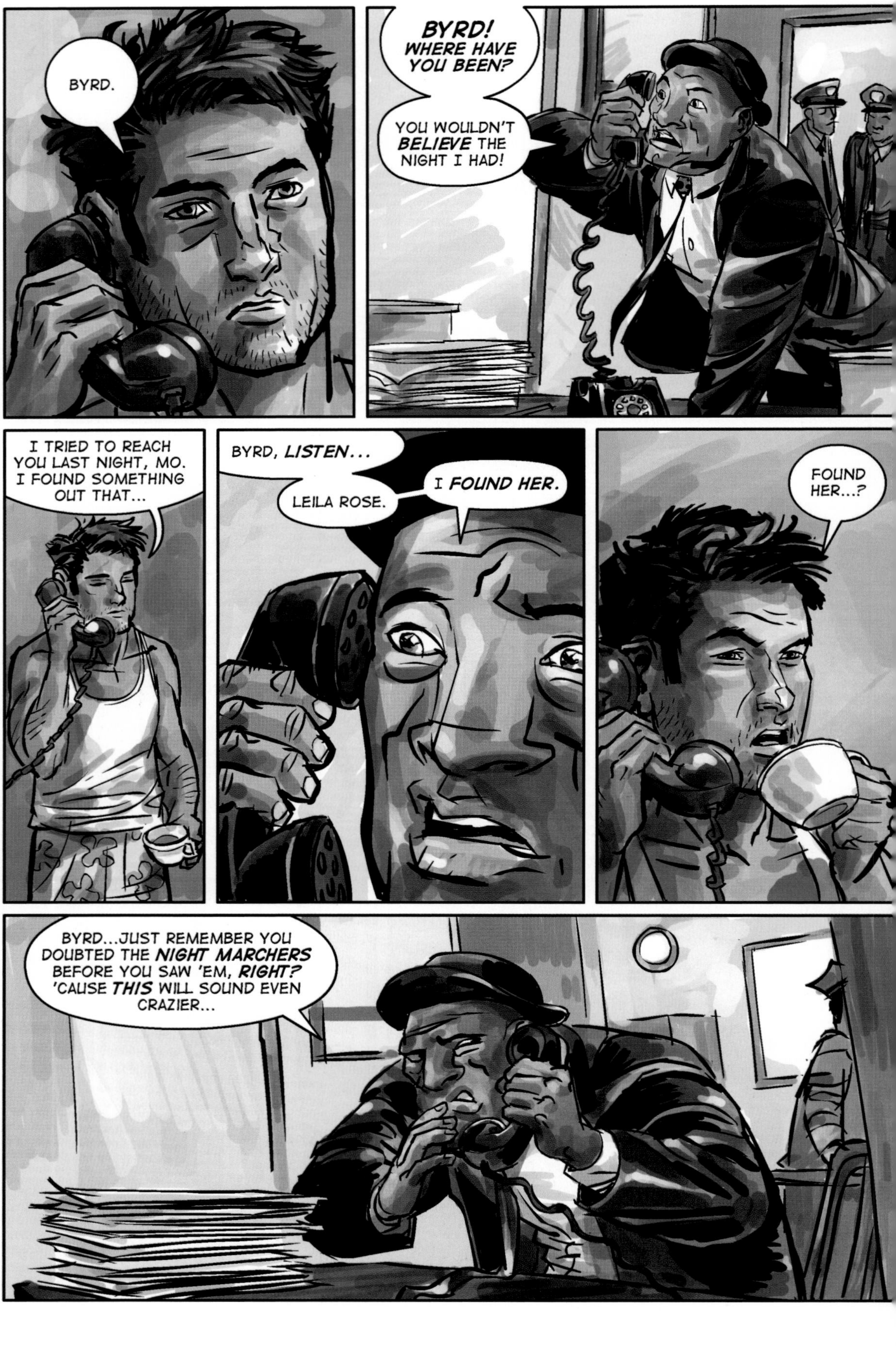

BYRD.
BYRD! WHERE HAVE YOU BEEN?
YOU WOULDN'T BELIEVE THE NIGHT I HAD!
I TRIED TO REACH YOU LAST NIGHT, MO. I FOUND SOMETHING OUT THAT...
BYRD, LISTEN...
LEILA ROSE.
I FOUND HER.
FOUND HER...?
BYRD...JUST REMEMBER YOU DOUBTED THE NIGHT MARCHERS BEFORE YOU SAW 'EM, RIGHT? 'CAUSE THIS WILL SOUND EVEN CRAZIER...

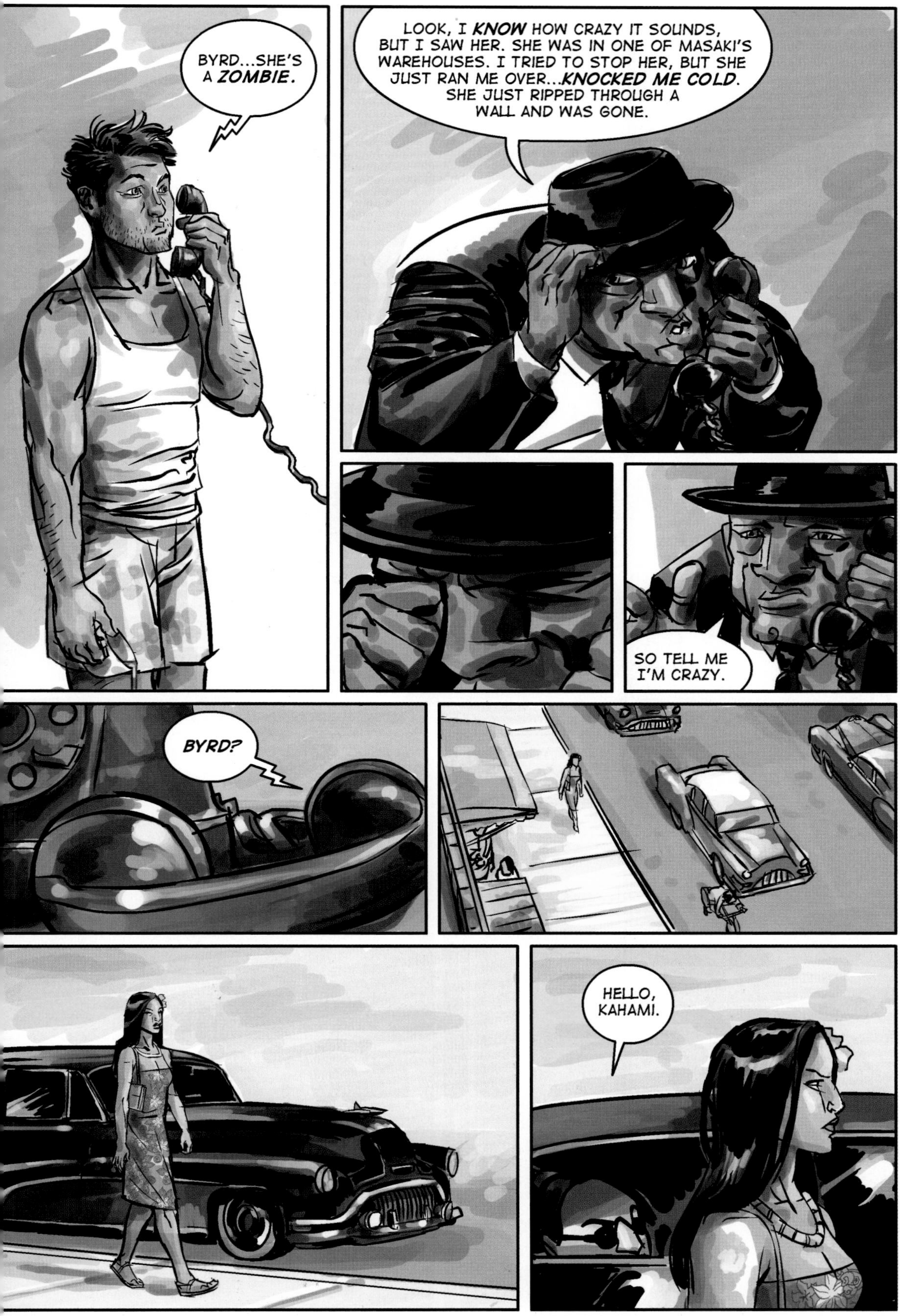
BYRD...SHE'S A ZOMBIE.
LOOK, I KNOW HOW CRAZY IT SOUNDS, BUT I SAW HER. SHE WAS IN ONE OF MASAKI'S WAREHOUSES. I TRIED TO STOP HER, BUT SHE JUST RAN ME OVER...KNOCKED ME COLD. SHE JUST RIPPED THROUGH A WALL AND WAS GONE.
SO TELL ME I'M CRAZY.
BYRD?
HELLO, KAHAMI.

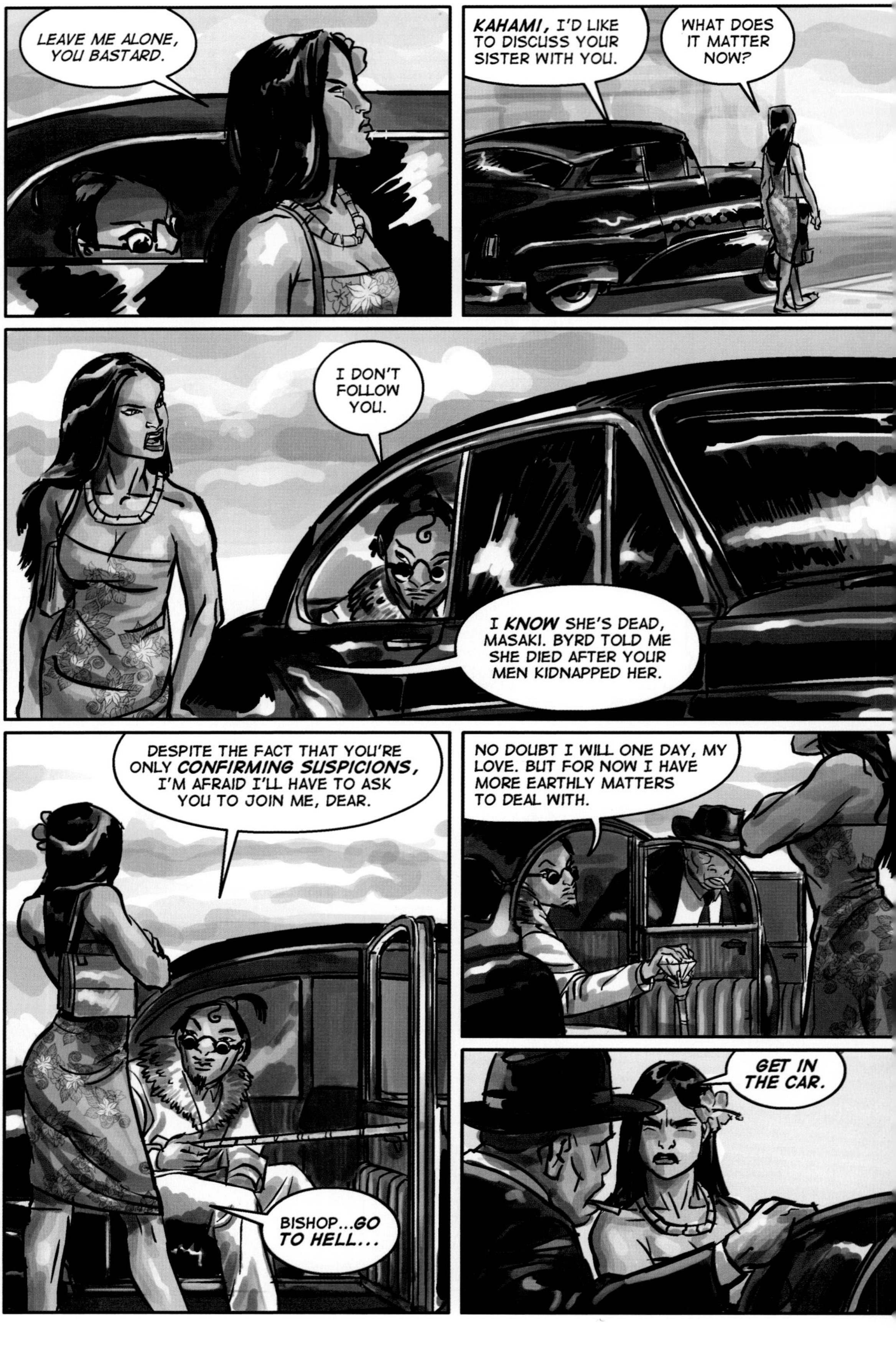
LEAVE ME ALONE, YOU BASTARD.
KAHAMI, I'D LIKE TO DISCUSS YOUR SISTER WITH YOU.
WHAT DOES IT MATTER NOW?
I DON'T FOLLOW YOU.
I KNOW SHE'S DEAD, MASAKI. BYRD TOLD ME SHE DIED AFTER YOUR MEN KIDNAPPED HER.
DESPITE THE FACT THAT YOU'RE ONLY CONFIRMING SUSPICIONS, I'M AFRAID I'LL HAVE TO ASK YOU TO JOIN ME, DEAR.
BISHOP...GO TO HELL...
NO DOUBT I WILL ONE DAY, MY LOVE. BUT FOR NOW I HAVE MORE EARTHLY MATTERS TO DEAL WITH.
GET IN THE CAR.

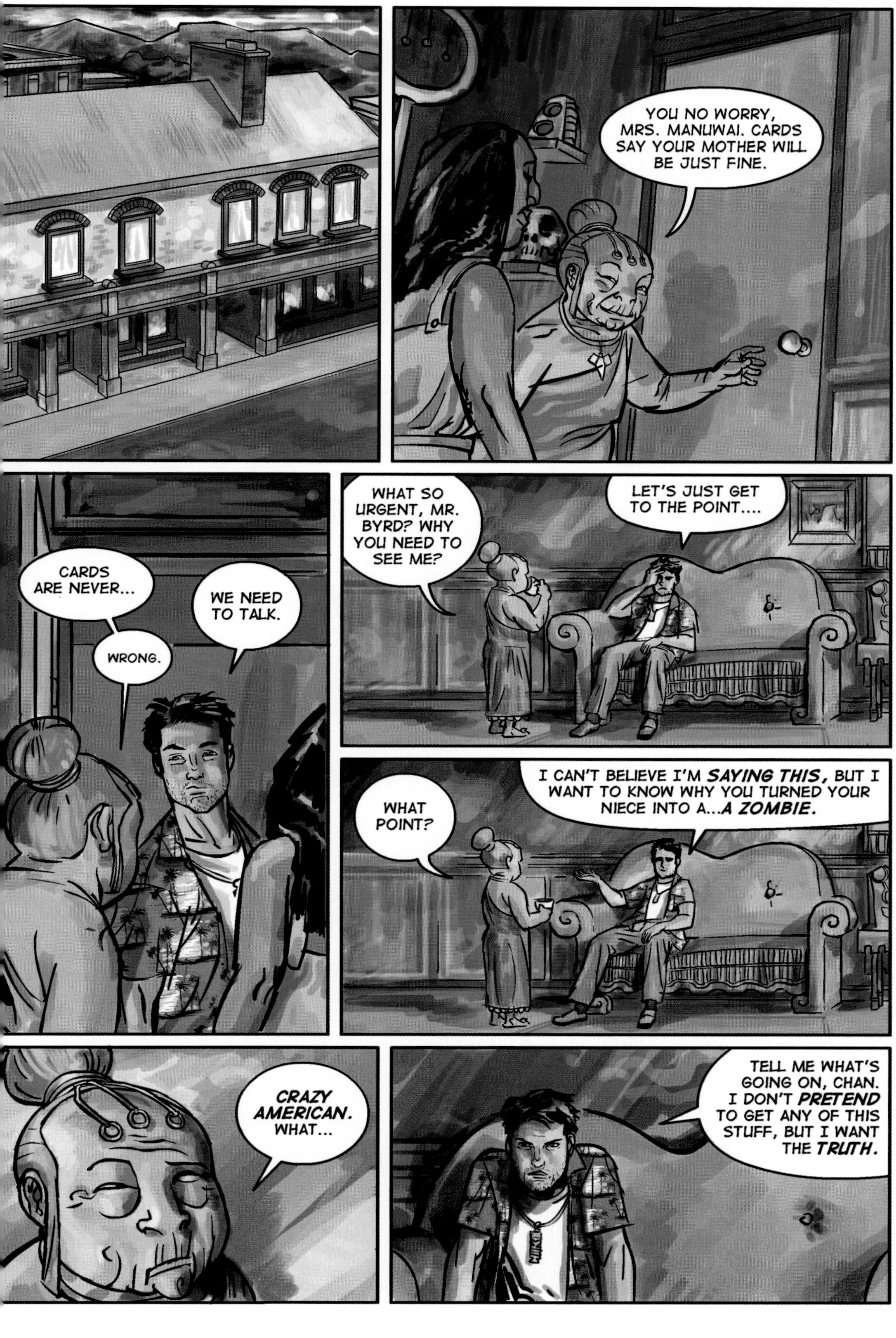
YOU NO WORRY, MRS. MANUWAI. CARDS SAY YOUR MOTHER WILL BE JUST FINE.
CARDS ARE NEVER...
WRONG.
WE NEED TO TALK.
WHAT SO URGENT, MR. BYRD? WHY YOU NEED TO SEE ME?
LET'S JUST GET TO THE POINT....
WHAT POINT?
I CAN'T BELIEVE I'M SAYING THIS, BUT I WANT TO KNOW WHY YOU TURNED YOUR NIECE INTO A...A ZOMBIE.
CRAZY AMERICAN. WHAT...
TELL ME WHAT'S GOING ON, CHAN. I DON'T PRETEND TO GET ANY OF THIS STUFF, BUT I WANT THE TRUTH.

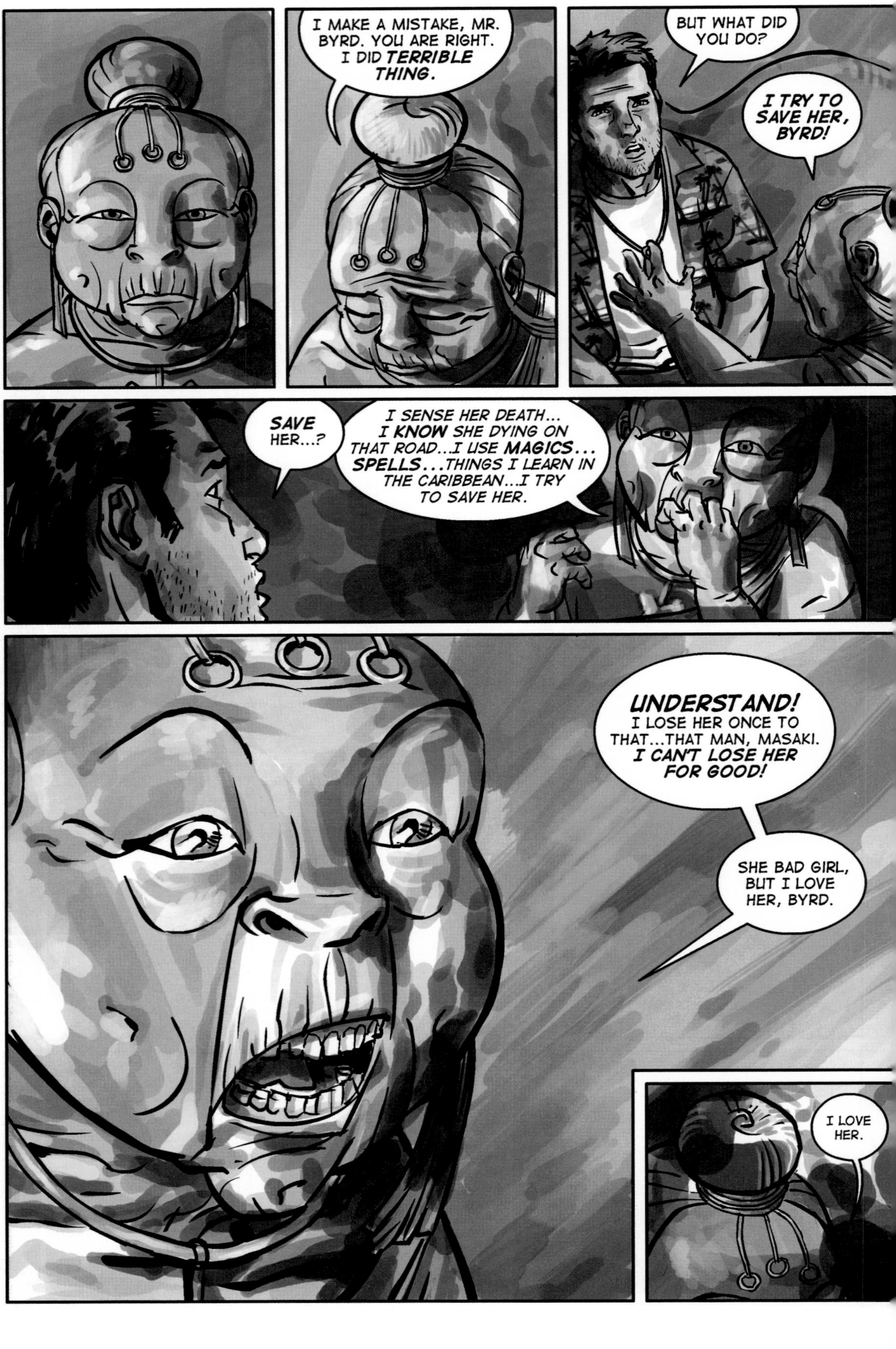
I MAKE A MISTAKE, MR. BYRD. YOU ARE RIGHT. I DID TERRIBLE THING.
BUT WHAT DID YOU DO?
I TRY TO SAVE HER, BYRD!
SAVE HER...?
I SENSE HER DEATH... I KNOW SHE DYING ON THAT ROAD...I USE MAGICS... SPELLS...THINGS I LEARN IN THE CARIBBEAN...I TRY TO SAVE HER.
UNDERSTAND! I LOSE HER ONCE TO THAT...THAT MAN, MASAKI. I CAN'T LOSE HER FOR GOOD!
SHE BAD GIRL, BUT I LOVE HER, BYRD.
I LOVE HER.

I KNOW THIS IS A STRANGE AND DIFFICULT THING, MA'AM... *BUT*...WHAT IS SHE DOING? WHY WAS SHE AT MASAKI'S WAREHOUSE LAST NIGHT? WHAT'S *DRIVING HER?*

MEMORIES.

SO-- *I MEAN*-- SHE REALLY *IS* A ZOMBIE?

SOME SAY ZOMBIE. SOME SAY LIVING DEAD.

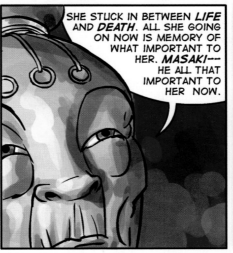

SHE STUCK IN BETWEEN *LIFE* AND *DEATH.* ALL SHE GOING ON NOW IS MEMORY OF WHAT IMPORTANT TO HER. *MASAKI*-- HE ALL THAT IMPORTANT TO HER NOW.

MO SAID SHE KNOCKED HIM OUT.

SHE *VERY STRONG.* HER WILL KEEP HER GOING--HARD TO STOP.

CAN SHE BE STOPPED?

STOP WHEN SHE FIND WHAT SHE LOOKING FOR. THEN SHE REST.

AND SHE WANTS *MASAKI...*

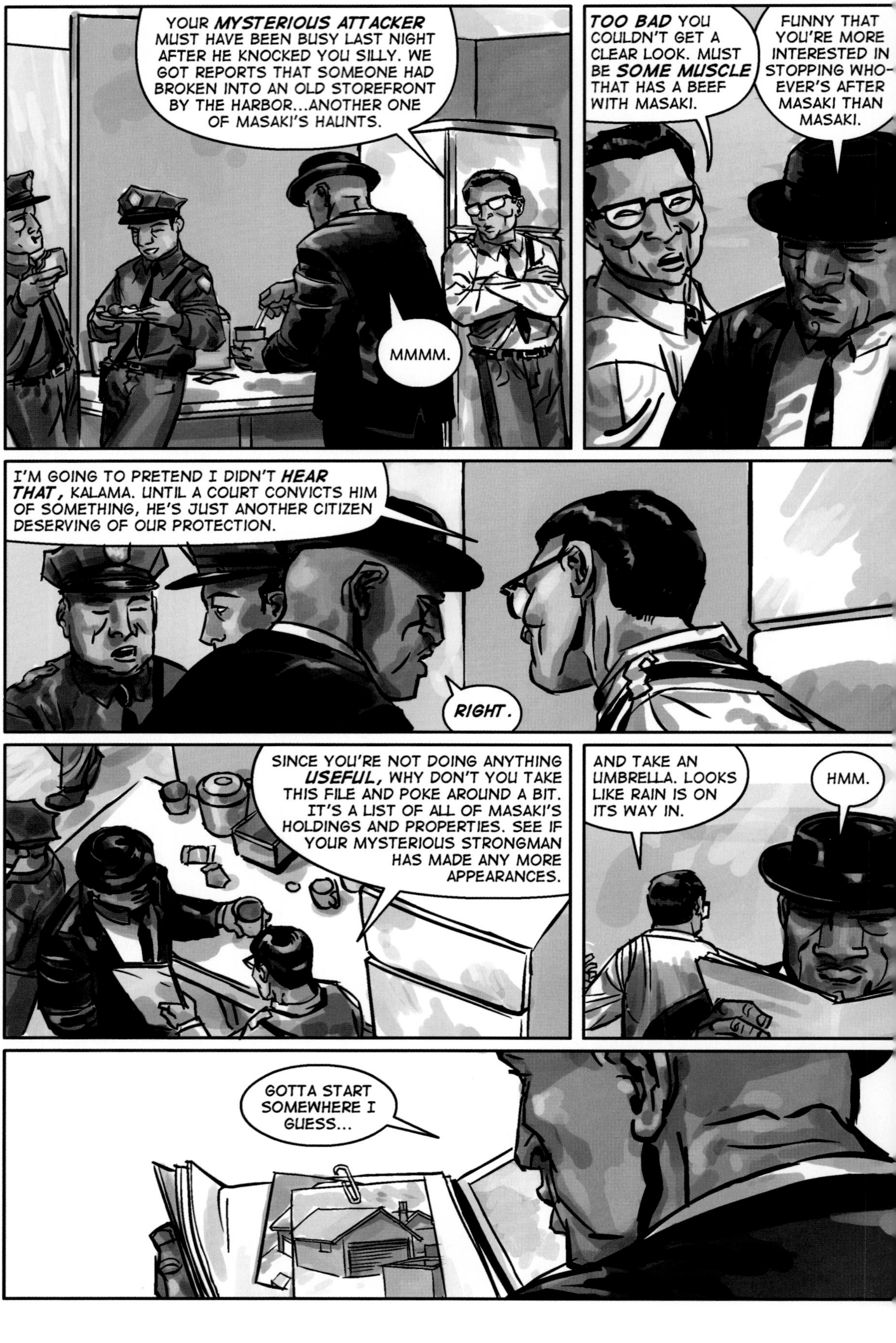
YOUR MYSTERIOUS ATTACKER MUST HAVE BEEN BUSY LAST NIGHT AFTER HE KNOCKED YOU SILLY. WE GOT REPORTS THAT SOMEONE HAD BROKEN INTO AN OLD STOREFRONT BY THE HARBOR...ANOTHER ONE OF MASAKI'S HAUNTS.
MMMM.
TOO BAD YOU COULDN'T GET A CLEAR LOOK. MUST BE SOME MUSCLE THAT HAS A BEEF WITH MASAKI.
FUNNY THAT YOU'RE MORE INTERESTED IN STOPPING WHO-EVER'S AFTER MASAKI THAN MASAKI.
I'M GOING TO PRETEND I DIDN'T HEAR THAT, KALAMA. UNTIL A COURT CONVICTS HIM OF SOMETHING, HE'S JUST ANOTHER CITIZEN DESERVING OF OUR PROTECTION.
RIGHT.
SINCE YOU'RE NOT DOING ANYTHING USEFUL, WHY DON'T YOU TAKE THIS FILE AND POKE AROUND A BIT. IT'S A LIST OF ALL OF MASAKI'S HOLDINGS AND PROPERTIES. SEE IF YOUR MYSTERIOUS STRONGMAN HAS MADE ANY MORE APPEARANCES.
AND TAKE AN UMBRELLA. LOOKS LIKE RAIN IS ON ITS WAY IN.
HMM.
GOTTA START SOMEWHERE I GUESS...

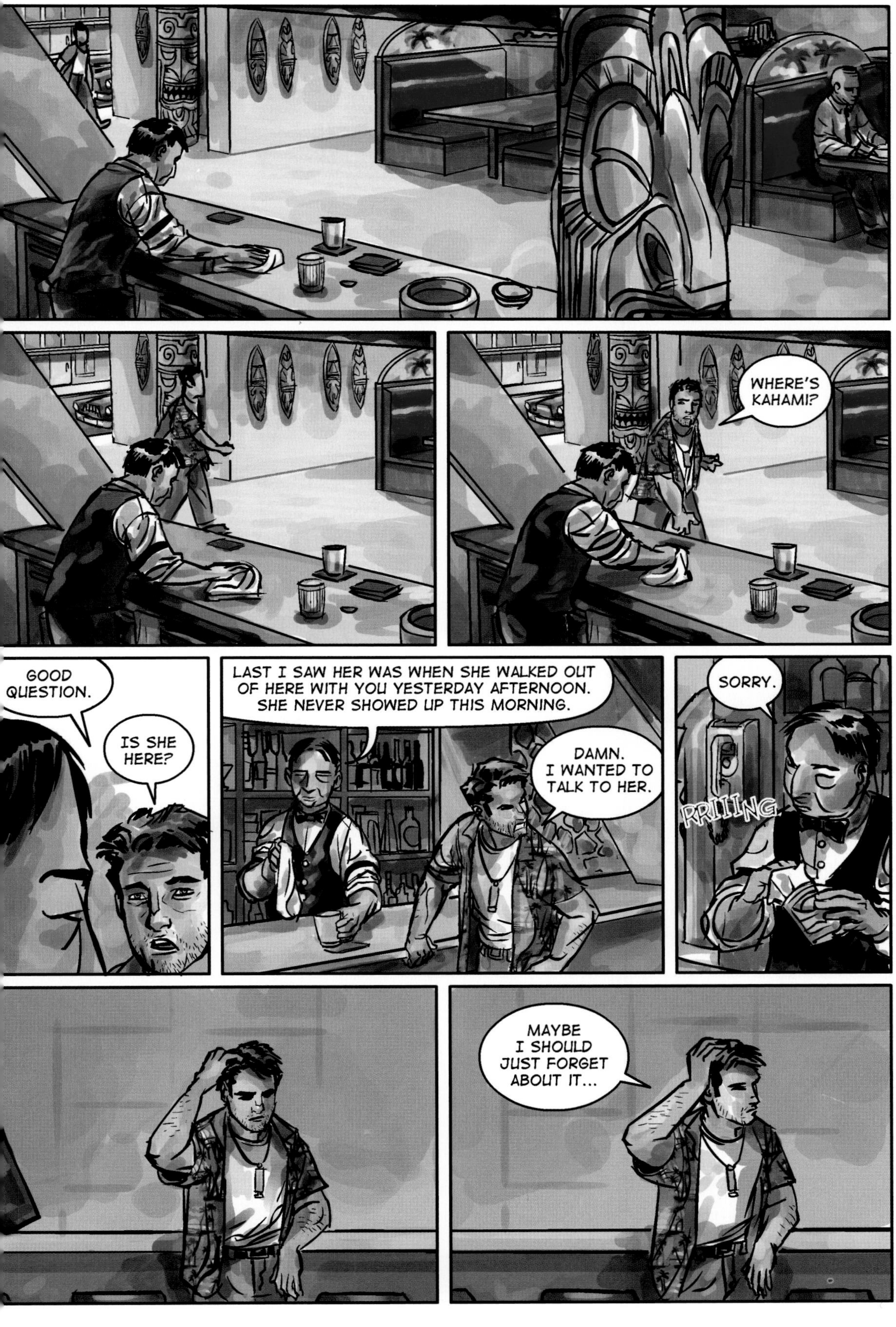
WHERE'S KAHAMI?
GOOD QUESTION.
IS SHE HERE?
LAST I SAW HER WAS WHEN SHE WALKED OUT OF HERE WITH YOU YESTERDAY AFTERNOON. SHE NEVER SHOWED UP THIS MORNING.
DAMN. I WANTED TO TALK TO HER.
SORRY.
RRIIING
MAYBE I SHOULD JUST FORGET ABOUT IT...

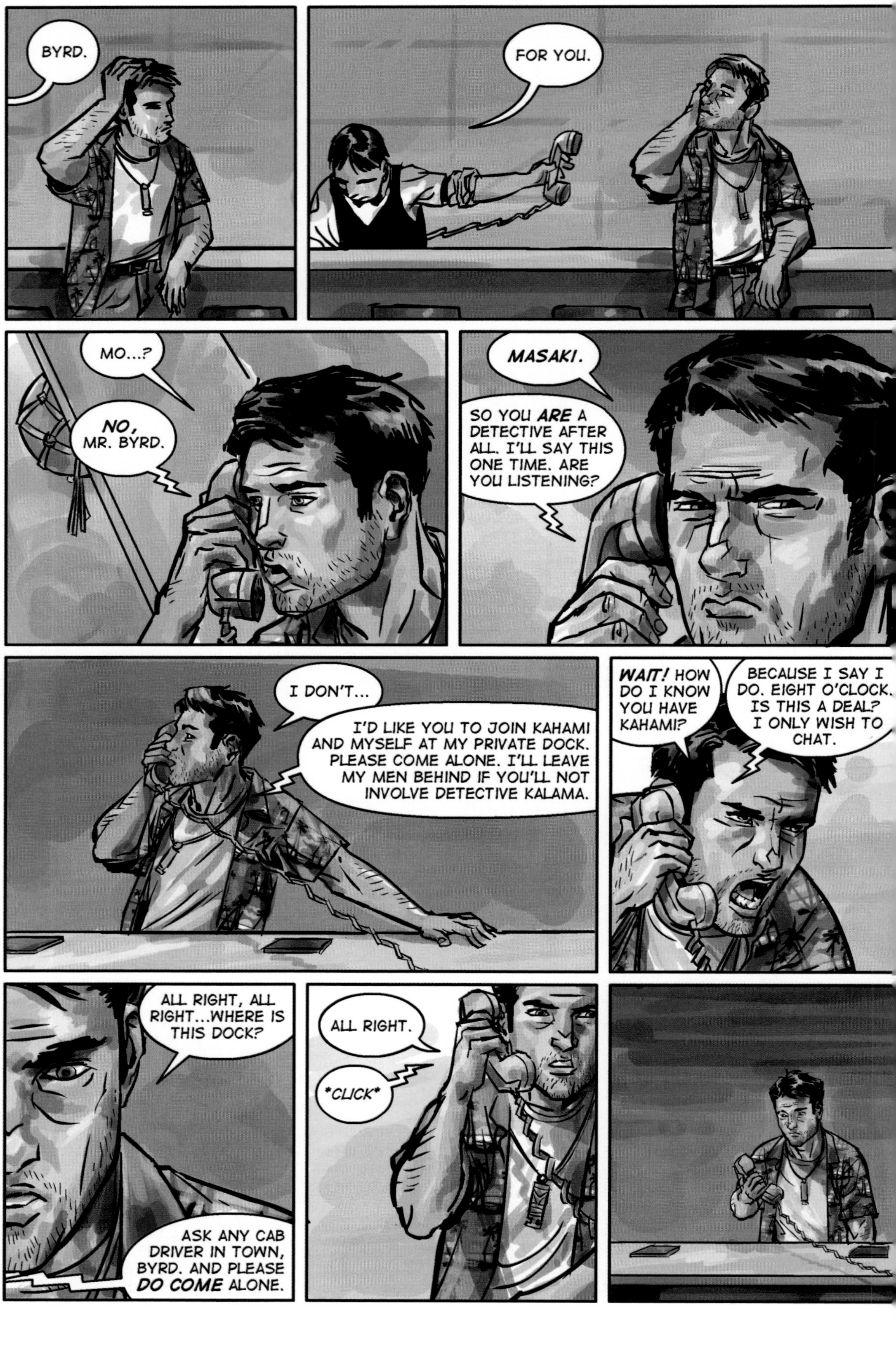
BYRD.
FOR YOU.
MO...?
NO, MR. BYRD.
MASAKI.
SO YOU ARE A DETECTIVE AFTER ALL. I'LL SAY THIS ONE TIME. ARE YOU LISTENING?
I DON'T...
I'D LIKE YOU TO JOIN KAHAMI AND MYSELF AT MY PRIVATE DOCK. PLEASE COME ALONE. I'LL LEAVE MY MEN BEHIND IF YOU'LL NOT INVOLVE DETECTIVE KALAMA.
WAIT! HOW DO I KNOW YOU HAVE KAHAMI?
BECAUSE I SAY I DO. EIGHT O'CLOCK. IS THIS A DEAL? I ONLY WISH TO CHAT.
ALL RIGHT, ALL RIGHT...WHERE IS THIS DOCK?
ASK ANY CAB DRIVER IN TOWN, BYRD. AND PLEASE DO COME ALONE.
ALL RIGHT.
CLICK

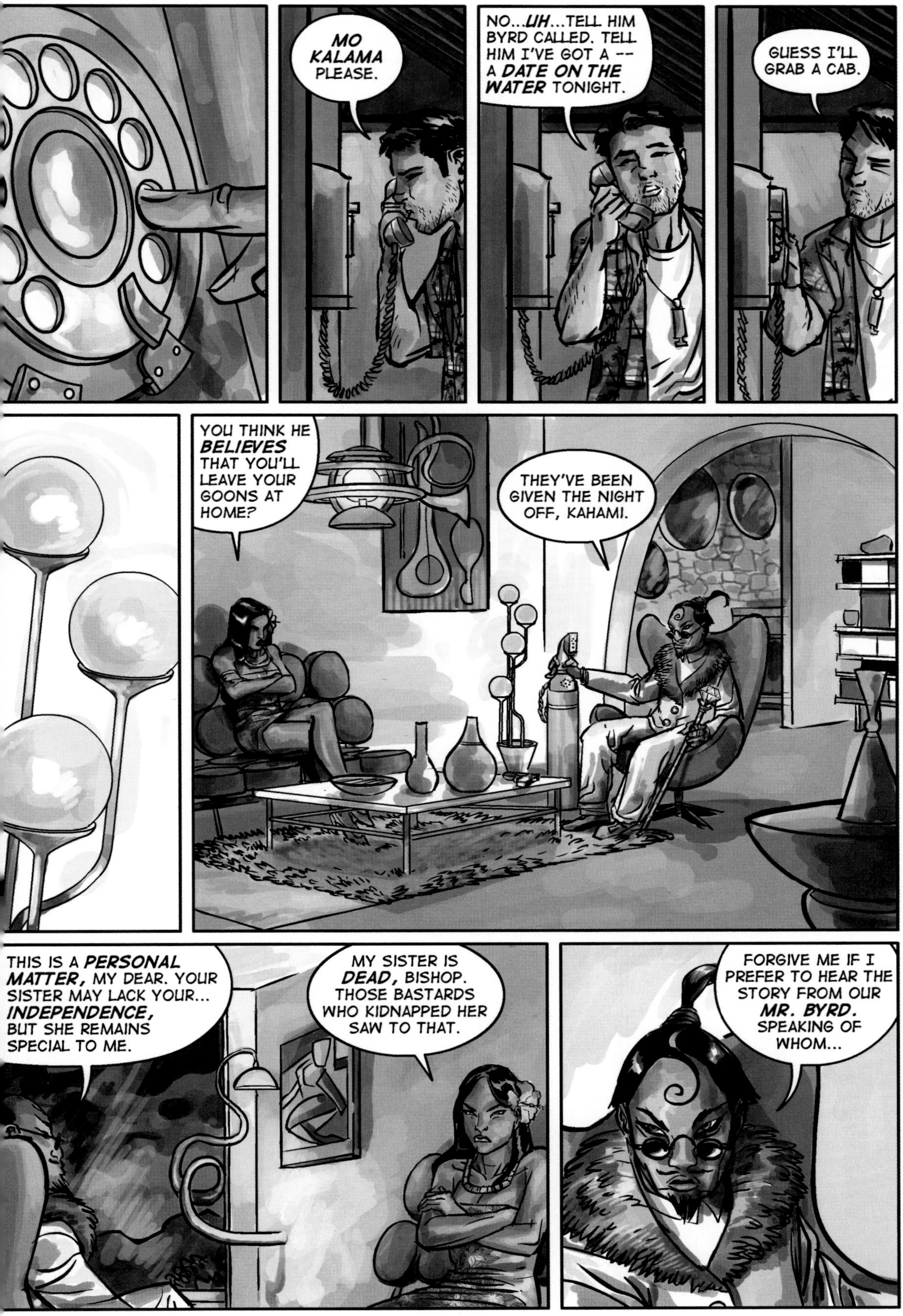
MO KALAMA PLEASE.
NO...UH...TELL HIM BYRD CALLED. TELL HIM I'VE GOT A -- A DATE ON THE WATER TONIGHT.
GUESS I'LL GRAB A CAB.
YOU THINK HE BELIEVES THAT YOU'LL LEAVE YOUR GOONS AT HOME?
THEY'VE BEEN GIVEN THE NIGHT OFF, KAHAMI.
THIS IS A PERSONAL MATTER, MY DEAR. YOUR SISTER MAY LACK YOUR... INDEPENDENCE, BUT SHE REMAINS SPECIAL TO ME.
MY SISTER IS DEAD, BISHOP. THOSE BASTARDS WHO KIDNAPPED HER SAW TO THAT.
FORGIVE ME IF I PREFER TO HEAR THE STORY FROM OUR MR. BYRD. SPEAKING OF WHOM...

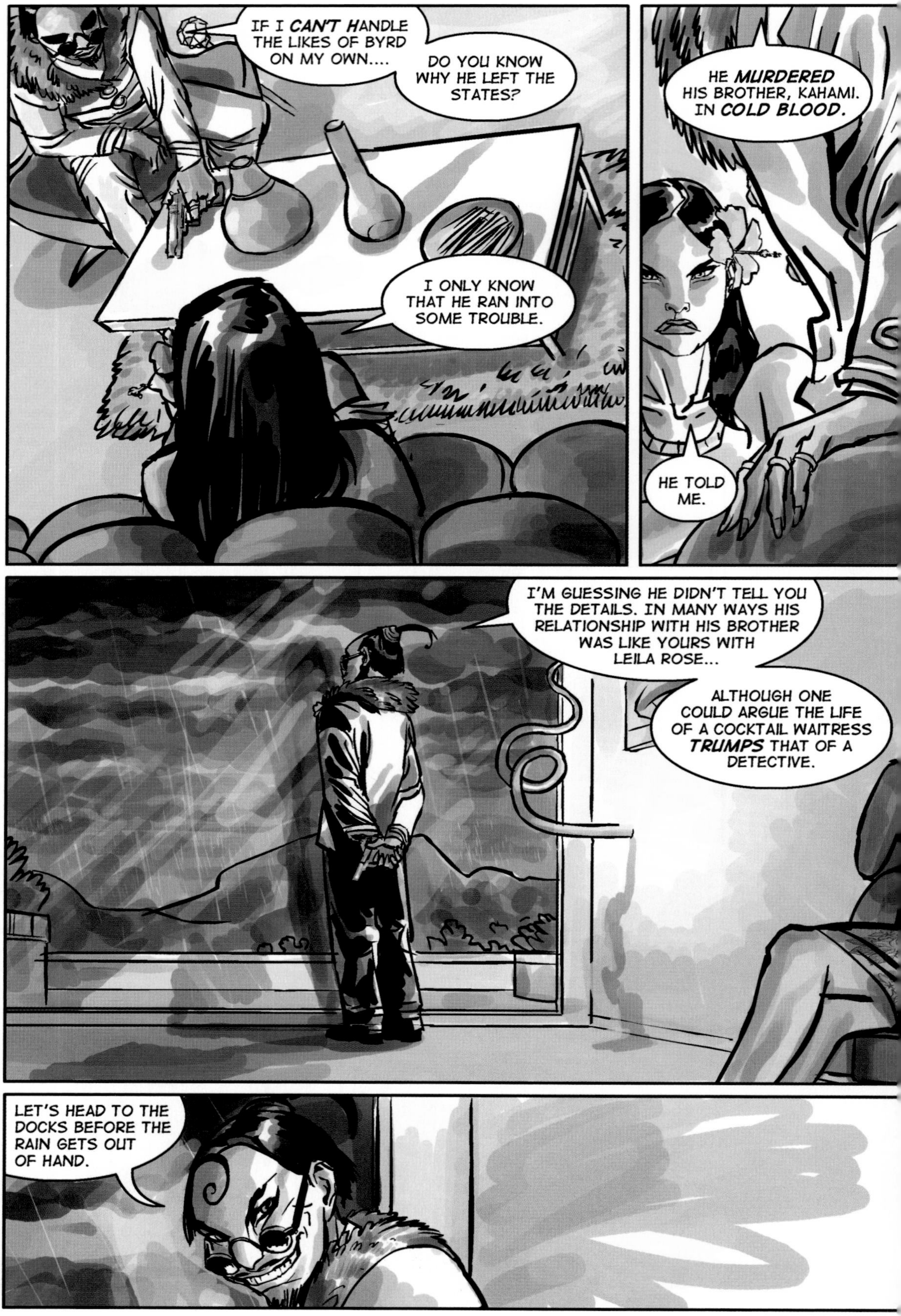

IF I ***CAN'T H***ANDLE THE LIKES OF BYRD ON MY OWN....
DO YOU KNOW WHY HE LEFT THE STATES?
I ONLY KNOW THAT HE RAN INTO SOME TROUBLE.
HE ***MURDERED*** HIS BROTHER, KAHAMI. IN ***COLD BLOOD.***
HE TOLD ME.
I'M GUESSING HE DIDN'T TELL YOU THE DETAILS. IN MANY WAYS HIS RELATIONSHIP WITH HIS BROTHER WAS LIKE YOURS WITH LEILA ROSE...
ALTHOUGH ONE COULD ARGUE THE LIFE OF A COCKTAIL WAITRESS ***TRUMPS*** THAT OF A DETECTIVE.
LET'S HEAD TO THE DOCKS BEFORE THE RAIN GETS OUT OF HAND.

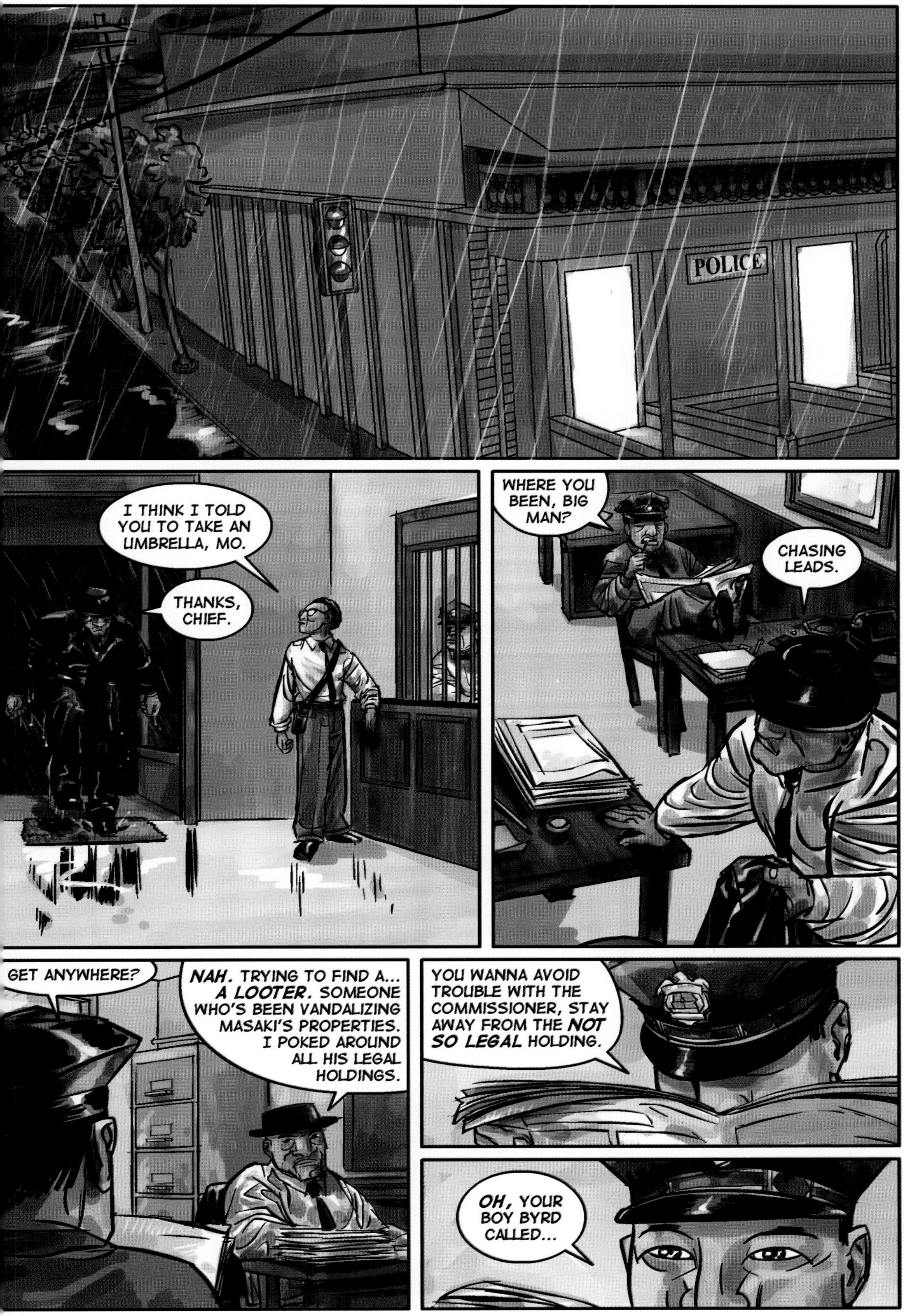

POLICE
I THINK I TOLD YOU TO TAKE AN UMBRELLA, MO.
THANKS, CHIEF.
WHERE YOU BEEN, BIG MAN?
CHASING LEADS.
GET ANYWHERE?
NAH. TRYING TO FIND A... A LOOTER. SOMEONE WHO'S BEEN VANDALIZING MASAKI'S PROPERTIES. I POKED AROUND ALL HIS LEGAL HOLDINGS.
YOU WANNA AVOID TROUBLE WITH THE COMMISSIONER, STAY AWAY FROM THE NOT SO LEGAL HOLDING.
OH, YOUR BOY BYRD CALLED...

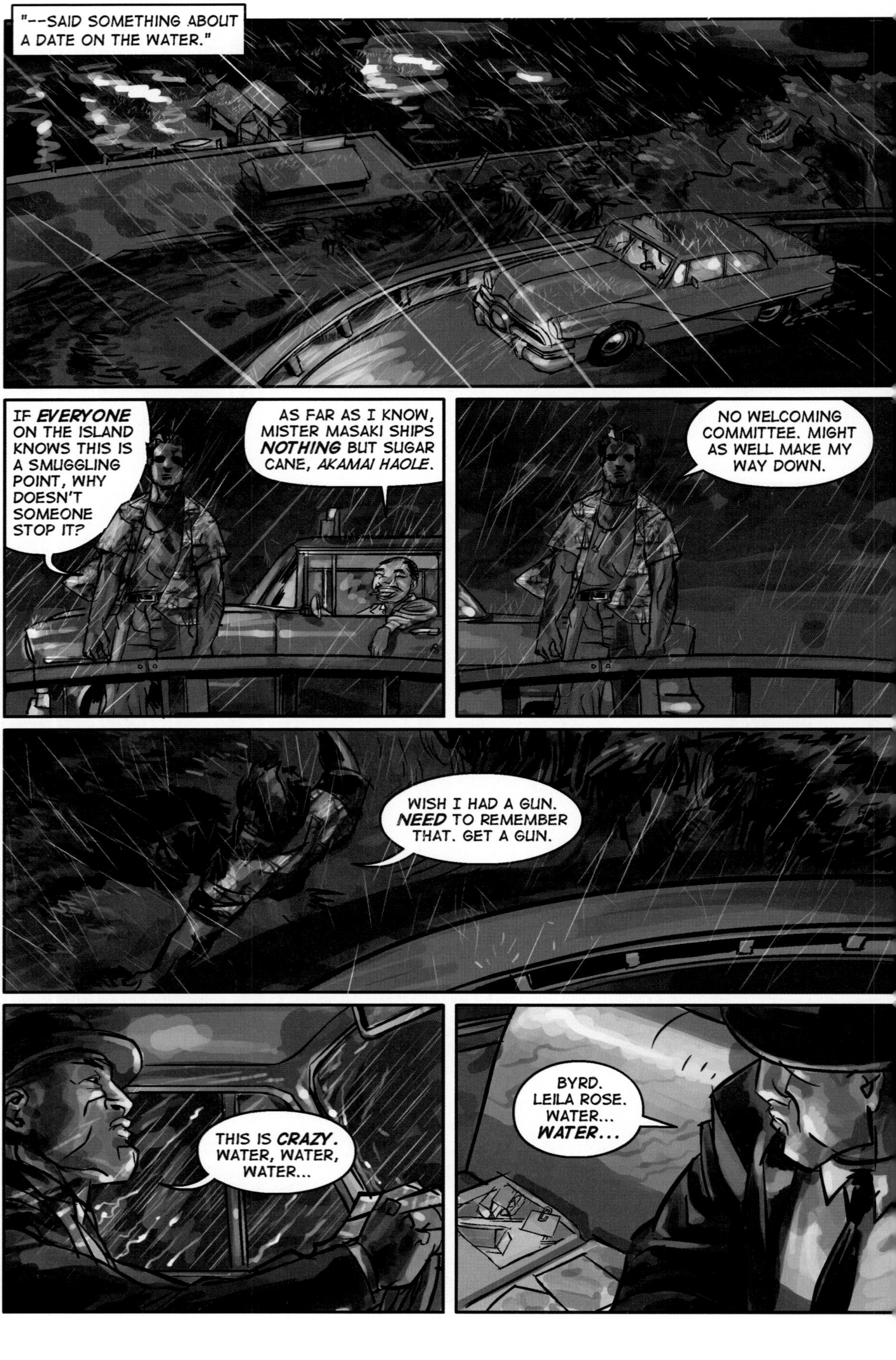

"--SAID SOMETHING ABOUT A DATE ON THE WATER."
IF EVERYONE ON THE ISLAND KNOWS THIS IS A SMUGGLING POINT, WHY DOESN'T SOMEONE STOP IT?
AS FAR AS I KNOW, MISTER MASAKI SHIPS NOTHING BUT SUGAR CANE, AKAMAI HAOLE.
NO WELCOMING COMMITTEE. MIGHT AS WELL MAKE MY WAY DOWN.
WISH I HAD A GUN. NEED TO REMEMBER THAT. GET A GUN.
THIS IS CRAZY. WATER, WATER, WATER...
BYRD. LEILA ROSE. WATER... WATER...

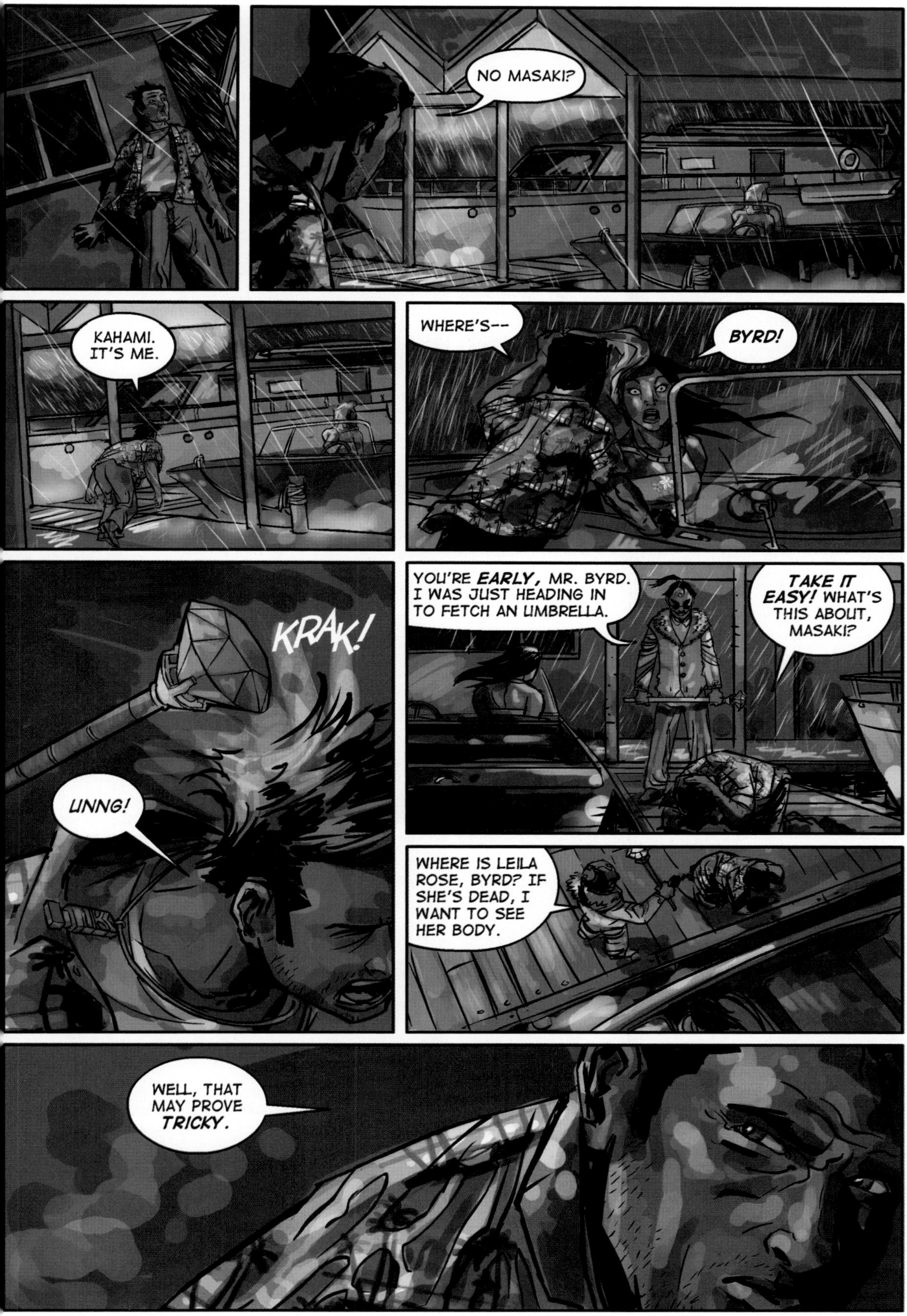
NO MASAKI?
KAHAMI. IT'S ME.
WHERE'S--
BYRD!
KRAK!
UNNG!
YOU'RE EARLY, MR. BYRD. I WAS JUST HEADING IN TO FETCH AN UMBRELLA.
TAKE IT EASY! WHAT'S THIS ABOUT, MASAKI?
WHERE IS LEILA ROSE, BYRD? IF SHE'S DEAD, I WANT TO SEE HER BODY.
WELL, THAT MAY PROVE TRICKY.

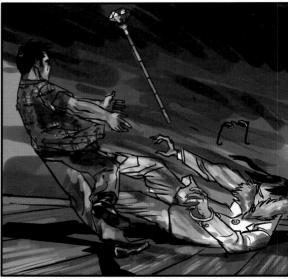

WELL, MR. BYRD. *CONGRATULATIONS.* YOU'VE WRINKLED A FINE SUIT.

I *COULD* EXTRACT THIS INFORMATION FROM DETECTIVE KALAMA, BUT I *HATE* TO TARNISH MY EXCELLENT RELATIONSHIP WITH THE LOCAL AUTHORITIES. *FEW PEOPLE* WOULD MISS A DISREPUTABLE AMERICAN WHO MURDERED HIS OWN BROTHER.

NO ONE WILL MISS *DRUG DEALING SCUM,* EITHER.

LEILA ROSE NOT *ENOUGH* FOR YOU, *PUA'A?* NOW YOU TAKE KAHAMI, TOO?

CHAN?

KRA-KA-KOW!

KRAK!

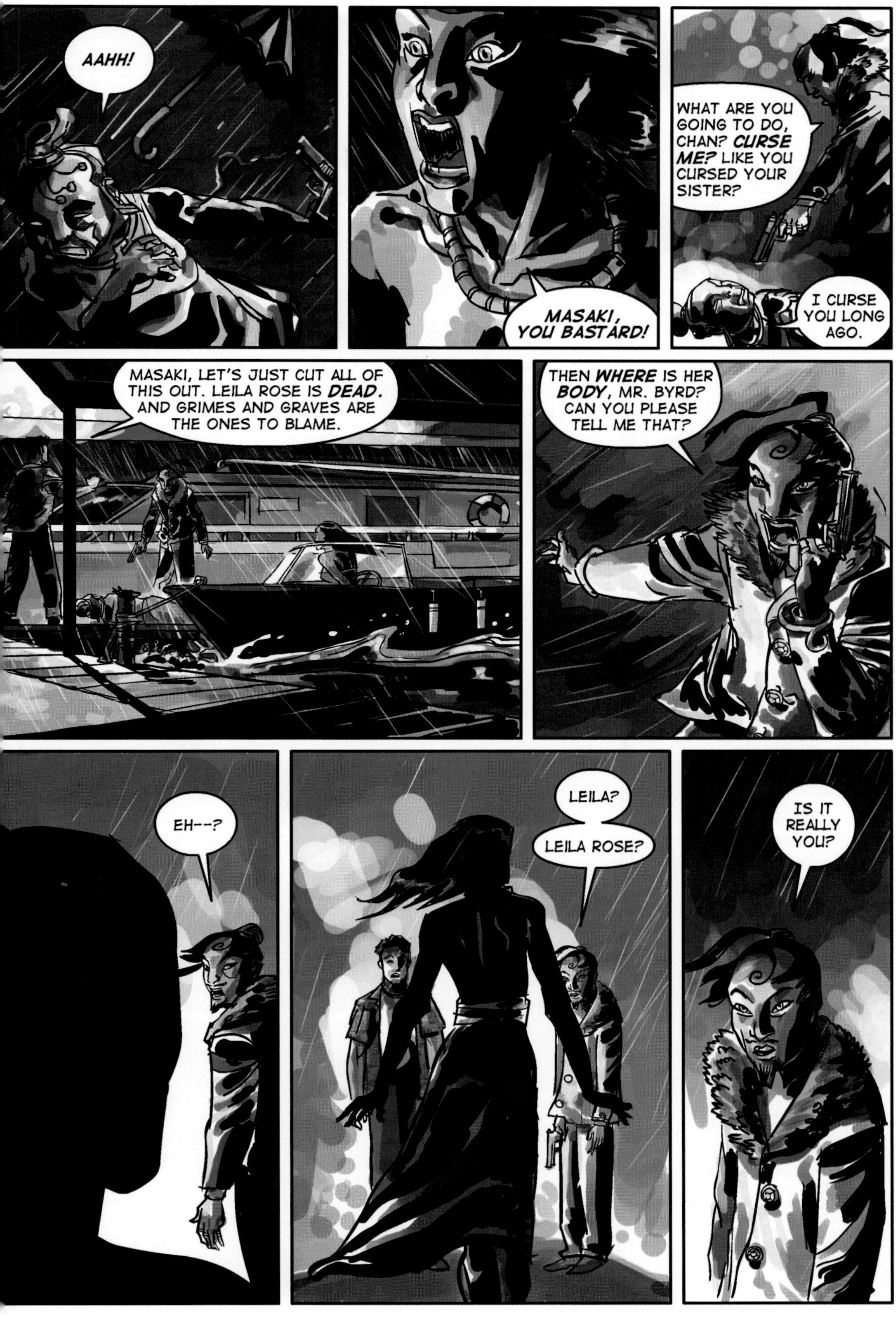
AAHH!
MASAKI, YOU BASTARD!
WHAT ARE YOU GOING TO DO, CHAN? CURSE ME? LIKE YOU CURSED YOUR SISTER?
I CURSE YOU LONG AGO.
MASAKI, LET'S JUST CUT ALL OF THIS OUT. LEILA ROSE IS DEAD. AND GRIMES AND GRAVES ARE THE ONES TO BLAME.
THEN WHERE IS HER BODY, MR. BYRD? CAN YOU PLEASE TELL ME THAT?
EH--?
LEILA?
LEILA ROSE?
IS IT REALLY YOU?

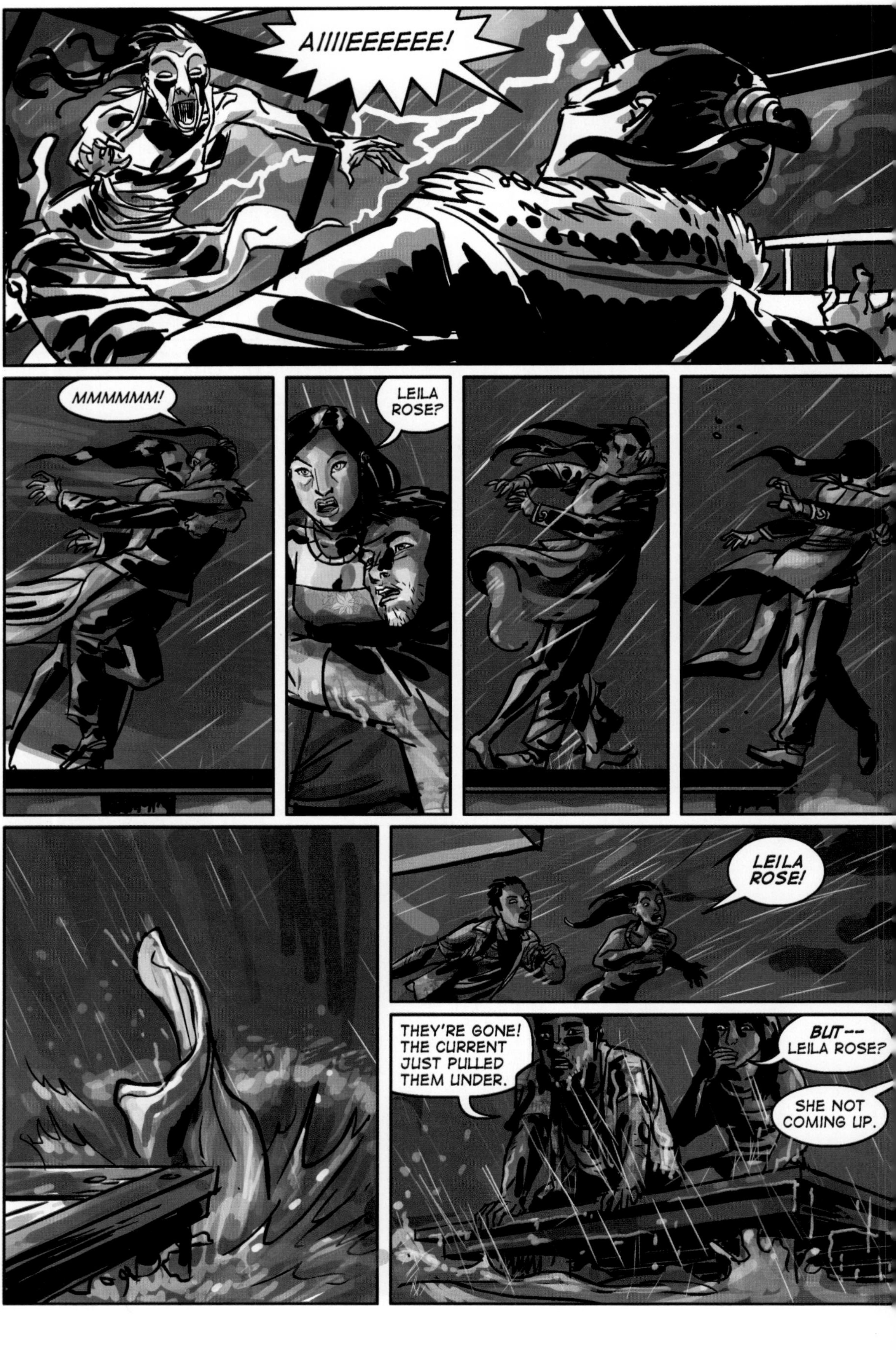
AIIIIEEEEEEE!
MMMMMMM!
LEILA ROSE?
LEILA ROSE!
THEY'RE GONE! THE CURRENT JUST PULLED THEM UNDER.
BUT--- LEILA ROSE?
SHE NOT COMING UP.

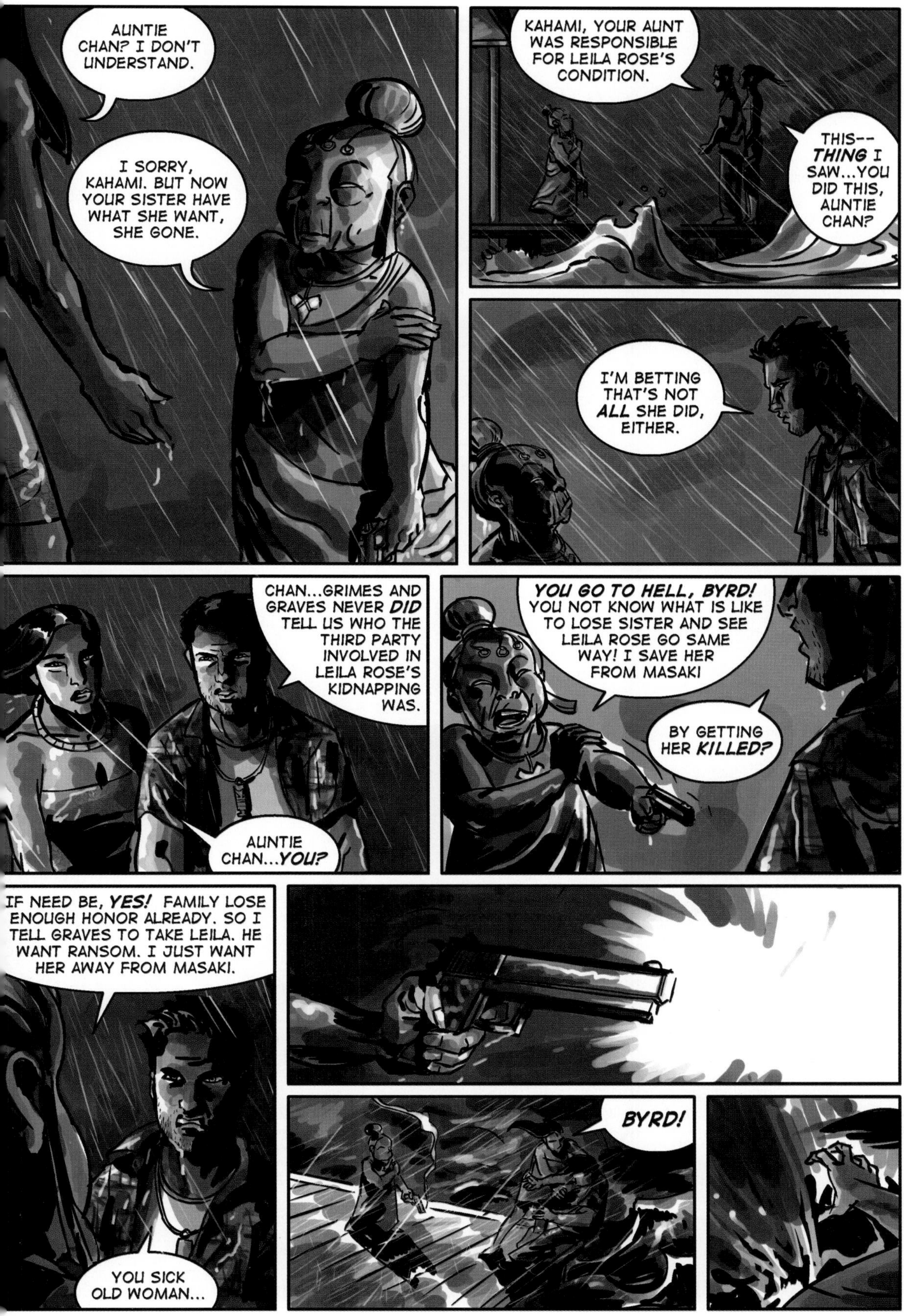
AUNTIE CHAN? I DON'T UNDERSTAND.
I SORRY, KAHAMI. BUT NOW YOUR SISTER HAVE WHAT SHE WANT, SHE GONE.
KAHAMI, YOUR AUNT WAS RESPONSIBLE FOR LEILA ROSE'S CONDITION.
THIS--*THING* I SAW...YOU DID THIS, AUNTIE CHAN?
I'M BETTING THAT'S NOT *ALL* SHE DID, EITHER.
CHAN...GRIMES AND GRAVES NEVER *DID* TELL US WHO THE THIRD PARTY INVOLVED IN LEILA ROSE'S KIDNAPPING WAS.
AUNTIE CHAN...*YOU?*
YOU GO TO HELL, BYRD! YOU NOT KNOW WHAT IS LIKE TO LOSE SISTER AND SEE LEILA ROSE GO SAME WAY! I SAVE HER FROM MASAKI
BY GETTING HER *KILLED?*
IF NEED BE, *YES!* FAMILY LOSE ENOUGH HONOR ALREADY. SO I TELL GRAVES TO TAKE LEILA. HE WANT RANSOM. I JUST WANT HER AWAY FROM MASAKI.
YOU SICK OLD WOMAN...
BYRD!

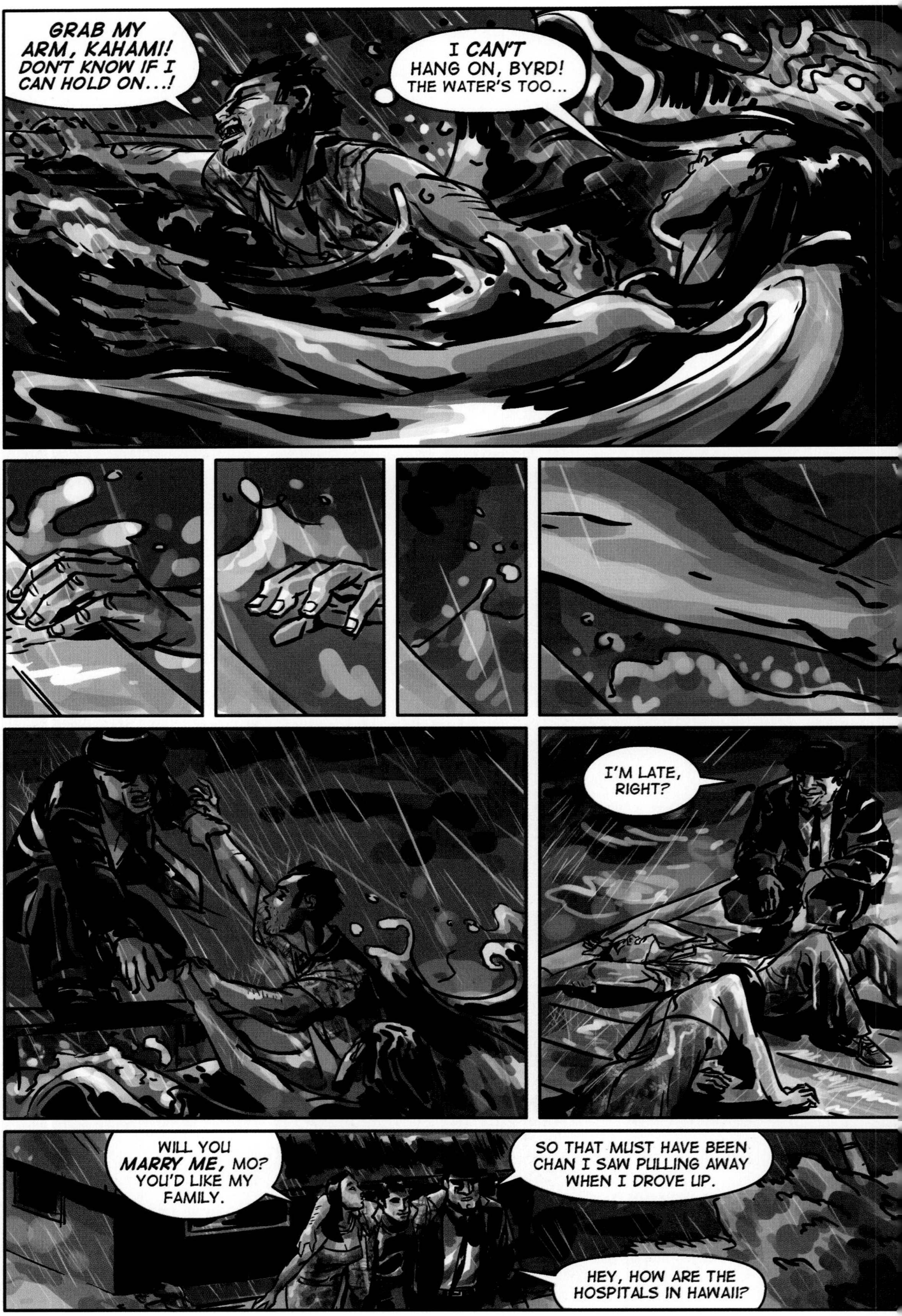
GRAB MY ARM, KAHAMI! DON'T KNOW IF I CAN HOLD ON...!
I CAN'T HANG ON, BYRD! THE WATER'S TOO...
I'M LATE, RIGHT?
WILL YOU MARRY ME, MO? YOU'D LIKE MY FAMILY.
SO THAT MUST HAVE BEEN CHAN I SAW PULLING AWAY WHEN I DROVE UP.
HEY, HOW ARE THE HOSPITALS IN HAWAII?

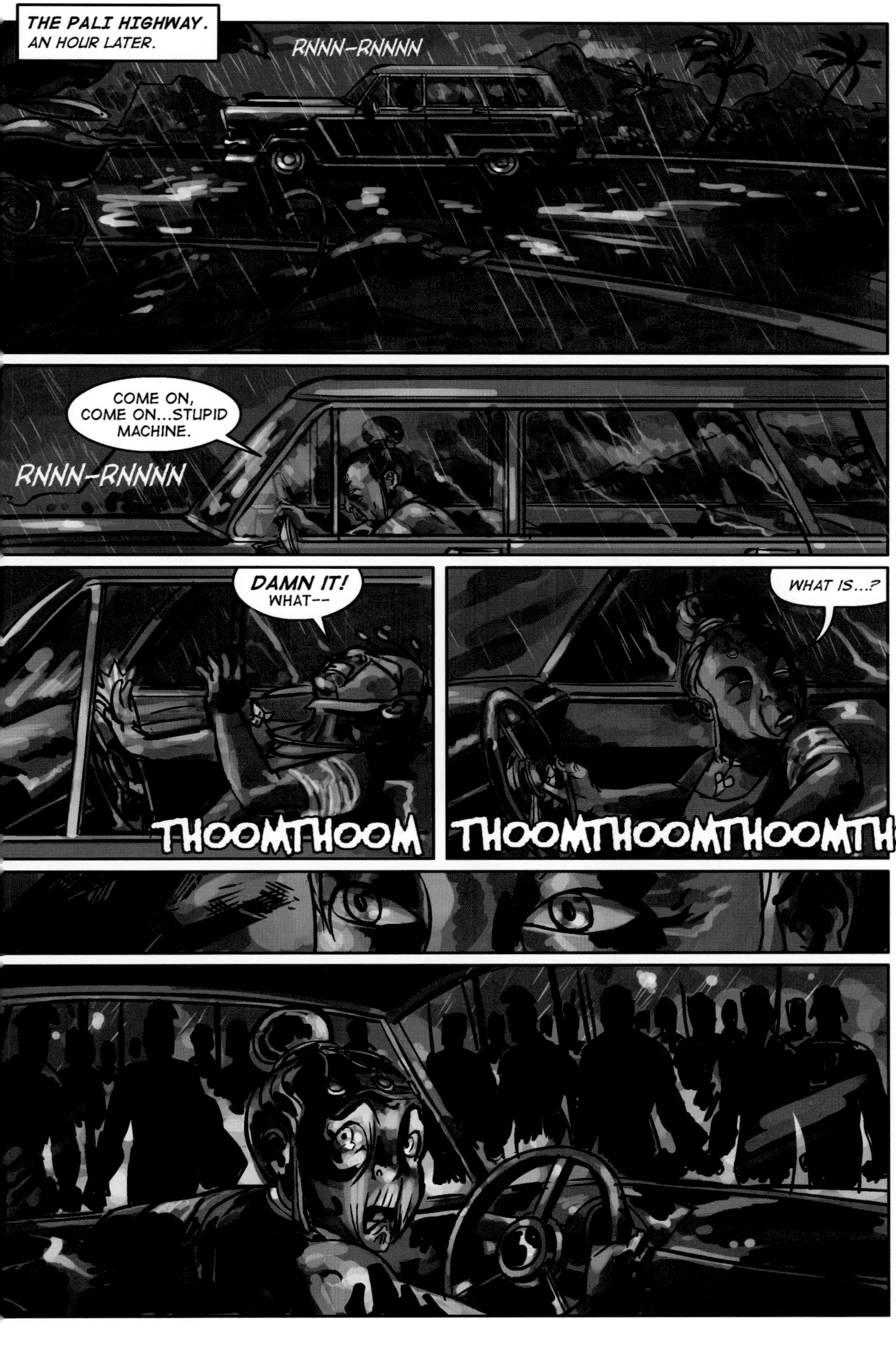
THE PALI HIGHWAY.
AN HOUR LATER.
RNNN-RNNNN
COME ON, COME ON...STUPID MACHINE.
RNNN-RNNNN
DAMN IT! WHAT--
THOOMTHOOM
WHAT IS...?
THOOMTHOOMTHOOMTHO

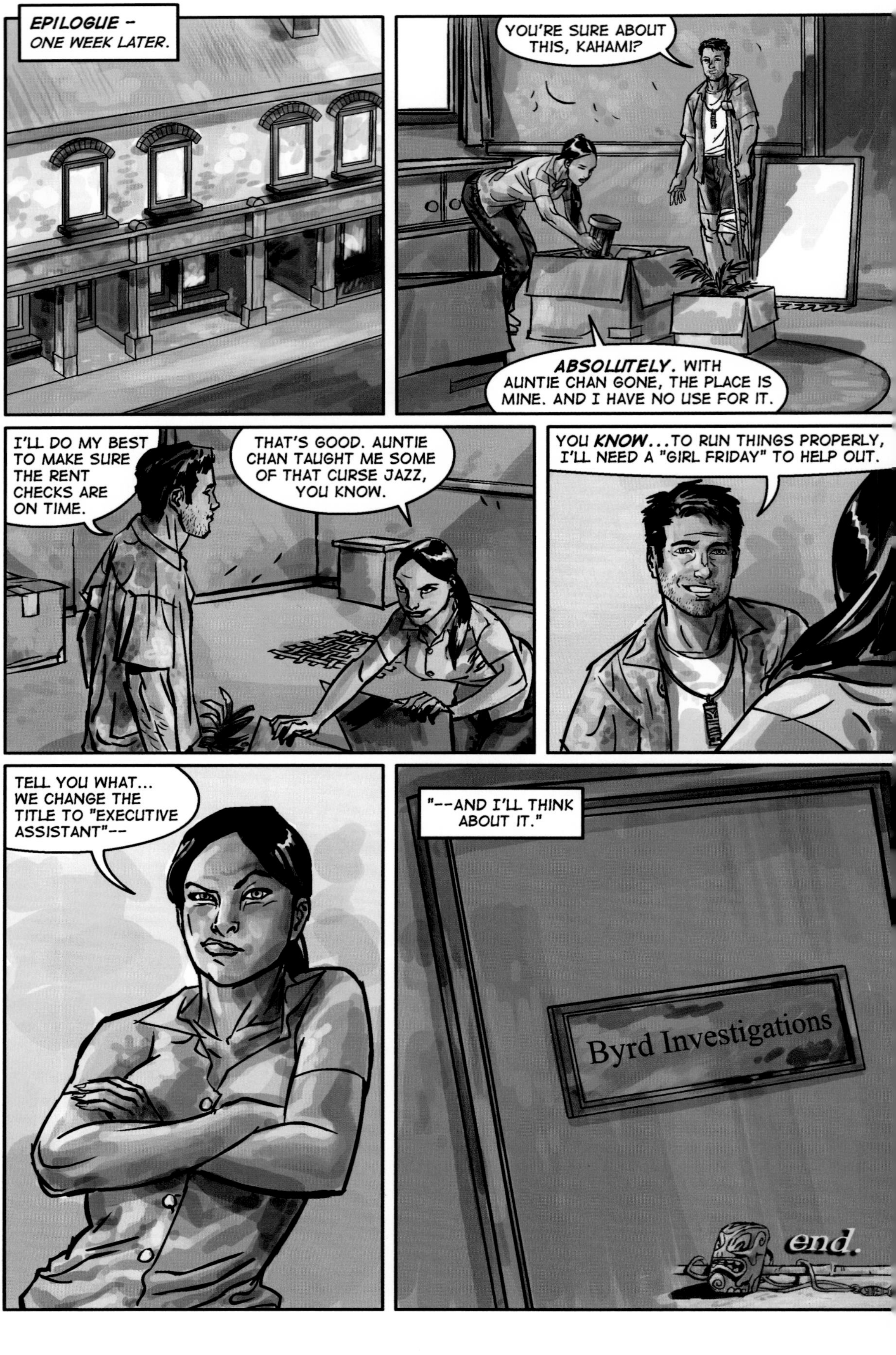
EPILOGUE - ONE WEEK LATER.
YOU'RE SURE ABOUT THIS, KAHAMI?
ABSOLUTELY. WITH AUNTIE CHAN GONE, THE PLACE IS MINE. AND I HAVE NO USE FOR IT.
I'LL DO MY BEST TO MAKE SURE THE RENT CHECKS ARE ON TIME.
THAT'S GOOD. AUNTIE CHAN TAUGHT ME SOME OF THAT CURSE JAZZ, YOU KNOW.
YOU KNOW...TO RUN THINGS PROPERLY, I'LL NEED A "GIRL FRIDAY" TO HELP OUT.
TELL YOU WHAT... WE CHANGE THE TITLE TO "EXECUTIVE ASSISTANT"--
"--AND I'LL THINK ABOUT IT."
Byrd Investigations
end.

AN INTRODUCTION OF SORTS

(For those who've been
curious as to how
Byrd met Mo)

January, 1945. Somewhere behind Japanese lines, the Philippines.

The raid had gone almost by the book.

The Rangers, after months of doing little more than securing islands already deserted by the Japanese, had been as efficient and skillful under fire as advertised. The prison camp had been reconned accurately by a combination of Filipino guerrillas and advance scouts, and the prison guards had withered under immediate, relentless fire. The liberation of the camp began with a burst of M-1 fire and the sound of exploding hand grenades, and within minutes the Rangers were inside the fence, pulling dazed and grinning shadows of men from makeshift beds inside the sun-beaten barracks buildings.

The prisoners of war inside the camp numbered just under 400, as all able-bodied prisoners had long ago been shipped to Japan for use as slave labor in factories and fields. What remained was a ragtag assemblage of emaciated soldiers, many closer to death than life.

Byrd's group had led the charge from the front of the camp, while another unit opened fire from the rear. As the camp's guards rushed to defend their flanks, Byrd's unit stormed the front gates, quickly overwhelming the surprised Japanese. The first targets had been the lookouts posted in turrets at each corner of the camp. The explosive concussion of Ranger fire had literally obliterated these men, and there was virtually no resistance to be offered from the Japanese troops.

So far, there hadn't been a single Ranger casualty, at least as far as Byrd could tell. And at the moment, he was focused on one thing: Keeping his head down and his rifle at the ready as he dashed madly forward, carried on by alternately surging waves of adrenaline and fear.

Byrd was now running through the back end of the camp, double-checking the deserted barracks for any prisoners who might be hiding from the sudden barrage of gunfire and the cries of wounded men. Here and there the body of a fallen Japanese soldier could be spotted crumpled in the dirt, but at the time of the raid only a handful of enemy troops had been stationed at the camp. Most of the Imperial Japanese Army was consumed with retreat, and only enough men as needed to maintain the camp were left behind.

Byrd pressed up against the last of the POW barracks and placed a hand on the exterior door handle. He unlatched the door and pushed it open with the muzzle of his rifle.

"Hello?" He called into the gloom. There was no immediate response, but that didn't mean anything. Many of the prisoners seemed to be in a state of shock at what was happening. Even those fully aware that they were being rescued could do little more than gape at the larger, well-conditioned men herding them out of the gates of the camp.

Some seemed almost afraid to leave the only home they'd known for months or even years.

Stepping cautiously into the room, he allowed a moment for his eyes to adjust to the darkness. When the shapes of the crudely constructed bunk beds became clearer, he relaxed a bit and walked forward, but saw none of the beds occupied. Here and there he noticed a frayed straw mat or an overturned wooden bowl, but beyond that...

"STOP!"

As the heavily accented voice reached his ears, he did just the opposite. Instinctively dropping into a crouch, he spun toward the front door, cursing himself for leaving the door wide open. He leveled his rifle and gripped the trigger. At first he wasn't sure what he was looking at. But standing behind the now half-closed door was a Japanese officer, his face blackened, no doubt by the smoke from grenades lobbed at the officer's quarters by the Rangers as they invaded the camp. As shocking as the Japanese officer's appearance was, it wasn't what most surprised Byrd. The officer was standing behind the biggest, baldest son-of-a-bitch Byrd had ever seen. At first Byrd thought the figure was that of another Japanese, but the tattered state of the man's clothes and the sunken flesh around his cheekbones indicated he was, in fact, a prisoner of war. Byrd judged him to be Samoan or, perhaps, the largest Filipino he'd ever seen.

For a straining instant, Byrd and the officer locked eyes, Byrd's rifle directed at the man's head. In the officer's eyes Byrd saw a desperate, ragged fear. And he was pretty sure the same could be seen in his own eyes. The only thing stopping Byrd from opening fire was the pistol pressed up against the prisoner's head.

As the two stood in the stifling heat of the barracks, nothing could be heard aside from the distant shouts of soldiers and the very sporadic sound of crackling gunfire. Byrd realized the camp was all but clear of resistance, and considered for a moment that he could die here, the only Ranger killed within the walls of the camp, after all other resistance had been subdued.

"Sorry about this." The sound of the prisoner's voice shocked Byrd, and seemed to momentarily panic the officer. The captor unleashed a torrent of Japanese, his voice emerging in a sort of strangled grasp. Byrd could see now that he was bleeding from his mouth.

The prisoner responded to Byrd's questioning look by shrugging. "I speak as much Japanese as you, brother." The word "brother" came out more like "brudder," and the deep, calm tone gave Byrd an irrational, fleeting sense of comfort.

Keeping his gun trained on the injured officer, he held a hand up slowly, and spoke as evenly as he could manage. "Listen, friend...I don't want to die here any more than you do. Just put down the gun and we'll take care of you."

"I don't think he speaks much English, either." The prisoner remained stock still, and was the only one in the room not drenched in sweat, despite the fetid stale air that seemed hotter in here, in the shade, than it had outside.

Another stream of Japanese, this time less panic-stricken. Byrd was paralyzed by uncertainty. He didn't like the sense that the Japanese officer was gaining composure. He knew all too well that the Japanese looked upon surrender as an act of shameful cowardice, and it seemed likely that the officer would rather see all of them dead than be captured. But he also knew he couldn't open fire on the man while that gun was pointed at the prisoner's head. And now, when his eyes locked on the officer's, he saw little of the earlier fear.

The prisoner spoke again, this time in a slow, deliberate cadence. "Listen. He's gaining courage. If he shoots me, be prepared to shoot him. Don't let him kill you, too."

Despite the gravity of the situation, the prisoner's relaxed manner struck a chord with Byrd. Here was a man who had suffered unimaginable torments at the hands of his captors, about to lose his life on a day his companions were already being escorted across the thick cogon grass, well on their way to safety, and he seemed willing to accept death if it came.

"He's not killing anyone," Byrd said, trying to match the prisoner's cool manner.

From outside, Byrd heard his name being called. It was Sergeant Baldelli, trying to round up stragglers for the long trek back to the Sixth Army Headquarters at Dagupan.

The prisoner, in the same relaxing tone he'd used before, asked, "You must be Byrd?"

Before another word was spoken, the Japanese officer made his move. Byrd saw him tensing, and he swung his rifle up, taking dead aim at the man's head. He assumed the man would shoot the prisoner and then try to shoot him. So he was taken off guard when the man quickly extended his arm toward Byrd and squeezed the trigger. Instead of firing, Byrd instinctively turned away from the gun, and as the shot echoed through the tiny barracks, he simply assumed both he and the prisoner were dead.

The bullet grazed the barrel of his rifle, tearing it from his grasp, but leaving him unharmed. He dropped to the floor and scrambled desperately for the damaged weapon. Across the room he could hear grunts and the sound of the men struggling. His rifle was within reach, and he pulled it toward him, assessing the damage in an instant. Aside from a black streak across the barrel, the gun looked fine. Although the act of dropping to the floor and locating the gun had taken no more than a few seconds, he felt as if he was moving at half-speed, driven by panic, sure that another bullet would come crashing through his head or his chest or his arm before he could defend himself. Grabbing the gun with his left hand, he rolled onto his stomach just as the crack of the officer's pistol rang out again. The prisoner gave a sharp cry, and Byrd swung his rifle wildly, taking shaky aim now at the Japanese officer, who was dropping the slumped figure of the prisoner onto the wooden floor.

Byrd aimed at the man's chest and pulled the trigger. But the trigger wouldn't pull. The gun was jammed. The Japanese officer smiled now, stepping across the prone figure of the prisoner, aiming his pistol squarely at Byrd.

"BYRD!" Sergeant Baldelli's voice was closer, but not close enough.

Byrd was still lying on the ground, in no position to defend himself. He looked straight into the steel of the pistol as the officer advanced. Just as he was certain it was over, a giant brown hand reached out and grabbed the officer's pant leg, sending the man tumbling forward. The pistol tumbled, too, landing halfway between Byrd and the officer. Byrd crawled toward the gun as the prisoner, bleeding now from a shoulder wound, held onto the officer's leg. The officer kicked at the larger man, landing blows to his head and the wounded shoulder, causing him to lose his grip. Byrd was an inch from the gun when the officer's hand reached out and swooped it up. The officer, breathing heavily now, scrambled to his feet and took aim at Byrd, lying face up on the floor, drained now of energy and hope.

Squinting up at the soldier, Byrd had trouble making sense of what happened next. Suddenly, light bathed the room and the Japanese soldier seemed startled, turning his head. The sound of a pistol shot shattered the still air. The officer stood in place for a moment, before falling over sideways, a widening spread of crimson soaking his blackened shirt.

Sergeant Baldelli stood in the doorway, his Colt .45 in his right hand, a concerned look on his ruddy face.

"What goes on in here, Byrd?"

Byrd closed his eyes and dropped his head back onto the grimy floor. He smiled despite himself. "Just keeping him busy for you, Sarge."

The prisoner gave a low moan and struggled to his feet, clutching his bloody shoulder. Putting aside his exhaustion, Byrd rose to meet him, extending a hand. Despite the pain of a damaged shoulder, the prisoner extended his own right hand, soaked in blood as it was. Byrd grasped it firmly.

"Private Mo Kalama."

"Corporal Byrd."

As the two Rangers helped the hulking private from the barracks, Byrd asked him where he was from...

THE ONLINE STRIPS

The first two strips here were the first two pieces of Hawaiian Dick continuity we produced. The initial strip was done as a sort of "trial run," to see how we worked together. The second was worked up to include in the initial pitch, and to show off Steven's use of color. Once the book was picked up, Image asked us to produce several more strips for the relaunched Image site, and here they are.

My favorite of these is probably the strip featuring Byrd in bed, answering a call from Mo. It was written to be drawn quickly, and the repeated shot of a hungover Byrd still makes me laugh.

- Clay

Two of these strips feature Byrd's local bar, a hangout with more Hawaiian culture and earthy feel than The Outrigger. It lacks Kahami, but also the tourists, which suits Byrd just fine.

The third strip features a sax player based on jazz legend, Lester Young, easily identifiable by the unique way he holds his instrument. I chose him simply because being different is always good.

- Steven

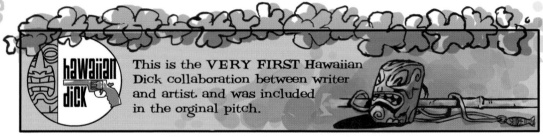

This is the **VERY FIRST** Hawaiian Dick collaboration between writer and artist and was included in the orginal pitch.

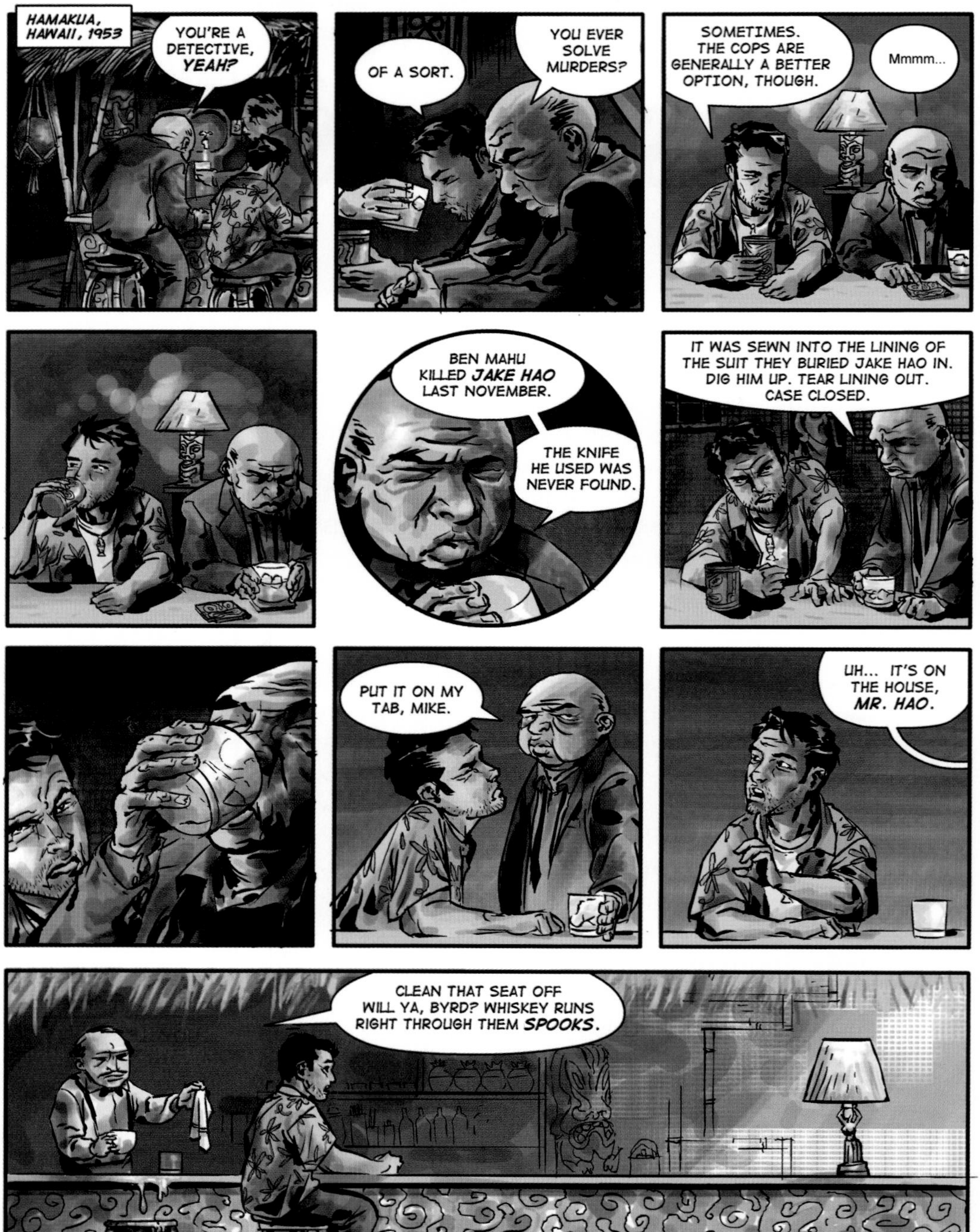

HAMAKUA, HAWAII, 1953
YOU'RE A DETECTIVE, YEAH?
OF A SORT.
YOU EVER SOLVE MURDERS?
SOMETIMES. THE COPS ARE GENERALLY A BETTER OPTION, THOUGH.
Mmmm...
BEN MAHU KILLED JAKE HAO LAST NOVEMBER.
THE KNIFE HE USED WAS NEVER FOUND.
IT WAS SEWN INTO THE LINING OF THE SUIT THEY BURIED JAKE HAO IN. DIG HIM UP. TEAR LINING OUT. CASE CLOSED.
PUT IT ON MY TAB, MIKE.
UH... IT'S ON THE HOUSE, MR. HAO.
CLEAN THAT SEAT OFF WILL YA, BYRD? WHISKEY RUNS RIGHT THROUGH THEM SPOOKS.

END.

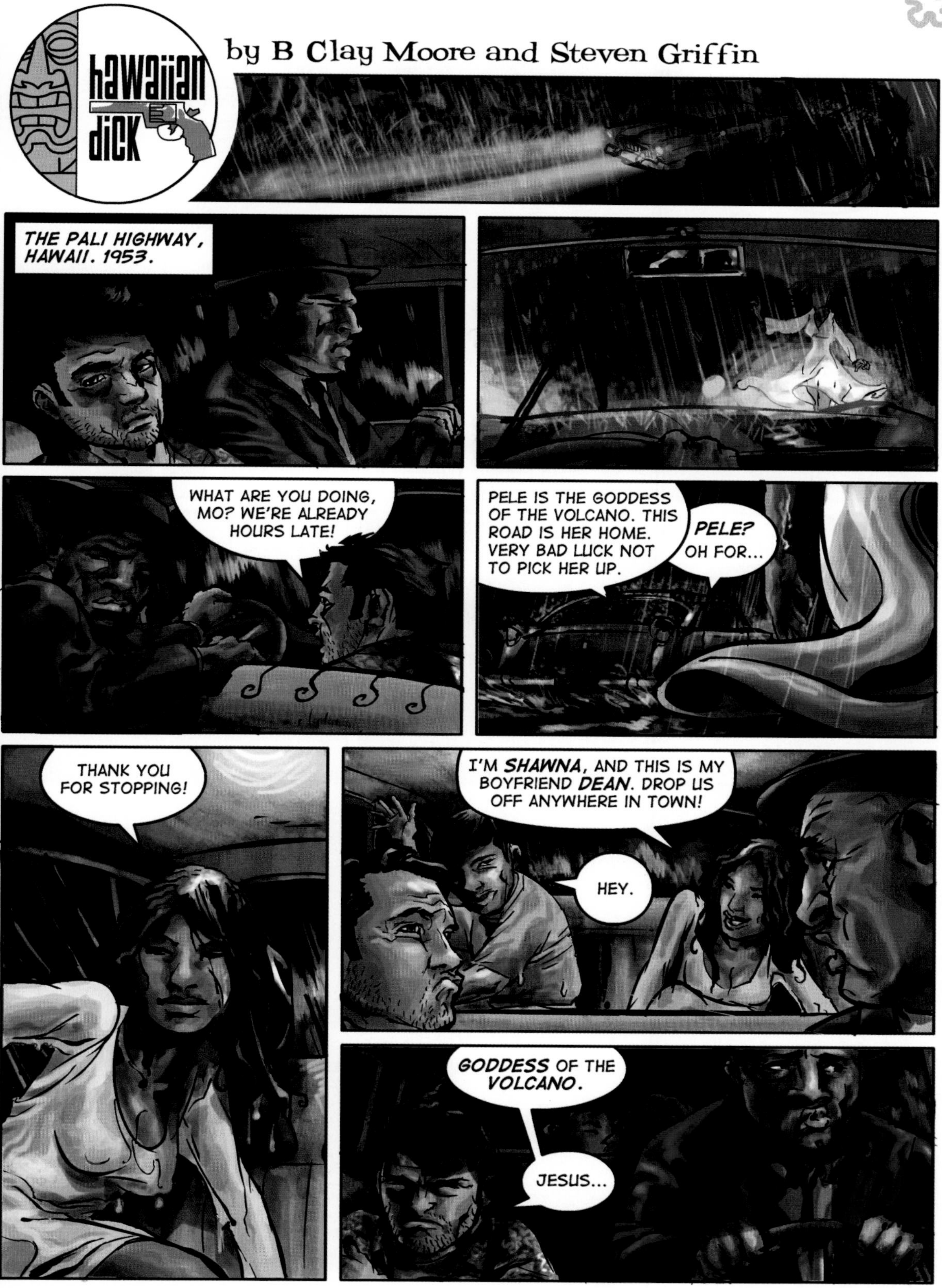

hawaiian dick
by B Clay Moore and Steven Griffin
THE PALI HIGHWAY, HAWAII. 1953.
WHAT ARE YOU DOING, MO? WE'RE ALREADY HOURS LATE!
PELE IS THE GODDESS OF THE VOLCANO. THIS ROAD IS HER HOME. VERY BAD LUCK NOT TO PICK HER UP.
PELE? OH FOR...
THANK YOU FOR STOPPING!
I'M SHAWNA, AND THIS IS MY BOYFRIEND DEAN. DROP US OFF ANYWHERE IN TOWN!
HEY.
GODDESS OF THE VOLCANO.
JESUS...

END.

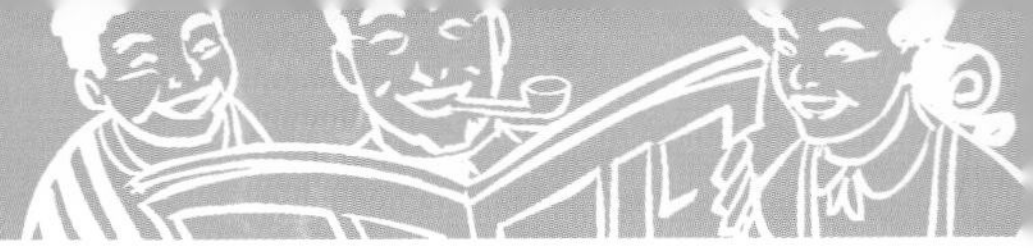

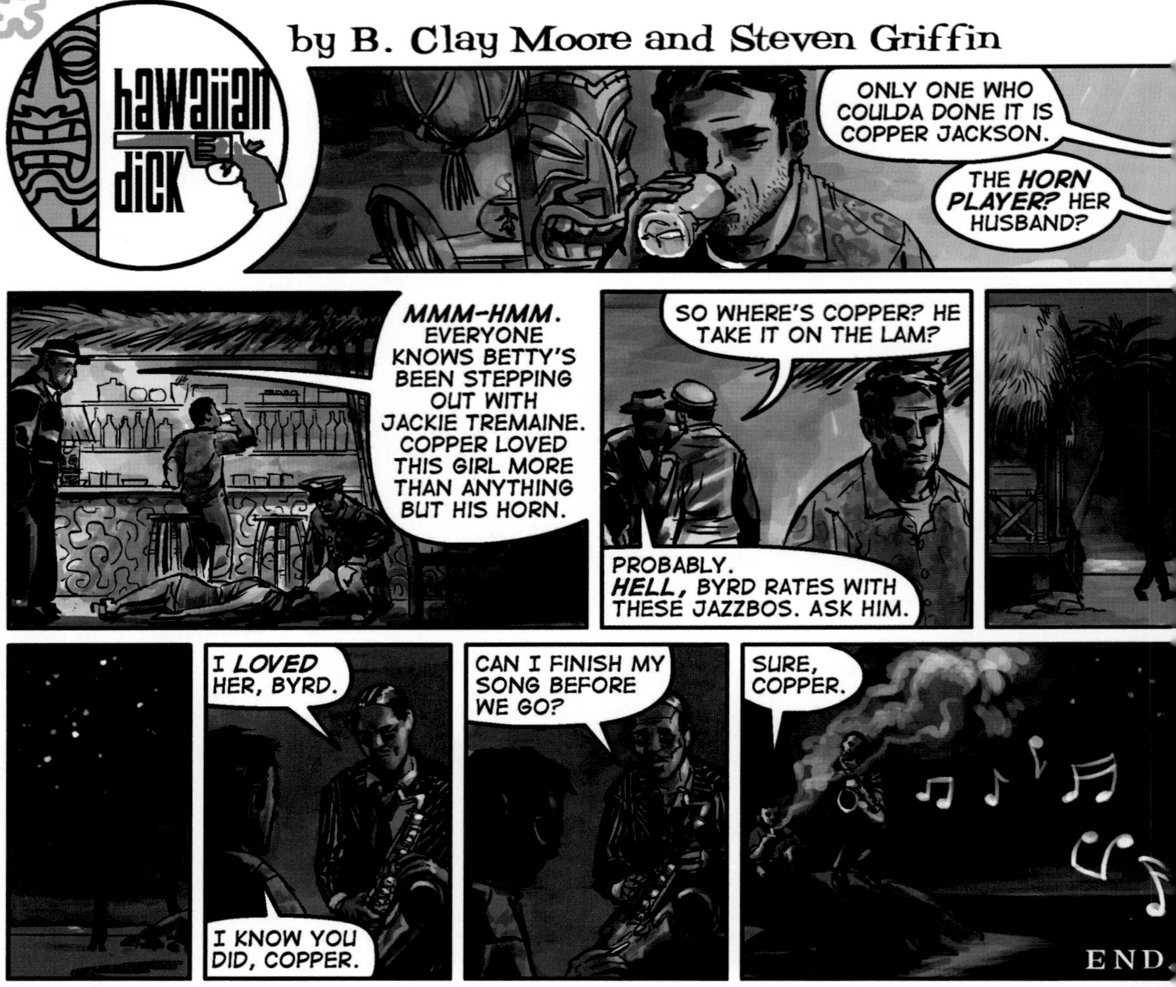

by B. Clay Moore and Steven Griffin
hawaiian dick
ONLY ONE WHO COULDA DONE IT IS COPPER JACKSON.
THE HORN PLAYER? HER HUSBAND?
MMM-HMM. EVERYONE KNOWS BETTY'S BEEN STEPPING OUT WITH JACKIE TREMAINE. COPPER LOVED THIS GIRL MORE THAN ANYTHING BUT HIS HORN.
SO WHERE'S COPPER? HE TAKE IT ON THE LAM?
PROBABLY. HELL, BYRD RATES WITH THESE JAZZBOS. ASK HIM.
I LOVED HER, BYRD.
I KNOW YOU DID, COPPER.
CAN I FINISH MY SONG BEFORE WE GO?
SURE, COPPER.
END

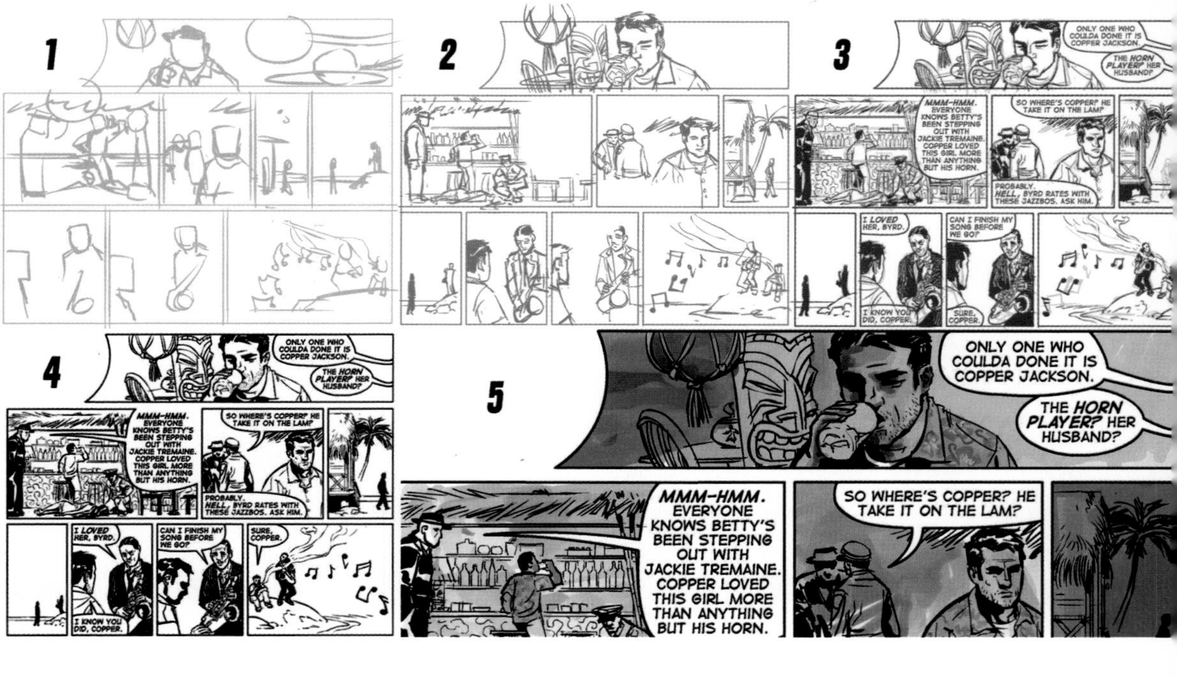

1
2
3
4
5

ONLY ONE WHO COULDA DONE IT IS COPPER JACKSON.
THE HORN PLAYER? HER HUSBAND?
MMM-HMM. EVERYONE KNOWS BETTY'S BEEN STEPPING OUT WITH JACKIE TREMAINE. COPPER LOVED THIS GIRL MORE THAN ANYTHING BUT HIS HORN.
SO WHERE'S COPPER? HE TAKE IT ON THE LAM?

by B. Clay Moore and Steven Griffin

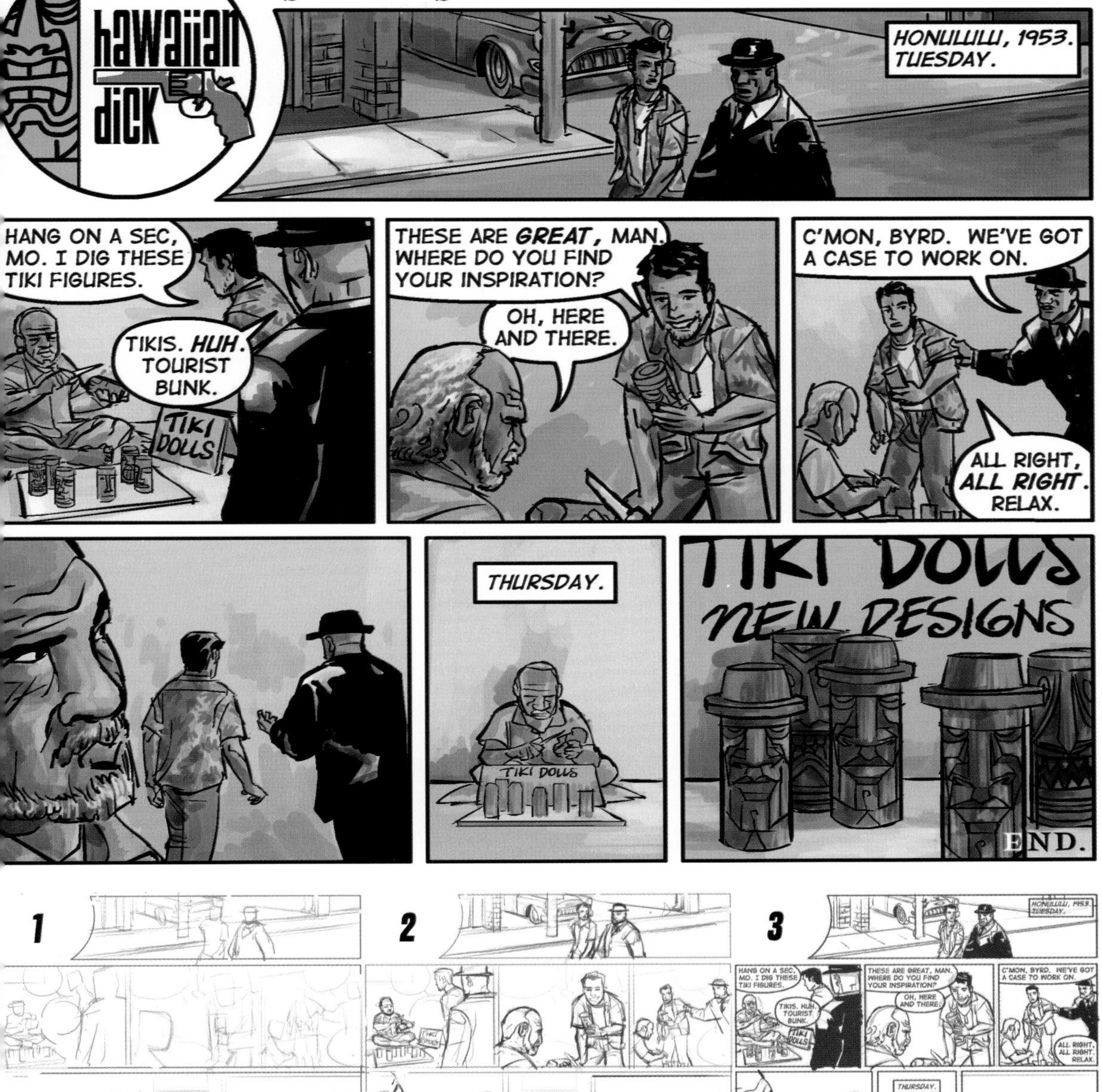
hawaiian dick
HONULULU, 1953. TUESDAY.
HANG ON A SEC, MO. I DIG THESE TIKI FIGURES.
TIKIS. HUH. TOURIST BUNK.
TIKI DOLLS
THESE ARE GREAT, MAN. WHERE DO YOU FIND YOUR INSPIRATION?
OH, HERE AND THERE.
C'MON, BYRD. WE'VE GOT A CASE TO WORK ON.
ALL RIGHT, ALL RIGHT. RELAX.
THURSDAY.
TIKI DOLLS
TIKI DOLLS NEW DESIGNS
END.

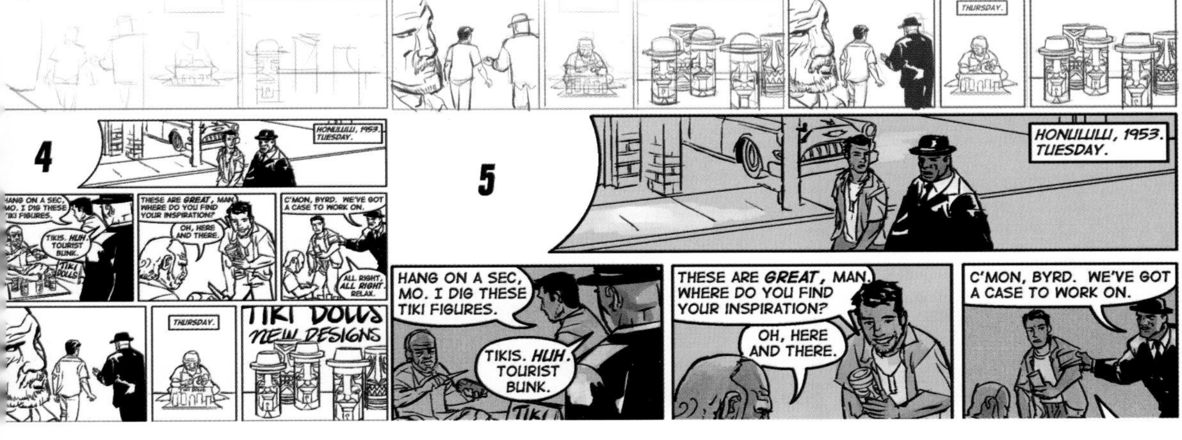
1
2
3
4
5
HONULULU, 1953. TUESDAY.
HANG ON A SEC, MO. I DIG THESE TIKI FIGURES.
TIKIS. HUH. TOURIST BUNK.
THESE ARE GREAT, MAN. WHERE DO YOU FIND YOUR INSPIRATION?
OH, HERE AND THERE.
C'MON, BYRD. WE'VE GOT A CASE TO WORK ON.

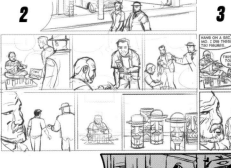

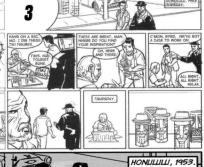

by B. Clay Moore and Steven Griffin

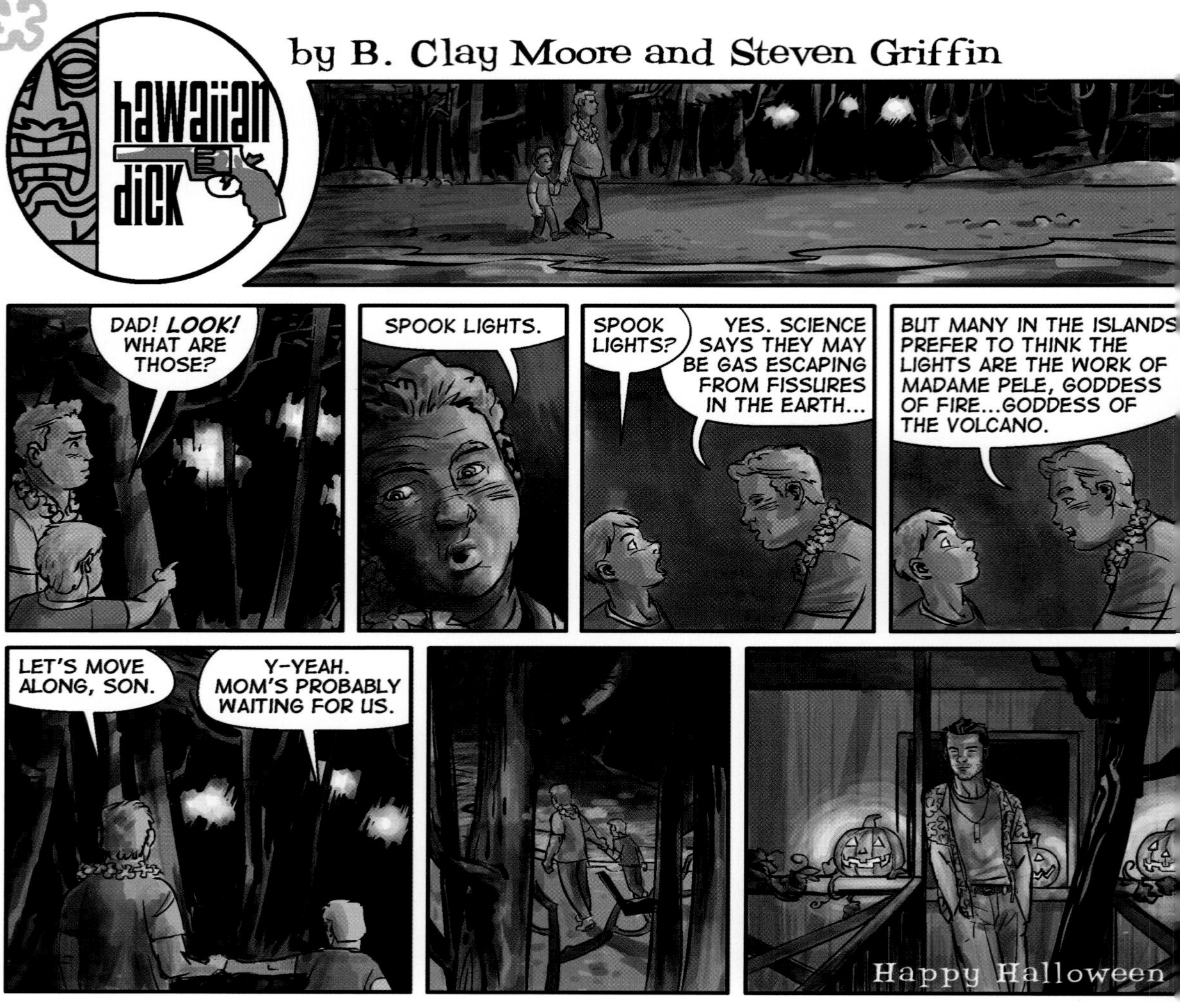
hawaiian dick
DAD! LOOK! WHAT ARE THOSE?
SPOOK LIGHTS.
SPOOK LIGHTS?
YES. SCIENCE SAYS THEY MAY BE GAS ESCAPING FROM FISSURES IN THE EARTH...
BUT MANY IN THE ISLANDS PREFER TO THINK THE LIGHTS ARE THE WORK OF MADAME PELE, GODDESS OF FIRE...GODDESS OF THE VOLCANO.
LET'S MOVE ALONG, SON.
Y-YEAH. MOM'S PROBABLY WAITING FOR US.
Happy Halloween

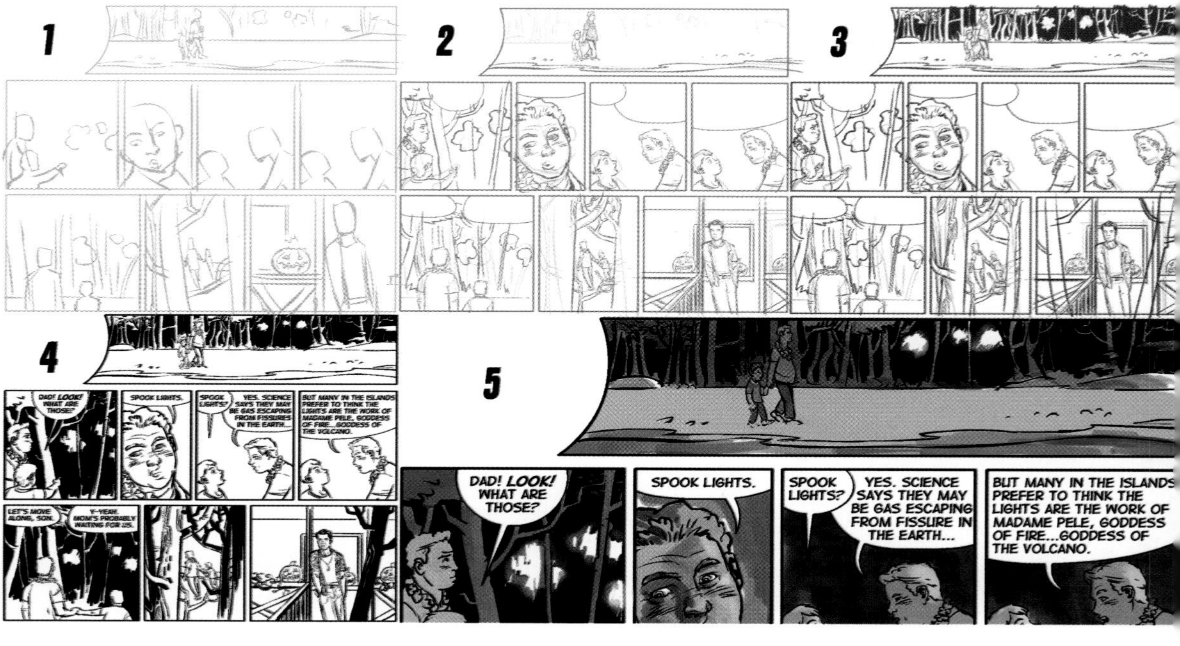
1
2
3
4
5
DAD! LOOK! WHAT ARE THOSE?
SPOOK LIGHTS.
SPOOK LIGHTS?
YES. SCIENCE SAYS THEY MAY BE GAS ESCAPING FROM FISSURE IN THE EARTH...
BUT MANY IN THE ISLANDS PREFER TO THINK THE LIGHTS ARE THE WORK OF MADAME PELE, GODDESS OF FIRE...GODDESS OF THE VOLCANO.

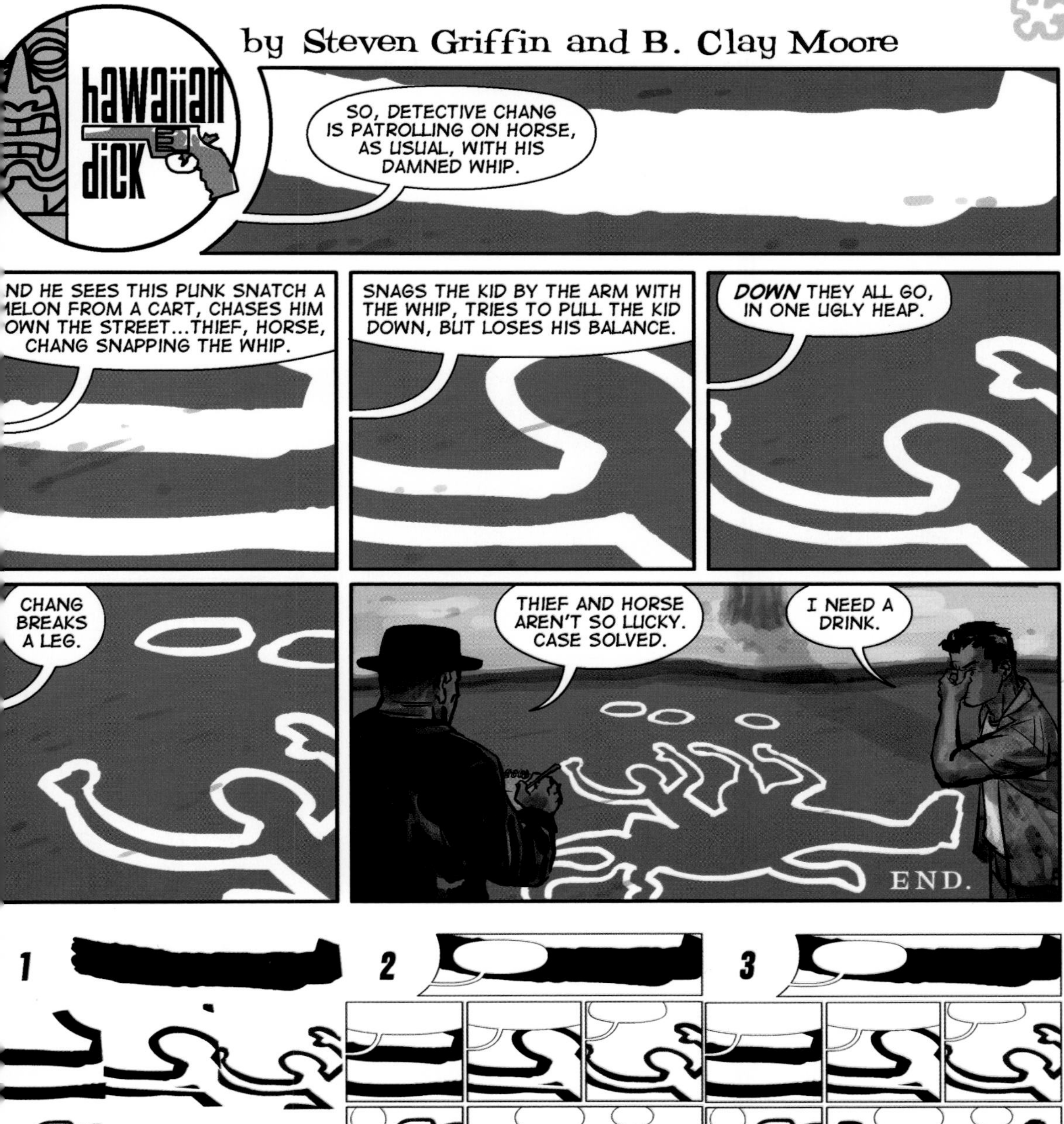

hawaiian dick
by Steven Griffin and B. Clay Moore
SO, DETECTIVE CHANG IS PATROLLING ON HORSE, AS USUAL, WITH HIS DAMNED WHIP.
ND HE SEES THIS PUNK SNATCH A MELON FROM A CART, CHASES HIM OWN THE STREET...THIEF, HORSE, CHANG SNAPPING THE WHIP.
SNAGS THE KID BY THE ARM WITH THE WHIP, TRIES TO PULL THE KID DOWN, BUT LOSES HIS BALANCE.
DOWN THEY ALL GO, IN ONE UGLY HEAP.
CHANG BREAKS A LEG.
THIEF AND HORSE AREN'T SO LUCKY. CASE SOLVED.
I NEED A DRINK.
END.

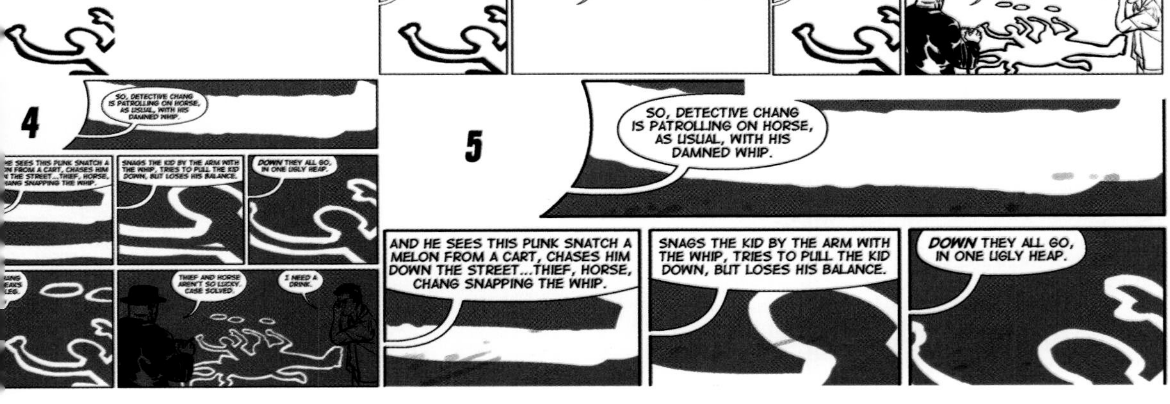

1
2
3
4
5
SO, DETECTIVE CHANG IS PATROLLING ON HORSE, AS USUAL, WITH HIS DAMNED WHIP.
AND HE SEES THIS PUNK SNATCH A MELON FROM A CART, CHASES HIM DOWN THE STREET...THIEF, HORSE, CHANG SNAPPING THE WHIP.
SNAGS THE KID BY THE ARM WITH THE WHIP, TRIES TO PULL THE KID DOWN, BUT LOSES HIS BALANCE.
DOWN THEY ALL GO, IN ONE UGLY HEAP.

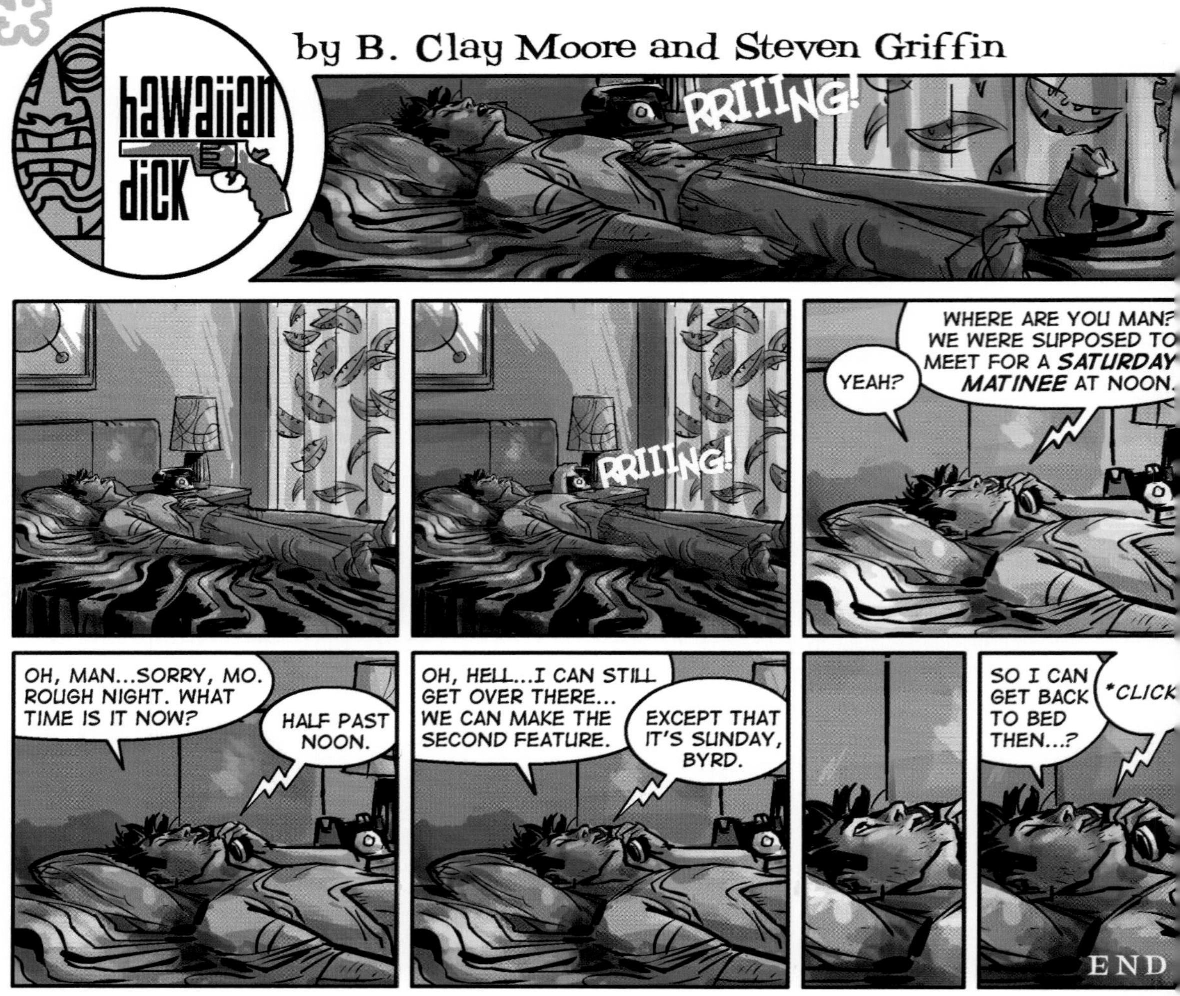
Hawaiian Dick
by B. Clay Moore and Steven Griffin
RRIIING!
RRIIING!
YEAH?
WHERE ARE YOU MAN? WE WERE SUPPOSED TO MEET FOR A *SATURDAY MATINEE* AT NOON.
OH, MAN...SORRY, MO. ROUGH NIGHT. WHAT TIME IS IT NOW?
HALF PAST NOON.
OH, HELL...I CAN STILL GET OVER THERE... WE CAN MAKE THE SECOND FEATURE.
EXCEPT THAT IT'S SUNDAY, BYRD.
SO I CAN GET BACK TO BED THEN...?
*CLICK
END

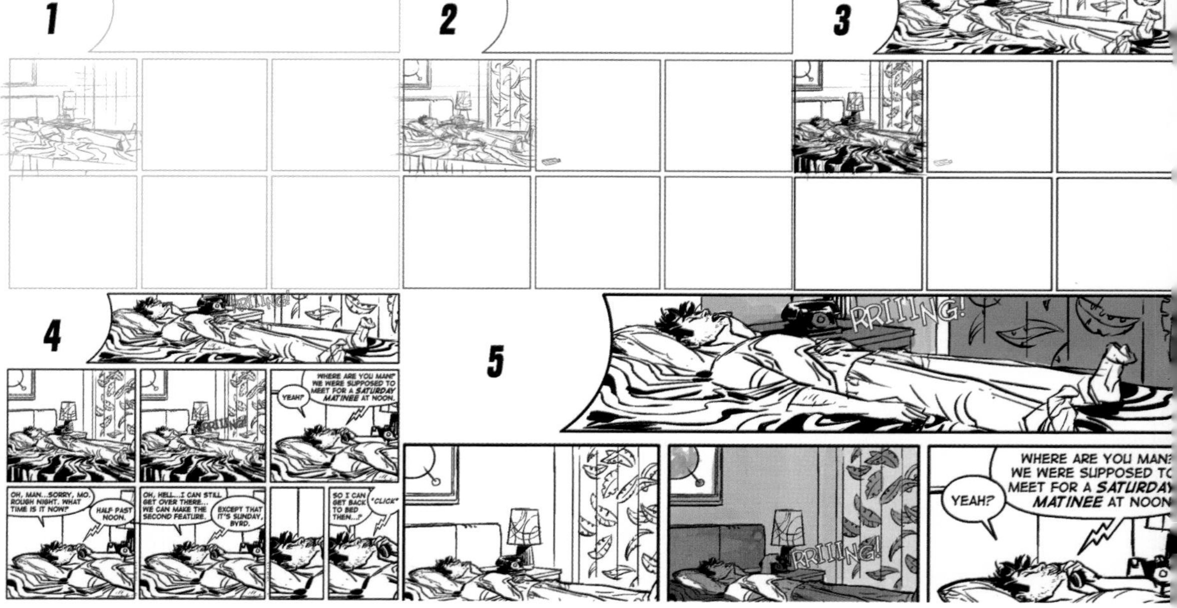
1
2
3
4
5
RRIIING!
RRIIING!
YEAH?
WHERE ARE YOU MAN? WE WERE SUPPOSED TO MEET FOR A *SATURDAY MATINEE* AT NOON.

CHARACTER DESIGN

Large amounts of research and discussion went into the story and art in Hawaiian Dick, and this section aims to give you a small glimpse behind that thought process.

Following are the original concept sketches for the series' characters along with excerpts from the actual emails they accompanied at the time. Some were sent only days after Clay and I had met (you can tell - I'm generally polite and respectful at this stage).

Hope you dig it!

- Steven

BYRD

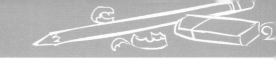

Subject: Hawaiian Dick

For the character of Byrd, were you thinking of a rough, unshaven, pulp detective look such as Bone's drawing, or more a groomed/shaven look (ie. the TV stars in the 50s)?

- Steven

...good point about fifties TV stars. But, no, he should be a little more scruffy than that. Not too rough, mind you. More like...rugged but still kind of handsome.

Byrd himself generally wears loud Hawaiian shirts.

- Clay

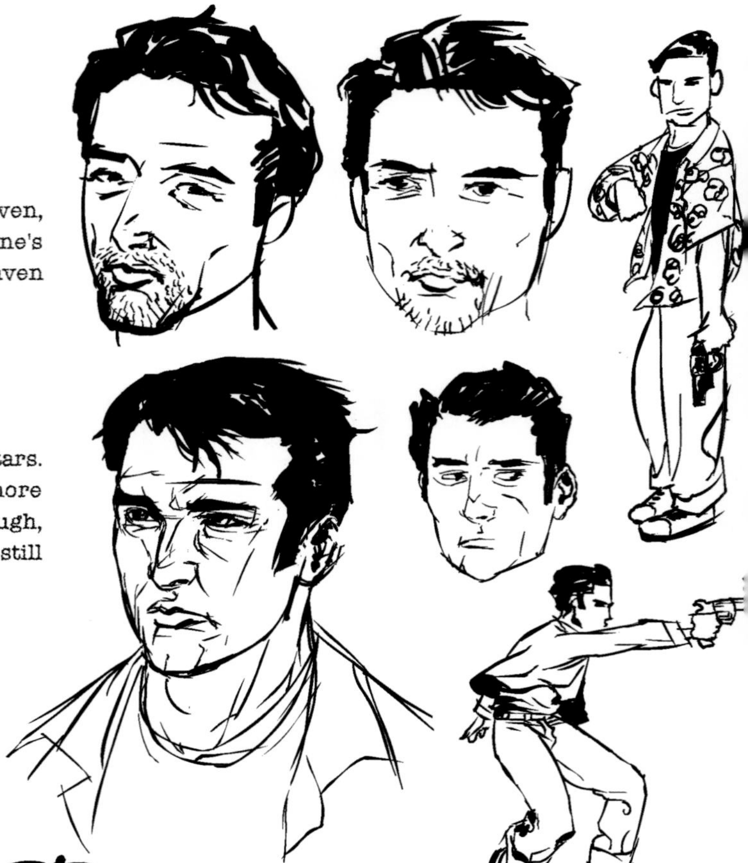

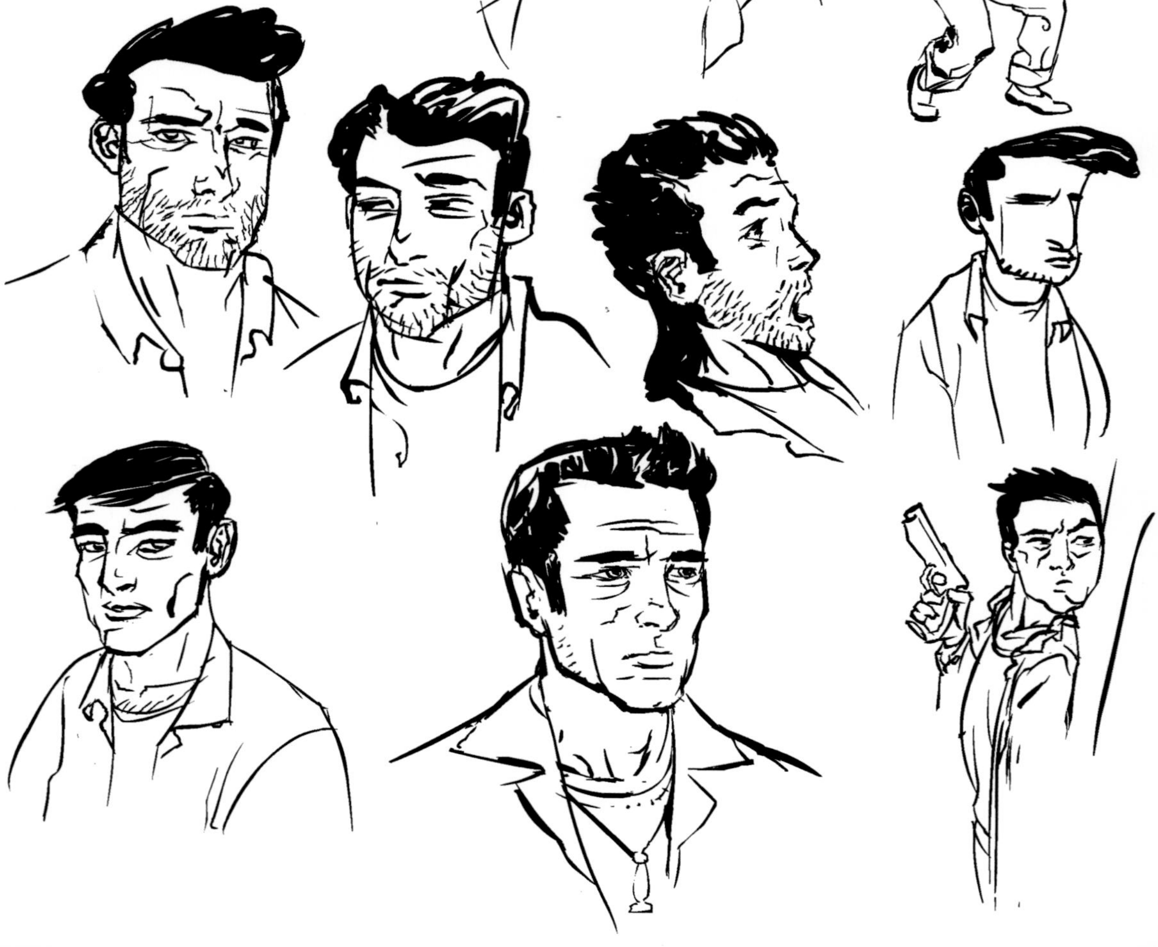

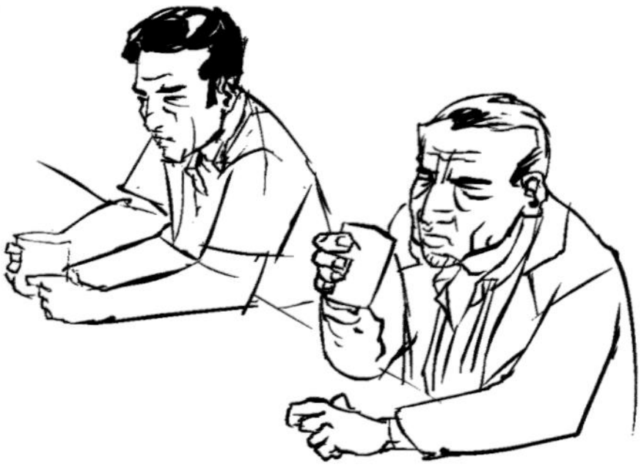

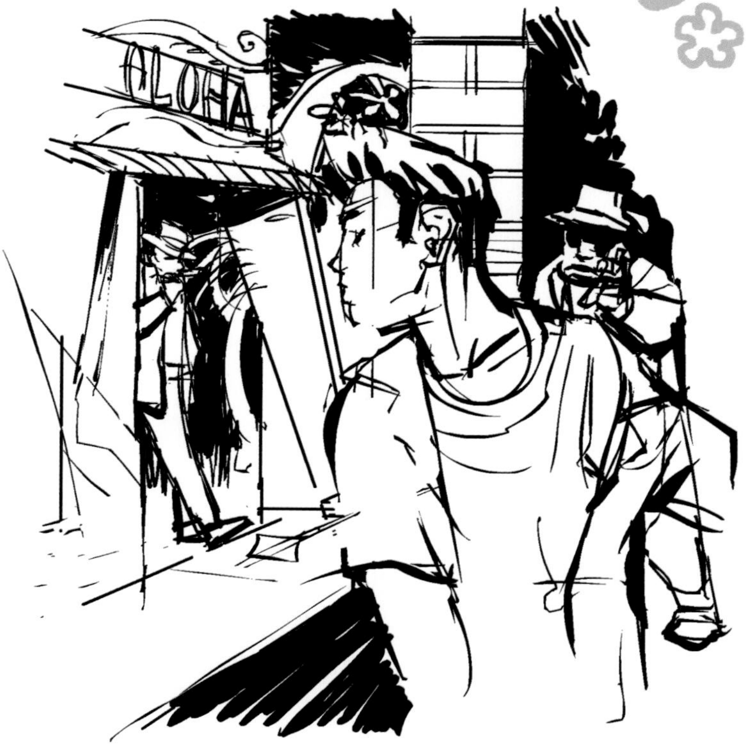

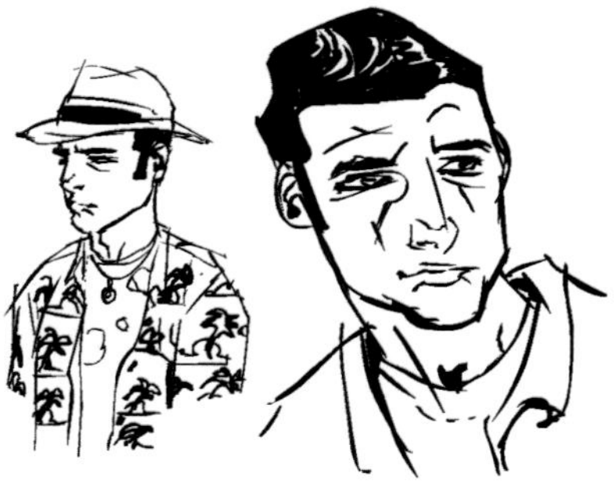

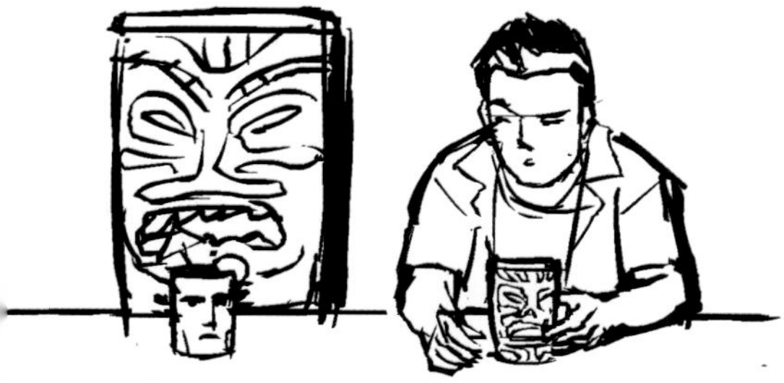

These are probably a bit late but I didn't get a chance to work over the weekend... I haven't finished the Mo designs yet, but I'll get them to you as soon as I do.

- Steven.

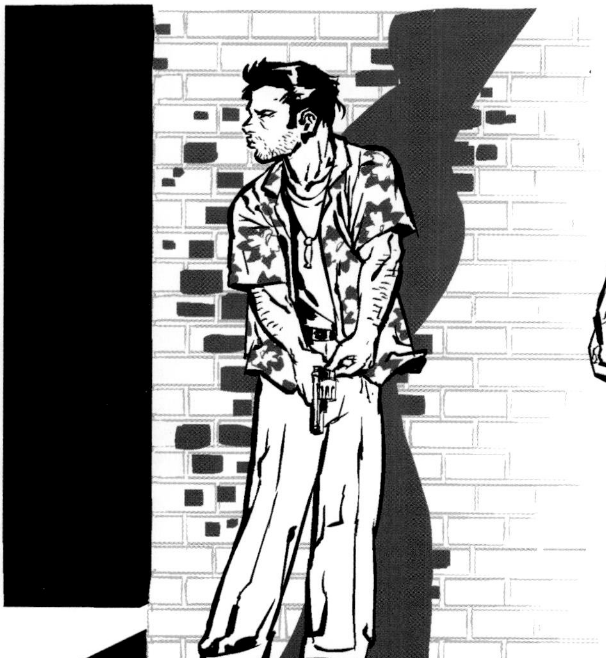

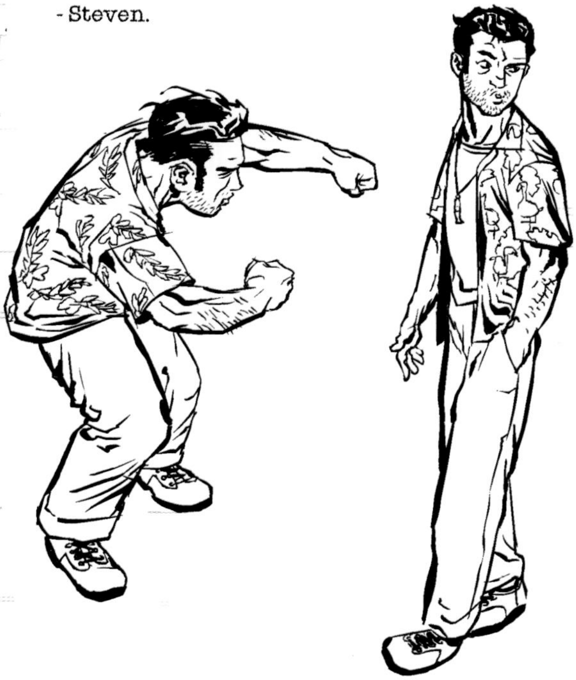

...as for the model sheets, by and large, nice work. I really dig the punching shot. Cool pose. Looks like he's just ducked a sucker punch and is responding in kind.

-Clay

Yay, that's pretty much what I was going for.

- Steven

I think there are a couple more characters who could benefit from this treatment, albeit on a lesser scale than Mo and Byrd. Perhaps just a design sketch a piece for Kahami, the zombie girl, Grimes, Bishop Masaki (whom we meet in issue two, and should be quite colorful), and maybe for Kahami's auntie, who also plays a role.

- Clay

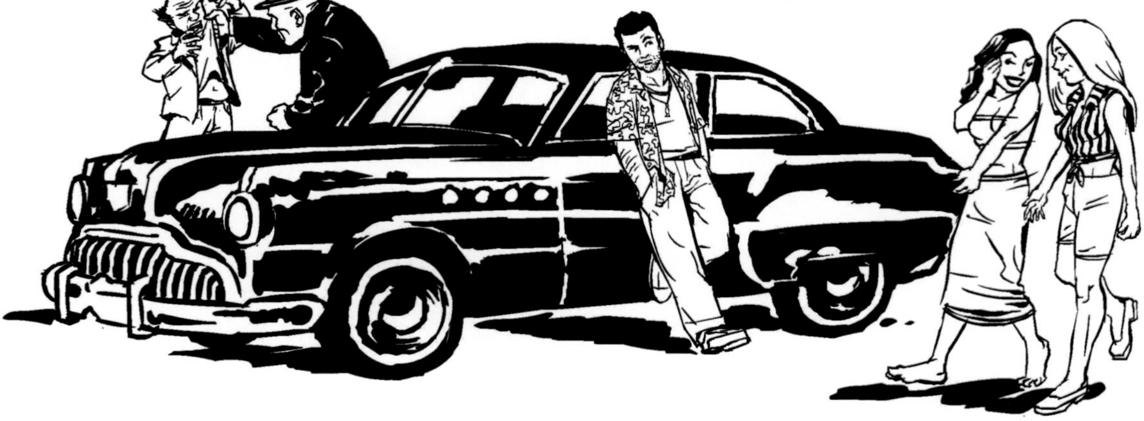

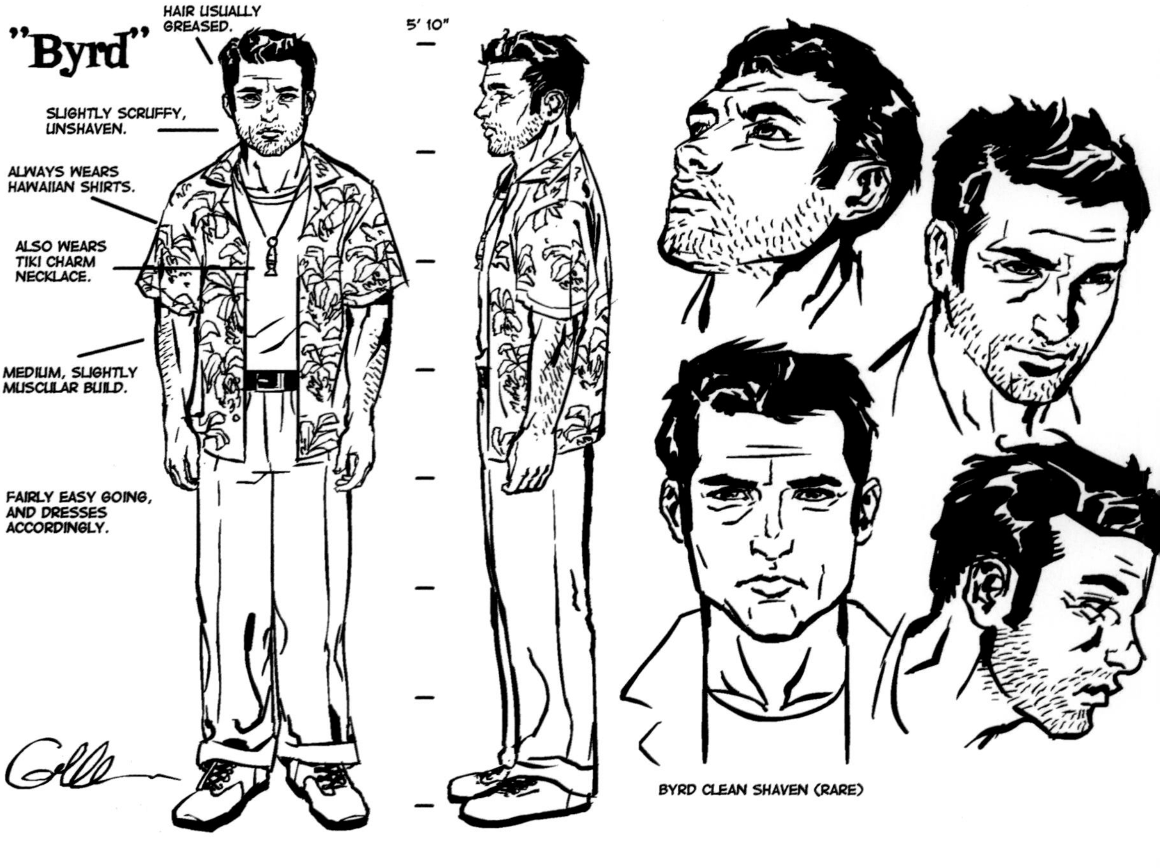
"Byrd"
HAIR USUALLY GREASED.
5' 10"
SLIGHTLY SCRUFFY, UNSHAVEN.
ALWAYS WEARS HAWAIIAN SHIRTS.
ALSO WEARS TIKI CHARM NECKLACE.
MEDIUM, SLIGHTLY MUSCULAR BUILD.
FAIRLY EASY GOING, AND DRESSES ACCORDINGLY.
BYRD CLEAN SHAVEN (RARE)

MO

Subject: Mo

By the way...I think I told you this, but I envision Mo as a big, burly Hawaiian/Samoan guy who wears tight-fitting blue suits and a porkpie hat all the time. He's a plainclothes detective. Very low key, kind of quiet, but doesn't mind using his fists when he thinks he has to.

- Clay

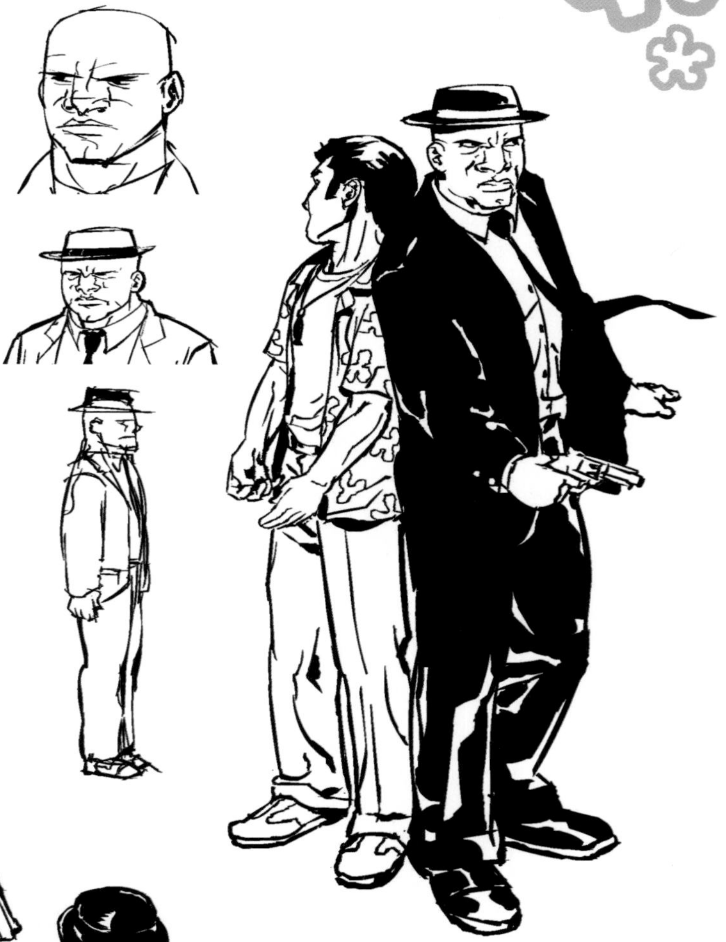

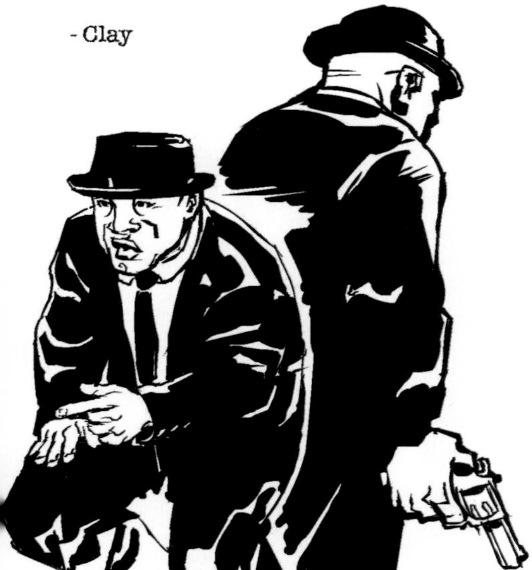

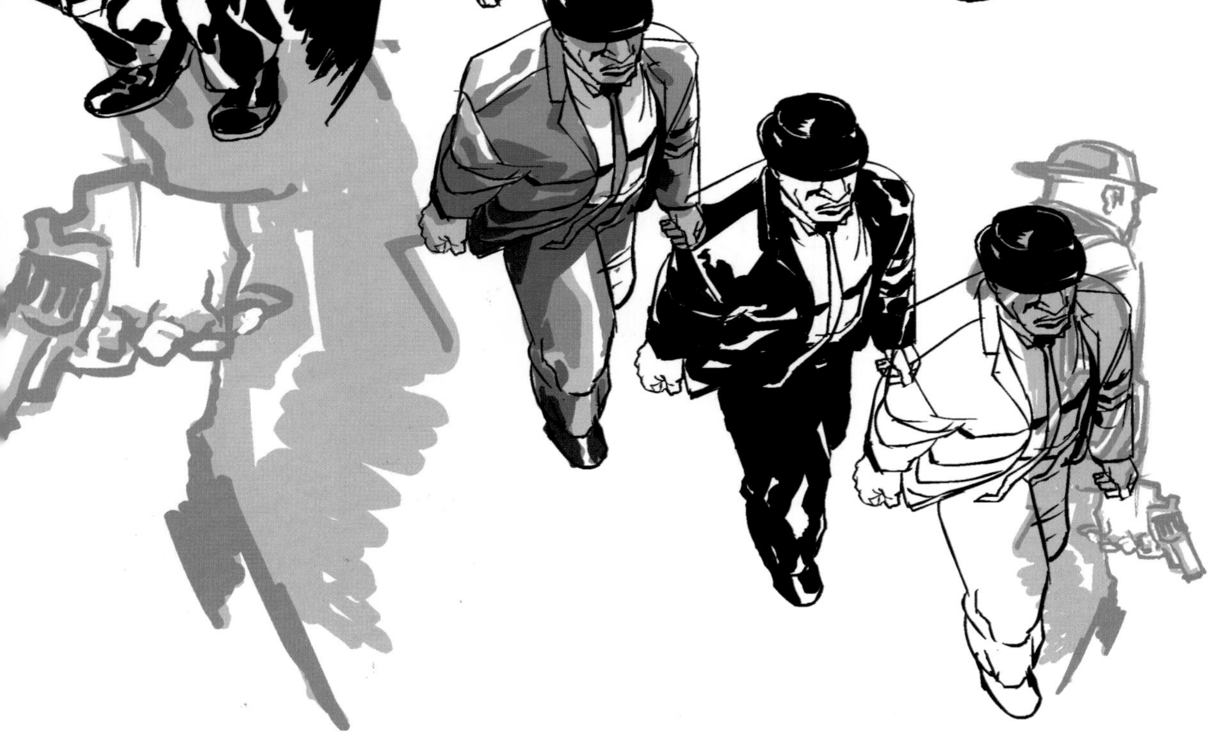

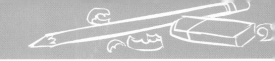

You around?

I'm just drawing up the character sheets for Mo, and trying to work out what look is best for him. Remember, if we're going with a black and white book, it's kinda hard to represent a blue suit :)

So, tell me what you think!

- Steven

I like the darkest option the best, I think. The one with highlights is kind of cool, but the middle suit in the "dark" sheet looks pretty solid!

- Clay

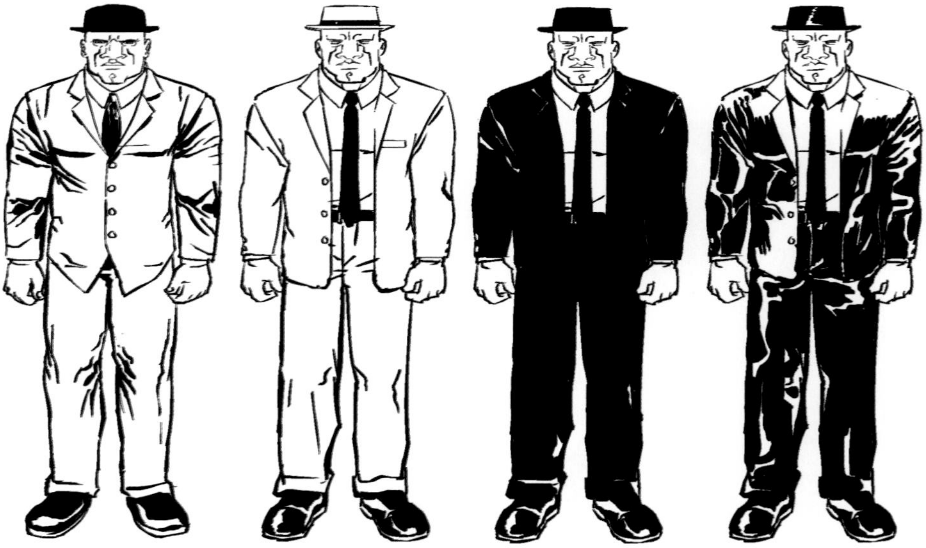

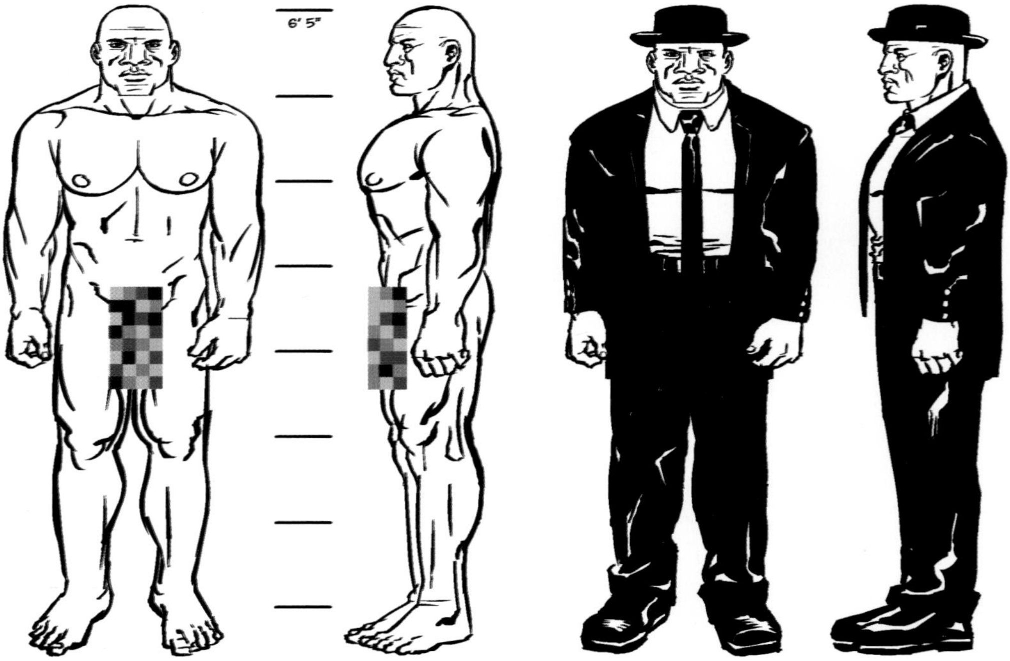
6' 5"

KAHAMI

Subject: couple of questions

...and BTW, what does Kahami wear? The stereotypical coconuts and grass skirts hardly seem her style.

- Steven

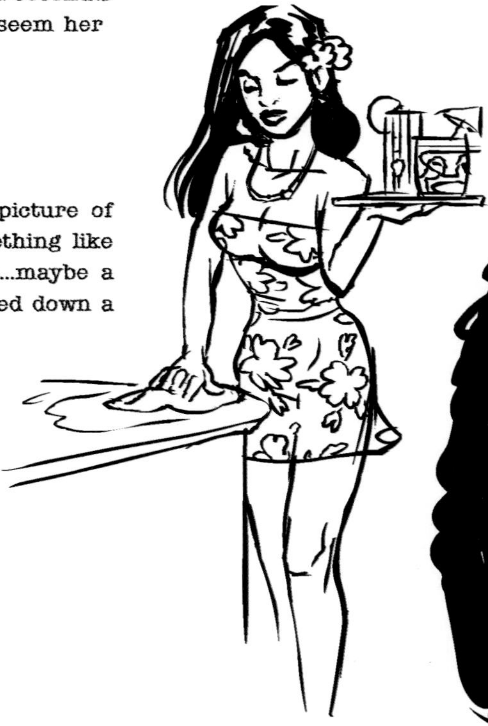

I've sent along an old picture of Dorothy Lamour. Something like this, with a floral print...maybe a flower in the hair. Toned down a bit, but still kinda sexy.

- Clay

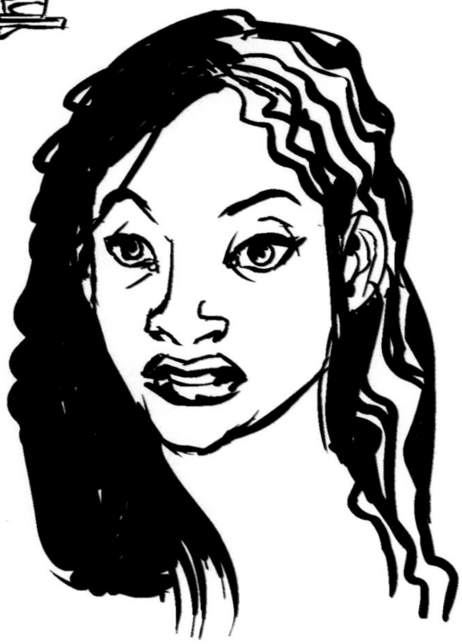

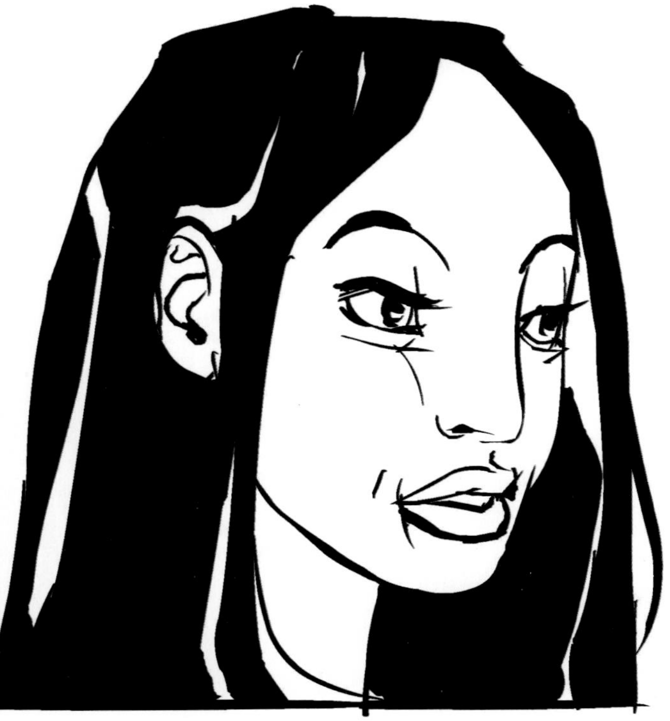

Okay, I'm sending some quick sketches of 3 different Kahamis I threw together. I've drawn them half asleep, so will probably get up tomorrow morning and realise I gave her three eyes or something...

I might have to de-Disneyize the one on the second page a bit though. Wasn't what I intended.

- Steven

Nah, she looks cute. :)

You're headed in the right direction, my man. Great shot of her with the tray, by the way!

- Clay

I still haven't worked out how I want Kahami to look... it's bugging me a bit. I can't decide if I want her face rounded, elegant, hair straight, hair curled... Anyway, here are a couple of pages of the latest faces...

- Steven

I like a more rounded look. She's sort of...she's not all wide eyed and innocent, but she's sexy and sort of sly. Her dead sister I picture as the more naive of the two. Kahami's the older sister, and has been down the road a bit.

- Clay

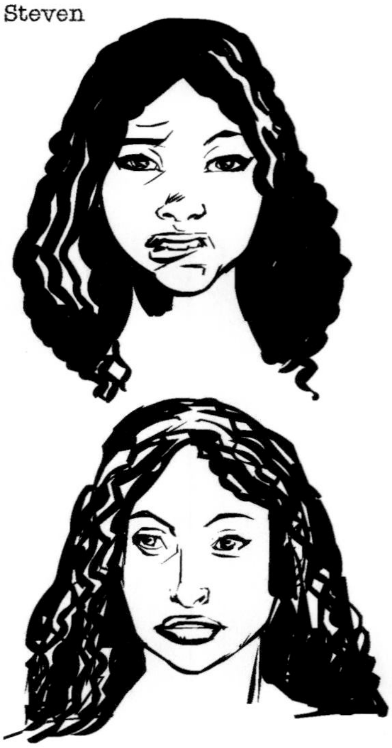

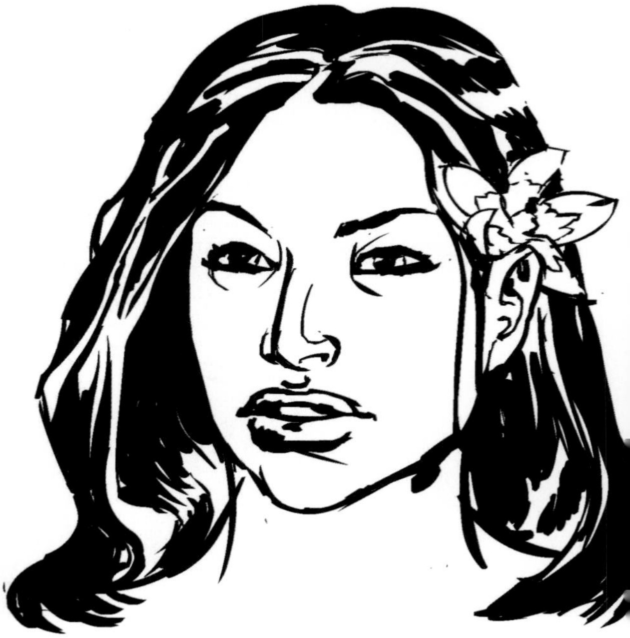

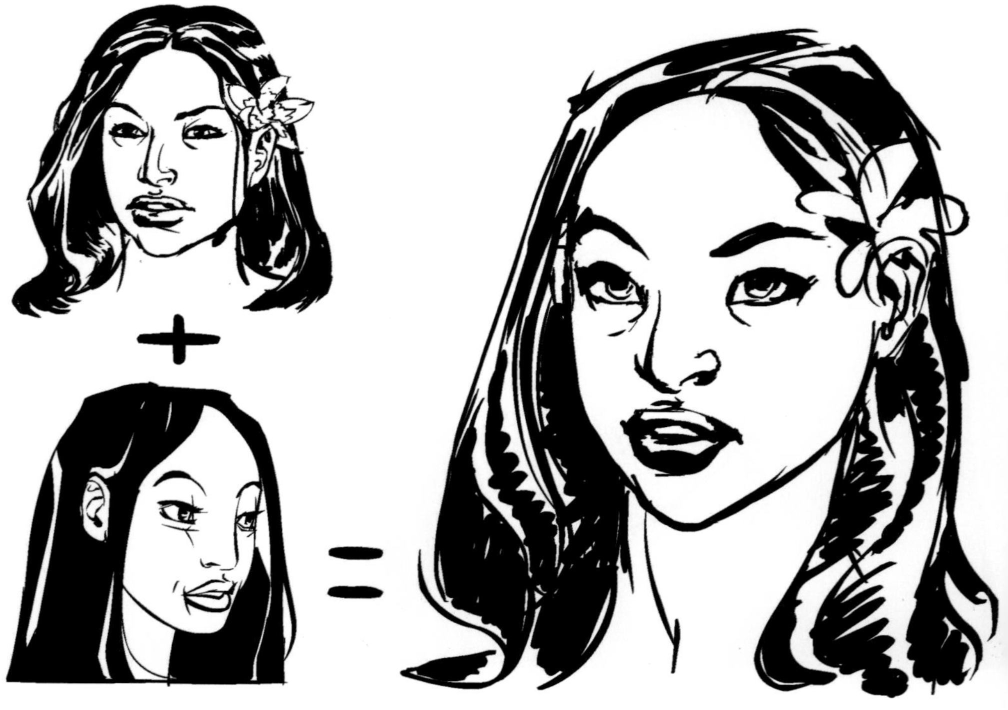

Another two pictures, hopefully I'm getting close at last. Although there's only subtle difference in each feature of the last two, I think I prefer the second out of all so far.

- Steven

I agree with you. I really have no problems with the second Kahami, either. She's my favorite, too. So long as you can get sly and flirty across, she looks great.

- Clay

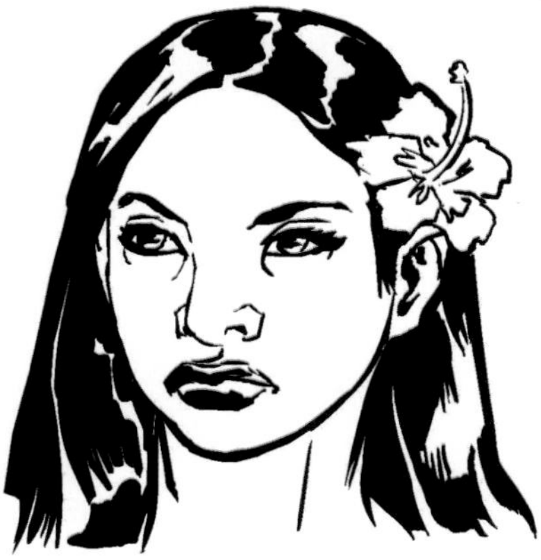

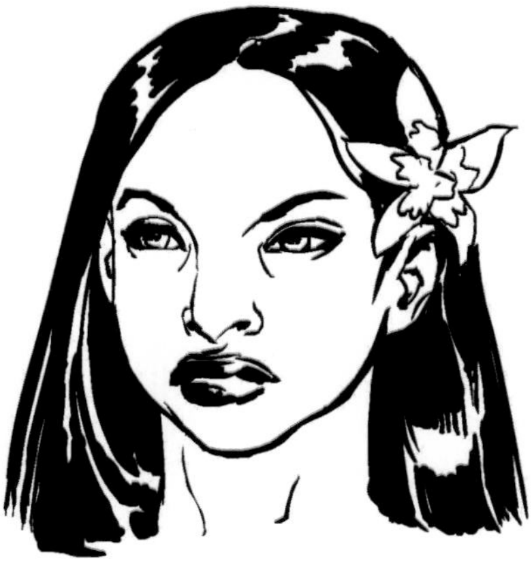

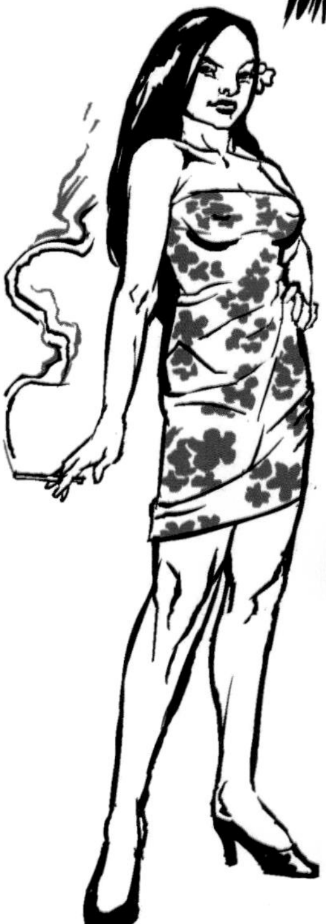

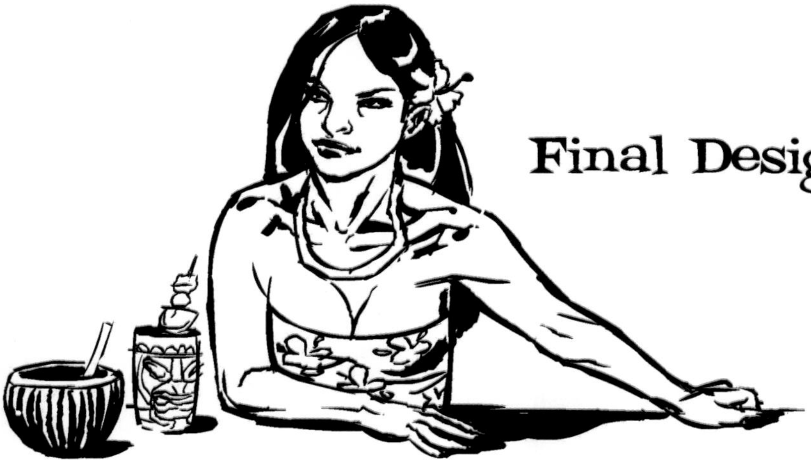

Final Design

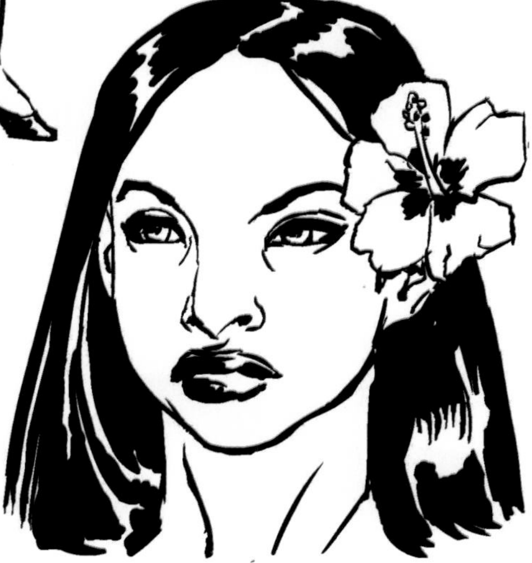

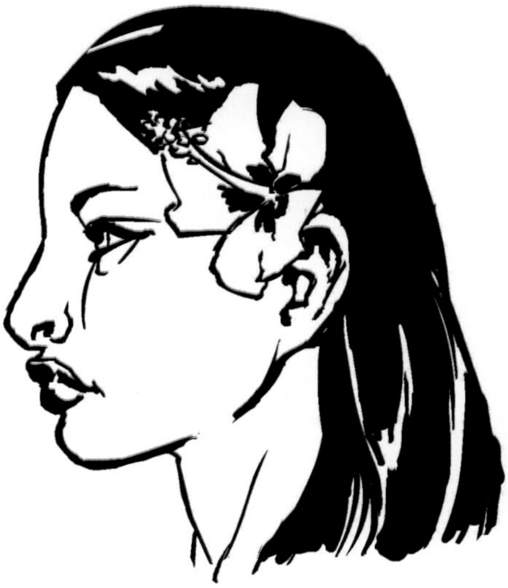

Subject: Re: couple of questions

What do you want Kahami's sister to wear? Gangster moll clothes?

- Steven

Something more "Western," in any event. I picture her sister being eager to kind of break away from the islands, and hanging with gangsters gives her that chance. Maybe something kind of fifties casual. Shorts and a blouse? pants and a blouse? I don't know. Or, hell, if you want to draw her in a cocktail dress, that might be fun...a sexy zombie ready for a night on the town. :) Sorry I'm not more specific here, but I'm not sure it matters that much. What do you think?

- Clay

That's okay. I was just checking in case you had any specific requests...

- Steven

What do you think about the plain black dress? I'm not 100% sure about keeping it, but the reason I went for flat black is that a) it's a black and white comic b) Kahami and Byrd already have Hawaiian print clothing. She might get lost against Mo's black suit though.

- Steven

The dress is okay. I'm not sure how common it would have been circa 1953, though. At this very moment I don't have a better solutions. I love the shot of her as a zombie. No doubt what's going on there.

- Clay

Kahami's sister

BEFORE

AFTER

Do you want her that zombified? ...Since I don't know yet whether she's going to act like a typical zombie, or just a dead girl with a bullet in the head.

- Steven

Yeah, I think that's good. The only thing I might change is that you might make her a bit more rigid...more upright. In the second issue, we'll open with her in the backseat, sitting up straight with that zombified look on her face.

- Clay

Here's some sketches for you to peruse and critique. First up is an alternate design of Kahami's sister, taking in some suggestions you made. I've given her a couple of different outfits as well...

...Tell me which versions you like or don't like for the various characters, and hopefully I'll get pages 5 and 6 to you soon as well, as I don't plan on going to bed tonight (this morning)...

- Steven

You're a maniac, Steven! I haven't looked at the art yet but will report back soon.

Clay

Okay...the girls look great. Keep doing your thing.

- Clay

Final Design

GRIMES

Do you have any specific way you see Grimes, besides the suit and fedora?

- Steven

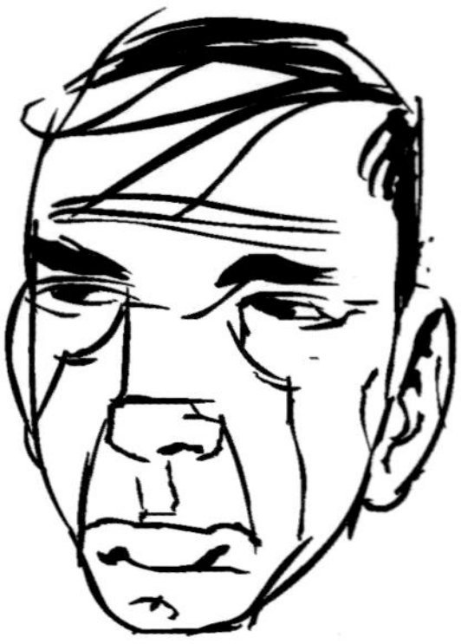

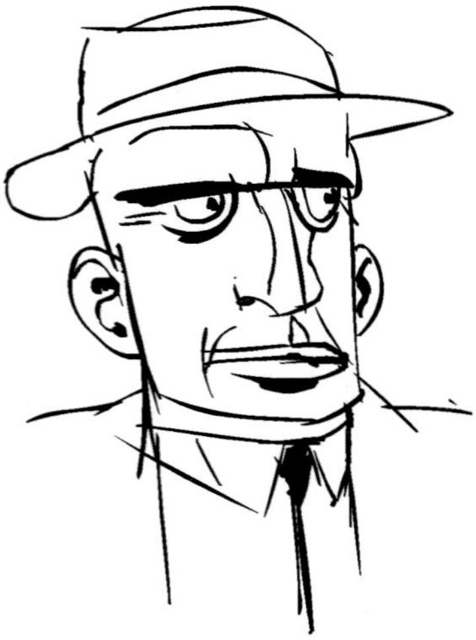

Slightly thuggish looking white guy...average size...don't know if this helps, but I imagine him as a hard guy...not ugly, but not quite handsome. His hat should probably fly off in the last scene to reveal a floppy strand of hair that looks like Lee Marvin's in the attached picture. I like the way in old film noir flicks the bad guys all have this slicked back hair that flies all over when the heat's on.

- Clay

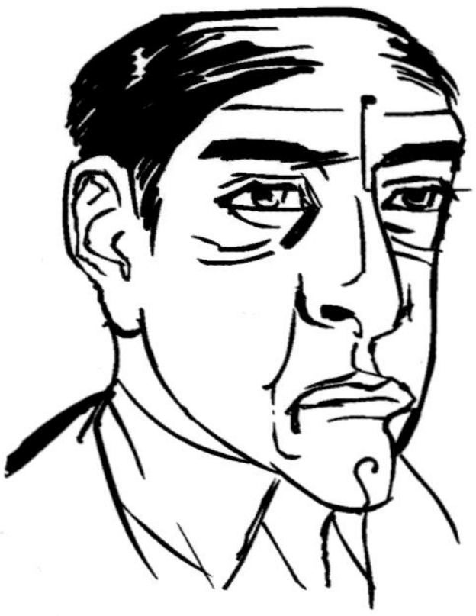

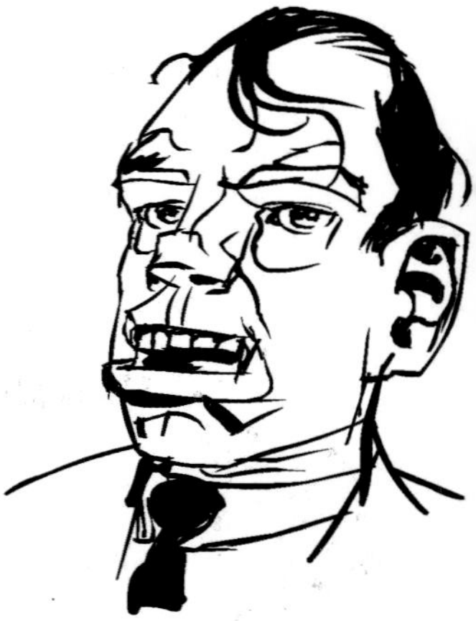

Actually, that character Lee Marvin's playing is pretty much how I envisioned Grimes. The white suit, startled look, bad hair, chimpy mouth, everything.

I've sent a file of a bunch of really rough Grimes sketches just for fun...

I'll send the Mo character sheets as well in a few minutes.

- Steven

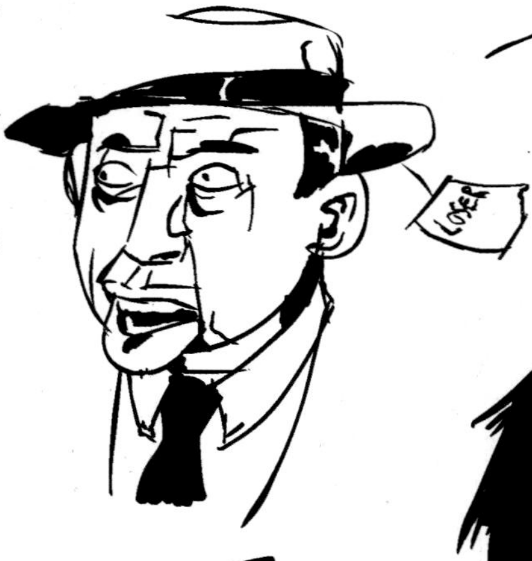
LOSER

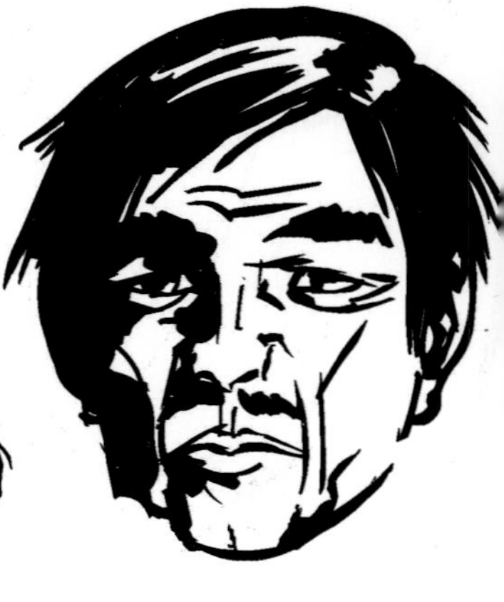

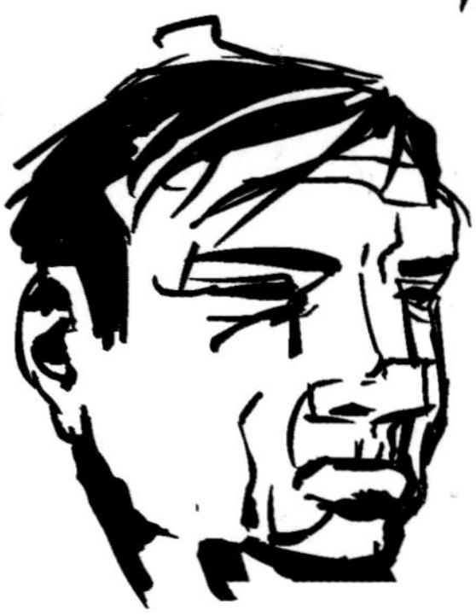

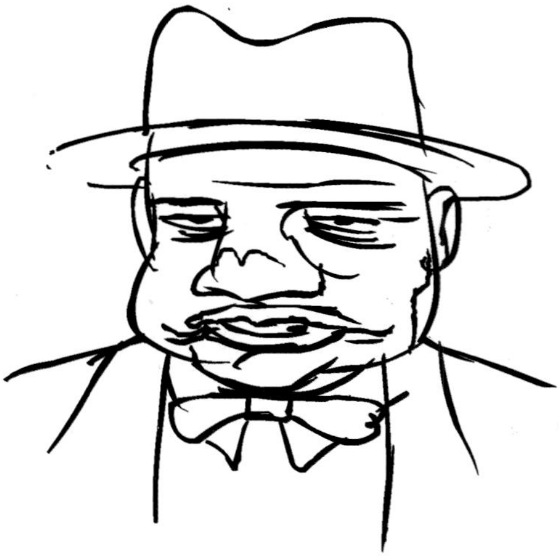

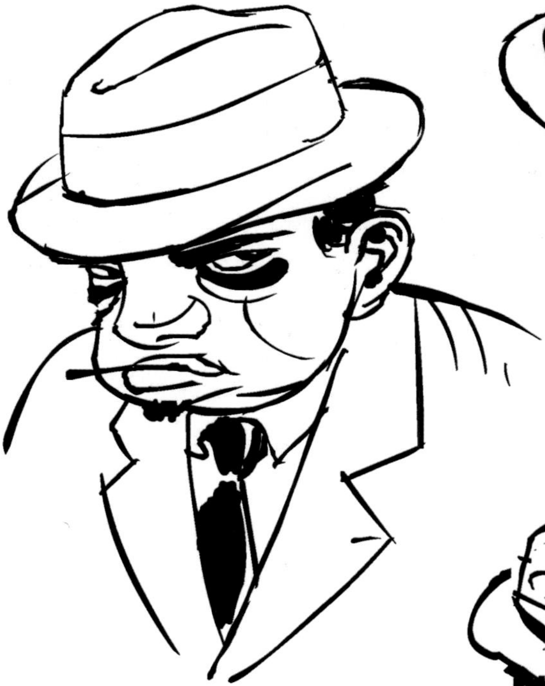

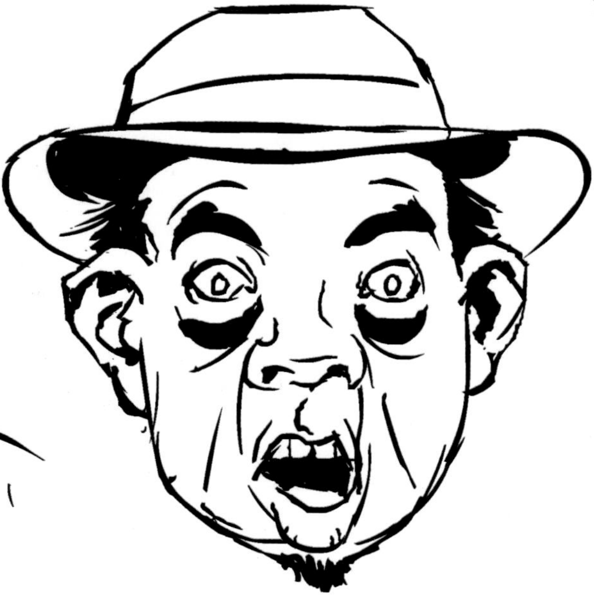

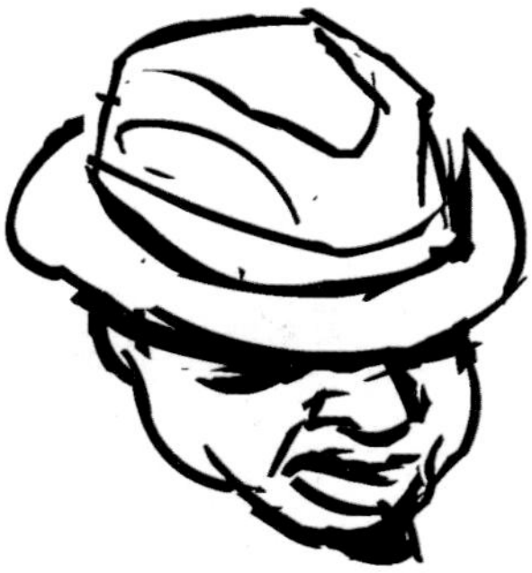

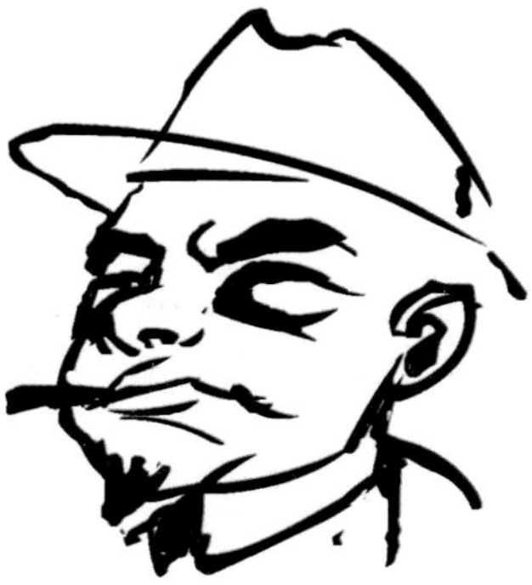

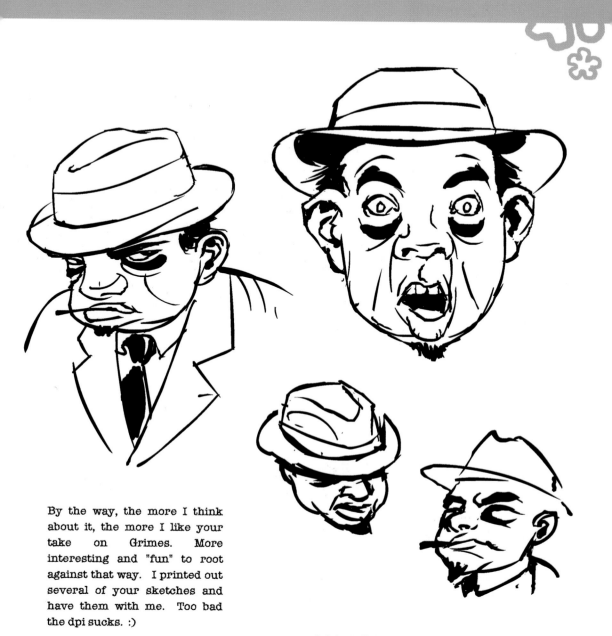

By the way, the more I think about it, the more I like your take on Grimes. More interesting and "fun" to root against that way. I printed out several of your sketches and have them with me. Too bad the dpi sucks. :)

- Clay

haha - The way the email word wrap is set, I was baffled for a second when I read that Grimes was "more interesting and fun to root", which sounds really bad if you live outside the United States. :) But it's all clear now...

- Steven

Subject: Grimes

Does he ever re-appear, or is he just dead?

- Steven

He's just dead.

- Clay

Subject: Masaki

All I have left to draw is Masaki (I think) ...if only I knew what he looks like. :)

- Steven

He's Japanese.
White suit, goatee, hip sunglasses. Carries a diamond headed cane at all times, has kind of an elegant style. Charming but diabolical and deadly. Smiles a wicked smile.

- Clay

Design 1

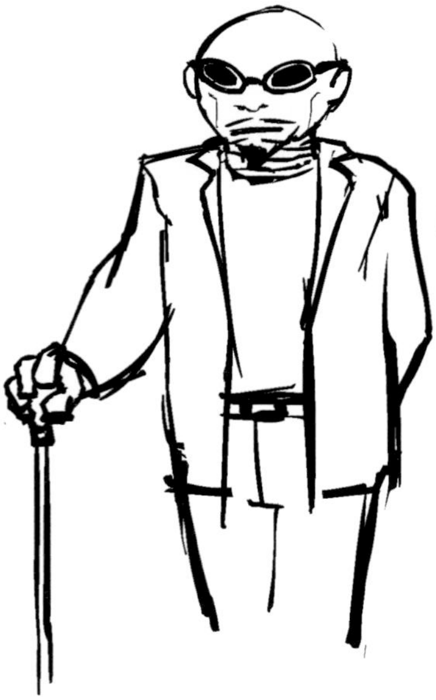

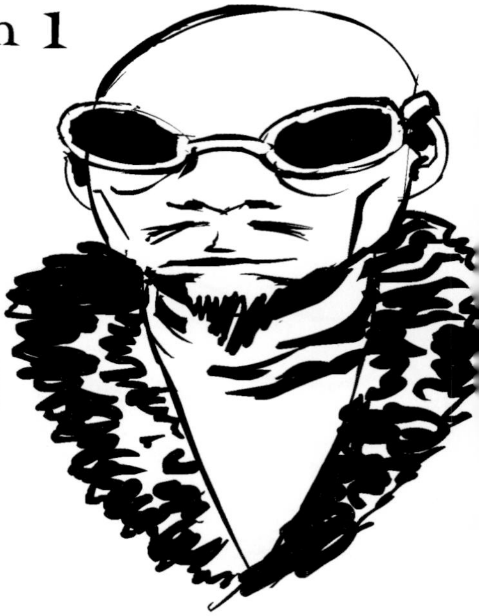

Design 2

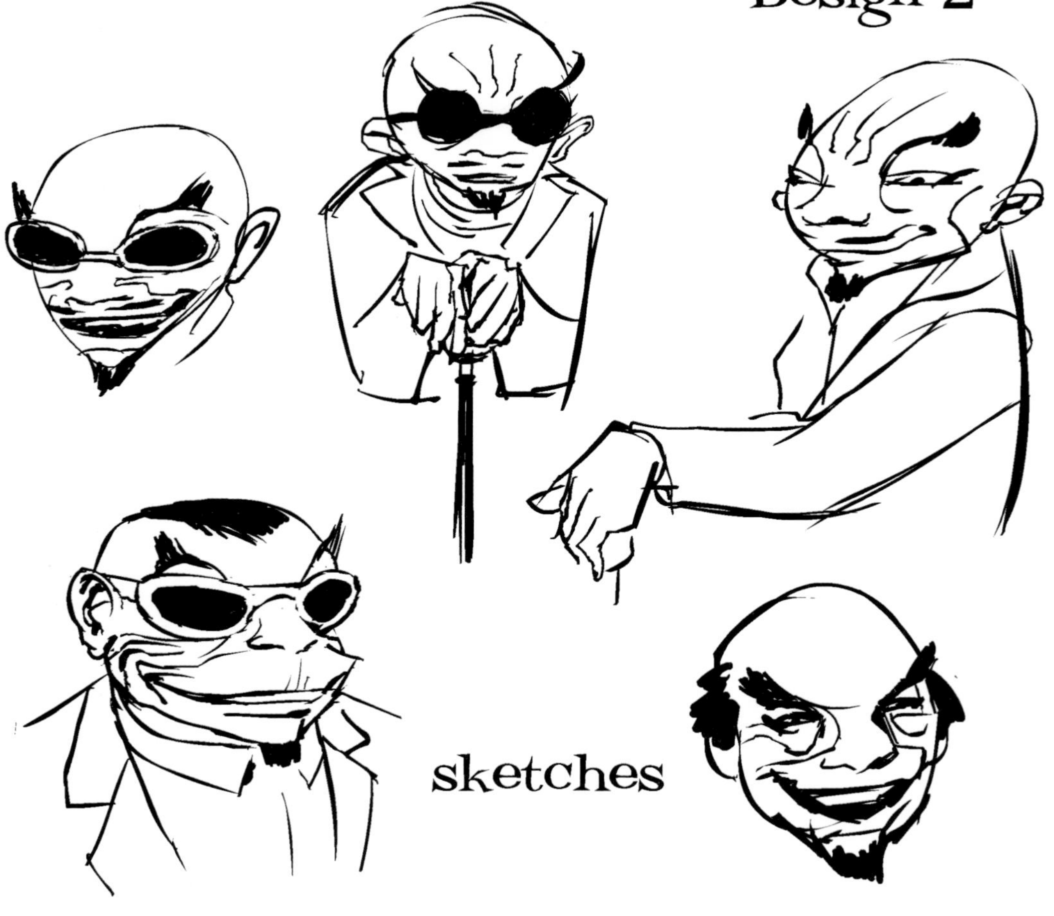

sketches

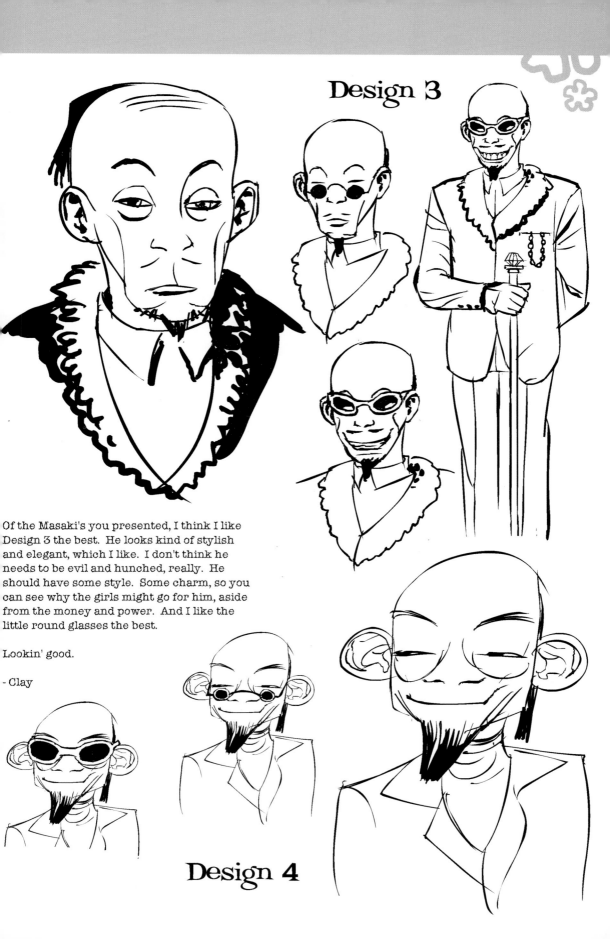

Design 3

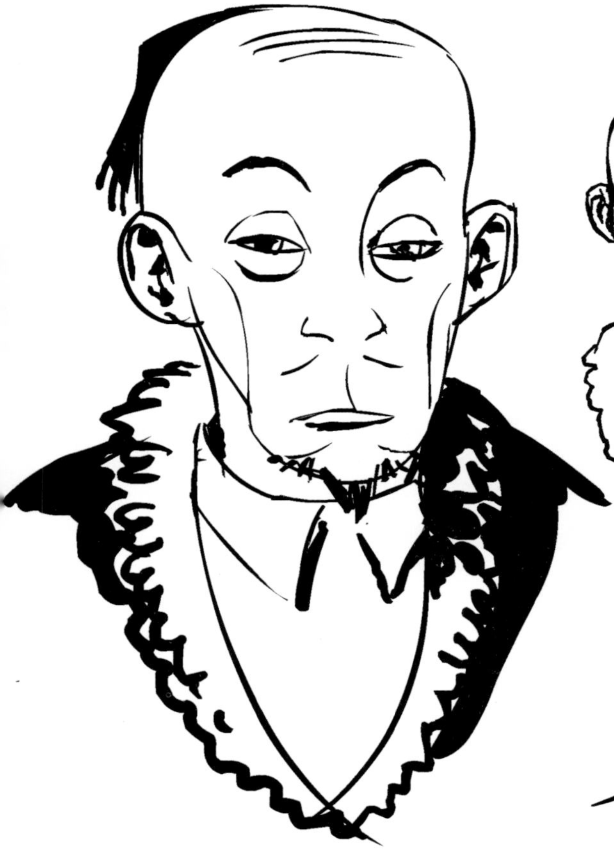

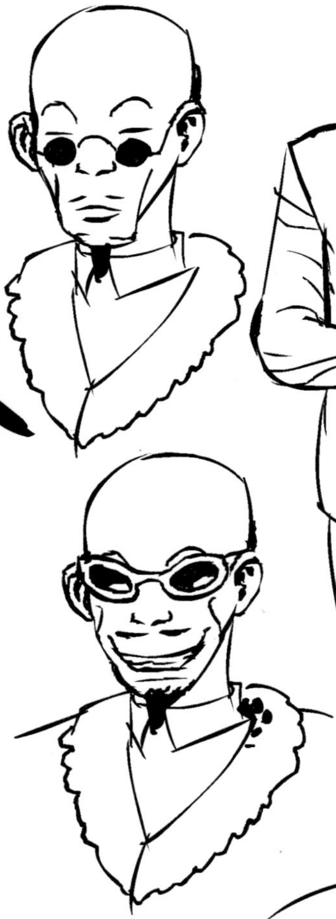

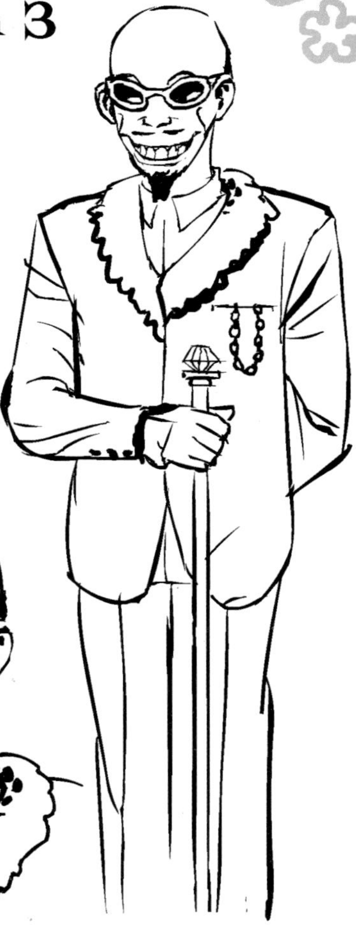

Of the Masaki's you presented, I think I like Design 3 the best. He looks kind of stylish and elegant, which I like. I don't think he needs to be evil and hunched, really. He should have some style. Some charm, so you can see why the girls might go for him, aside from the money and power. And I like the little round glasses the best.

Lookin' good.

- Clay

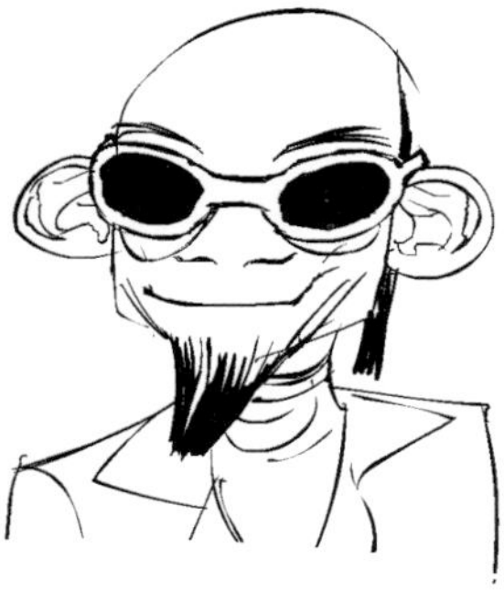

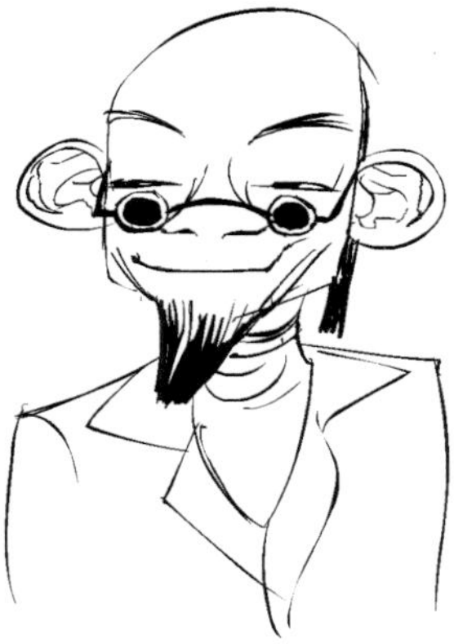

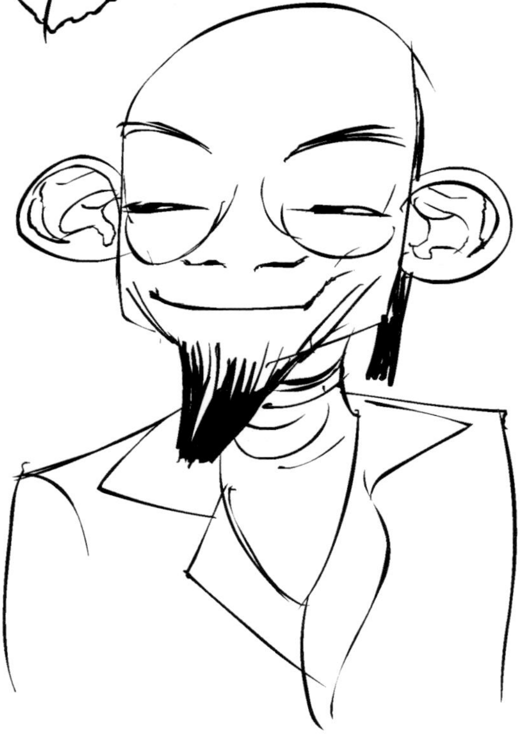

Design 4

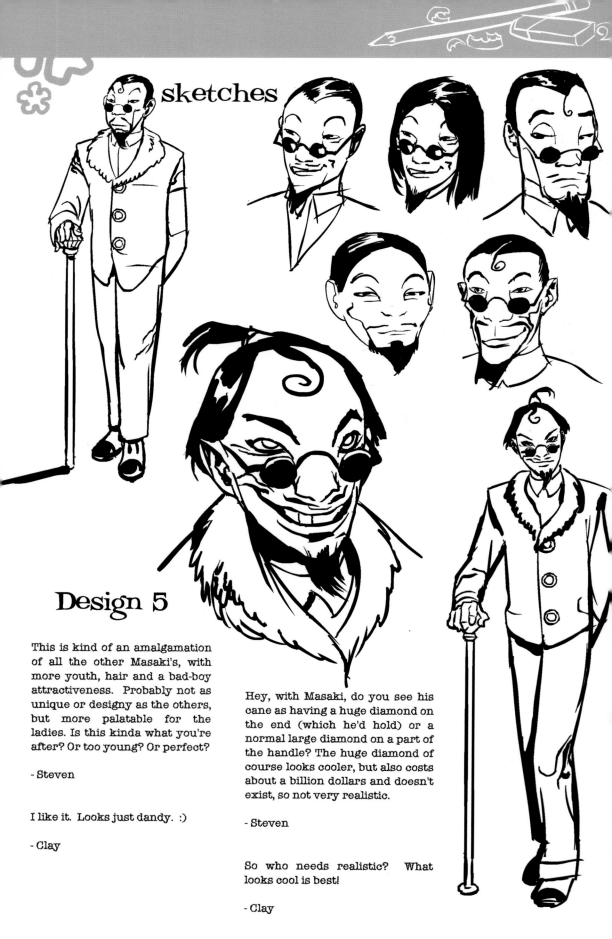

sketches

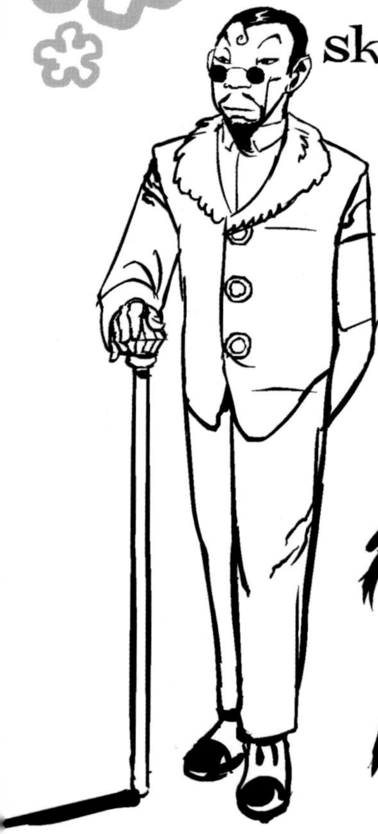

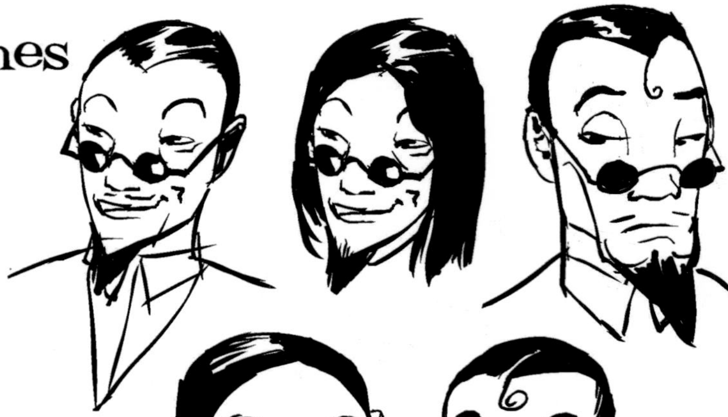

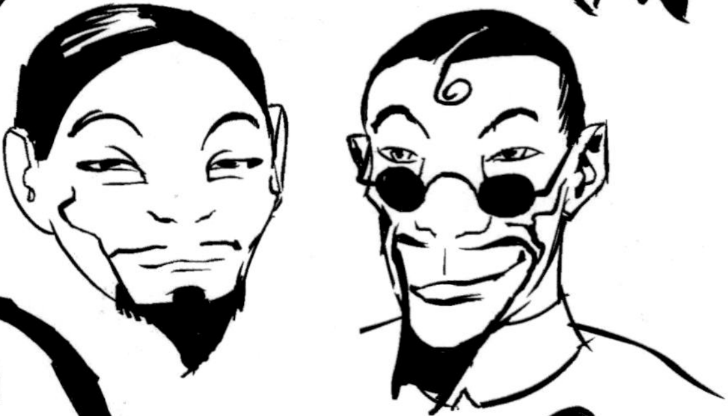

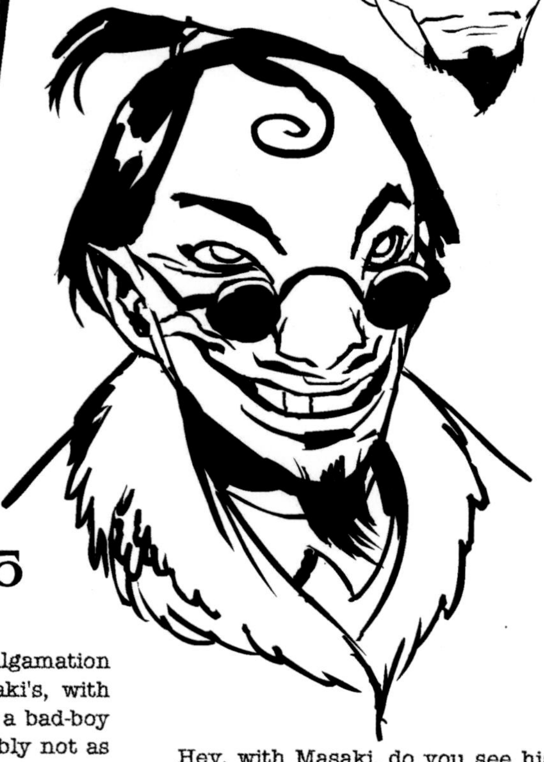

Design 5

This is kind of an amalgamation of all the other Masaki's, with more youth, hair and a bad-boy attractiveness. Probably not as unique or designy as the others, but more palatable for the ladies. Is this kinda what you're after? Or too young? Or perfect?

- Steven

I like it. Looks just dandy. :)

- Clay

Hey, with Masaki, do you see his cane as having a huge diamond on the end (which he'd hold) or a normal large diamond on a part of the handle? The huge diamond of course looks cooler, but also costs about a billion dollars and doesn't exist, so not very realistic.

- Steven

So who needs realistic? What looks cool is best!

- Clay

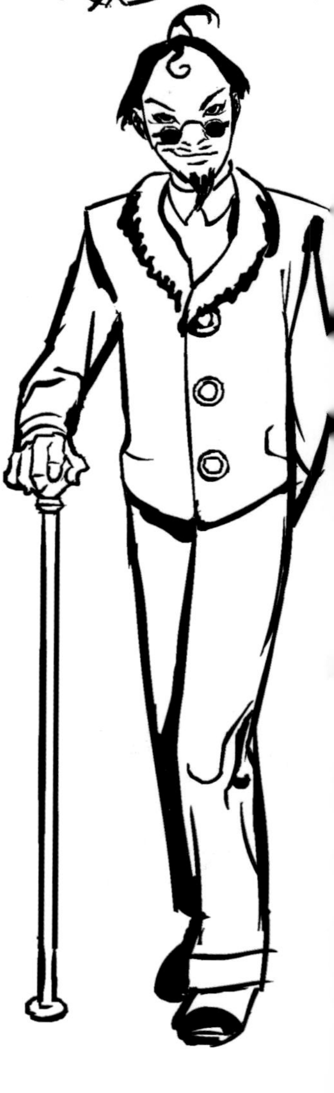

NIGHT MARCHERS

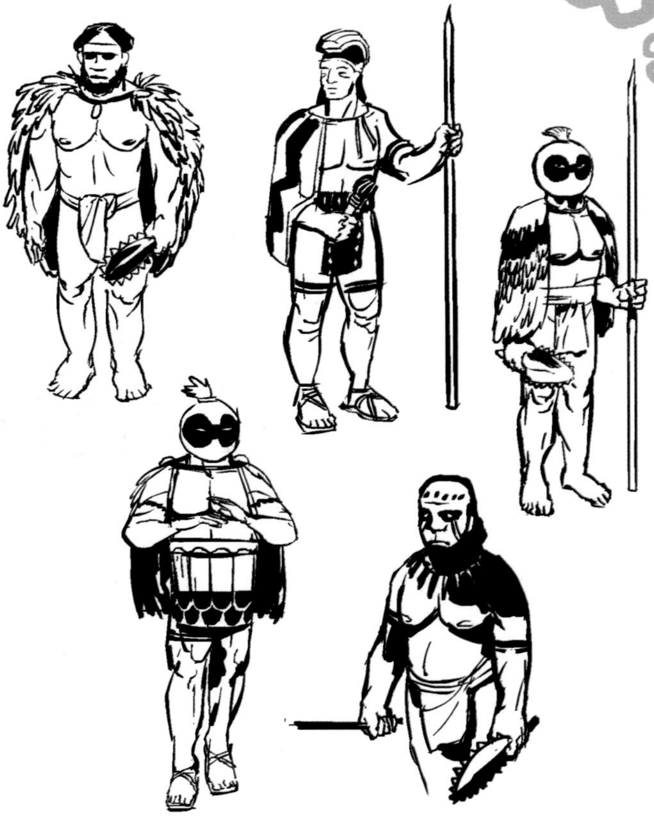

Subject: Night Marchers

A couple of stories have the Night Marchers floating without legs. And a few also say they're high-ranking warriors (which would mean they all had feather helmets and capes). However, I first read that they were the warriors of a certain battle they lost and now forever tread the same path they marched that day (which is why in my group shot, I tried to draw them as proper army. With the king (full length cape) in front, a couple of high ranking guys around him and regular soldiers in the back). Do you have any better idea what the deal is? I think being legless is kinda cool, and I could just fog or blacken out their lower half to give that ghostly appearance.

- Steven

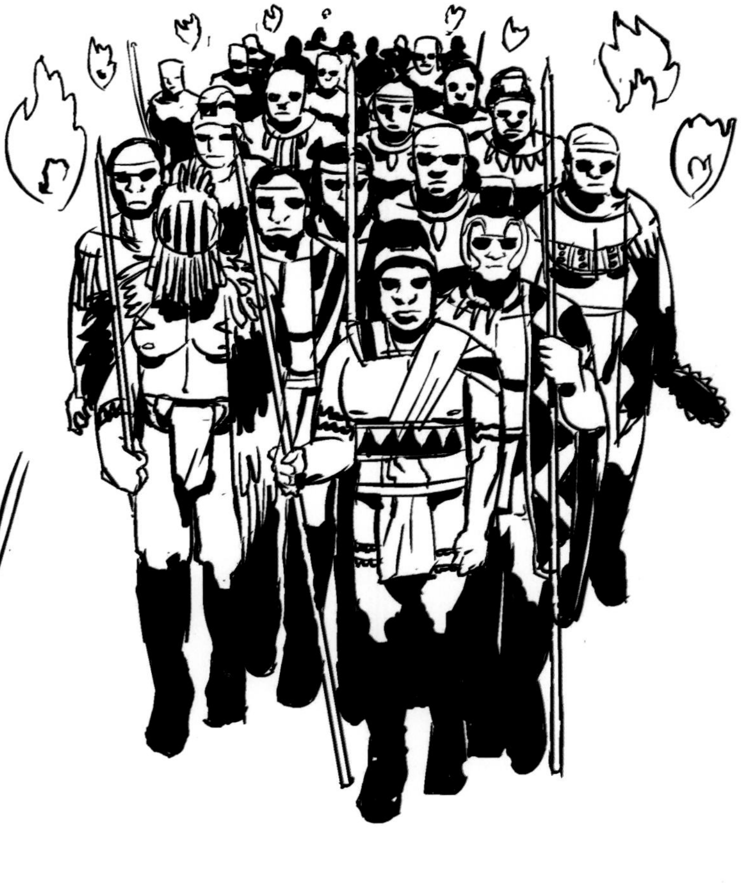

If you want to play around and draw them that way, go for it. I recently watched a show on the Night Marchers, and I don't recall any mention of specific origins, or of them being legless, but if you can make it work, do it.

- Clay

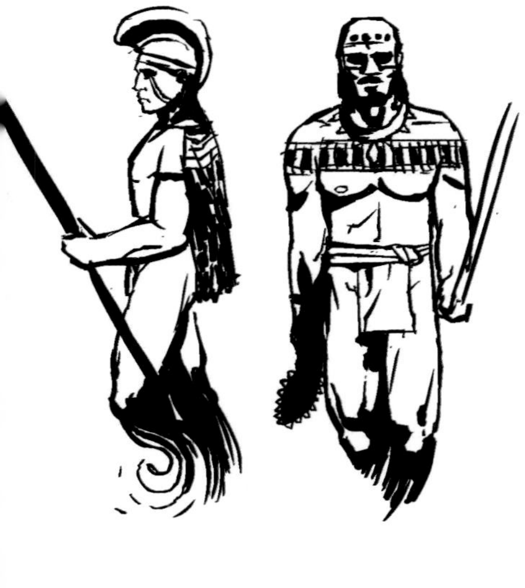

COVER DESIGN

My process for creating covers is different to story pages - it's pretty much anything goes. I like to throw things around, make a big mess, produce a whole bunch of options and finally settle on a design minutes before it's due.

- Steven

Development process of covers

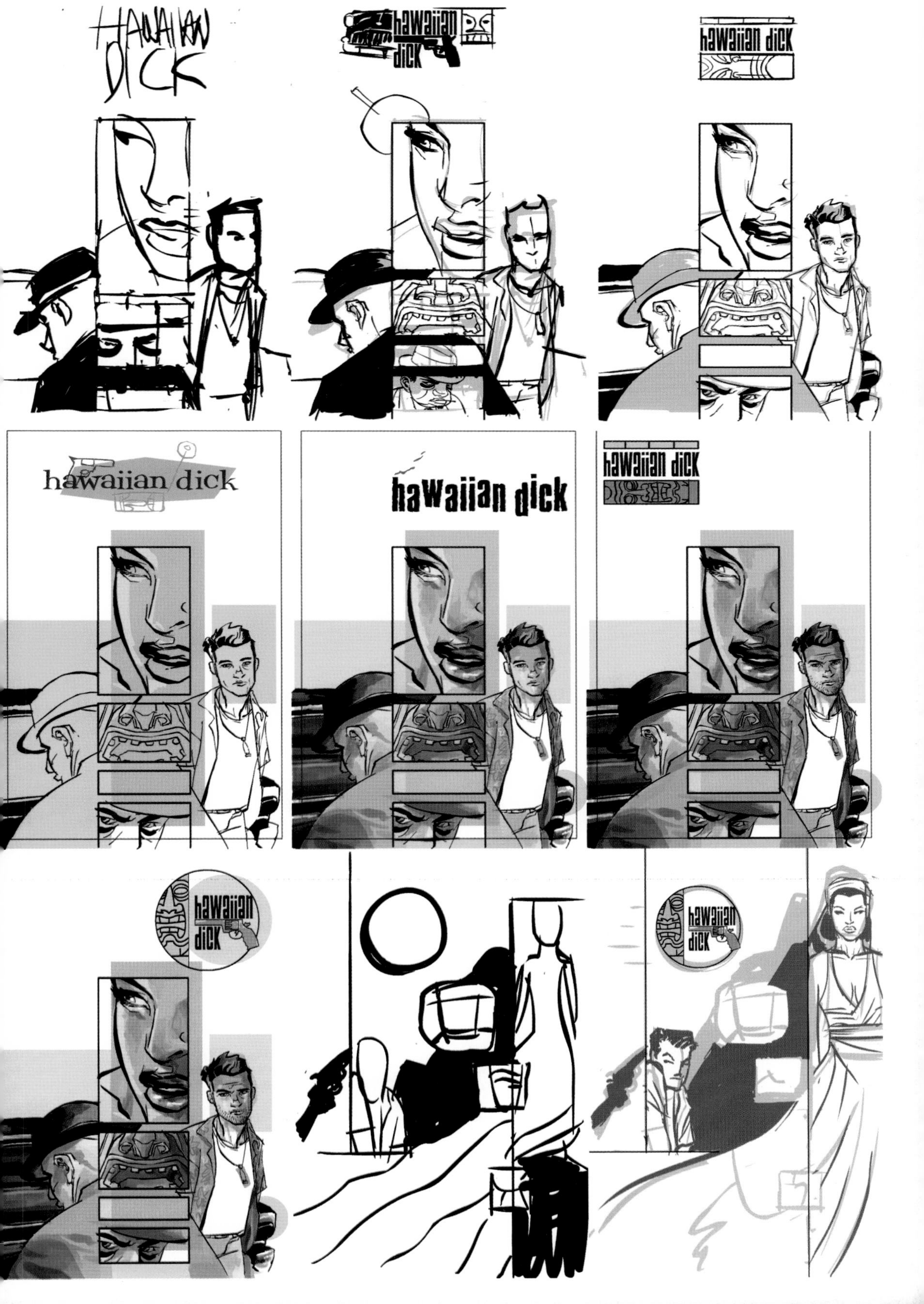
HAWAIIAN DICK
hawaiian dick
hawaiian dick
hawaiian dick
hawaiian dick
hawaiian dick
hawaiian dick
hawaiian dick

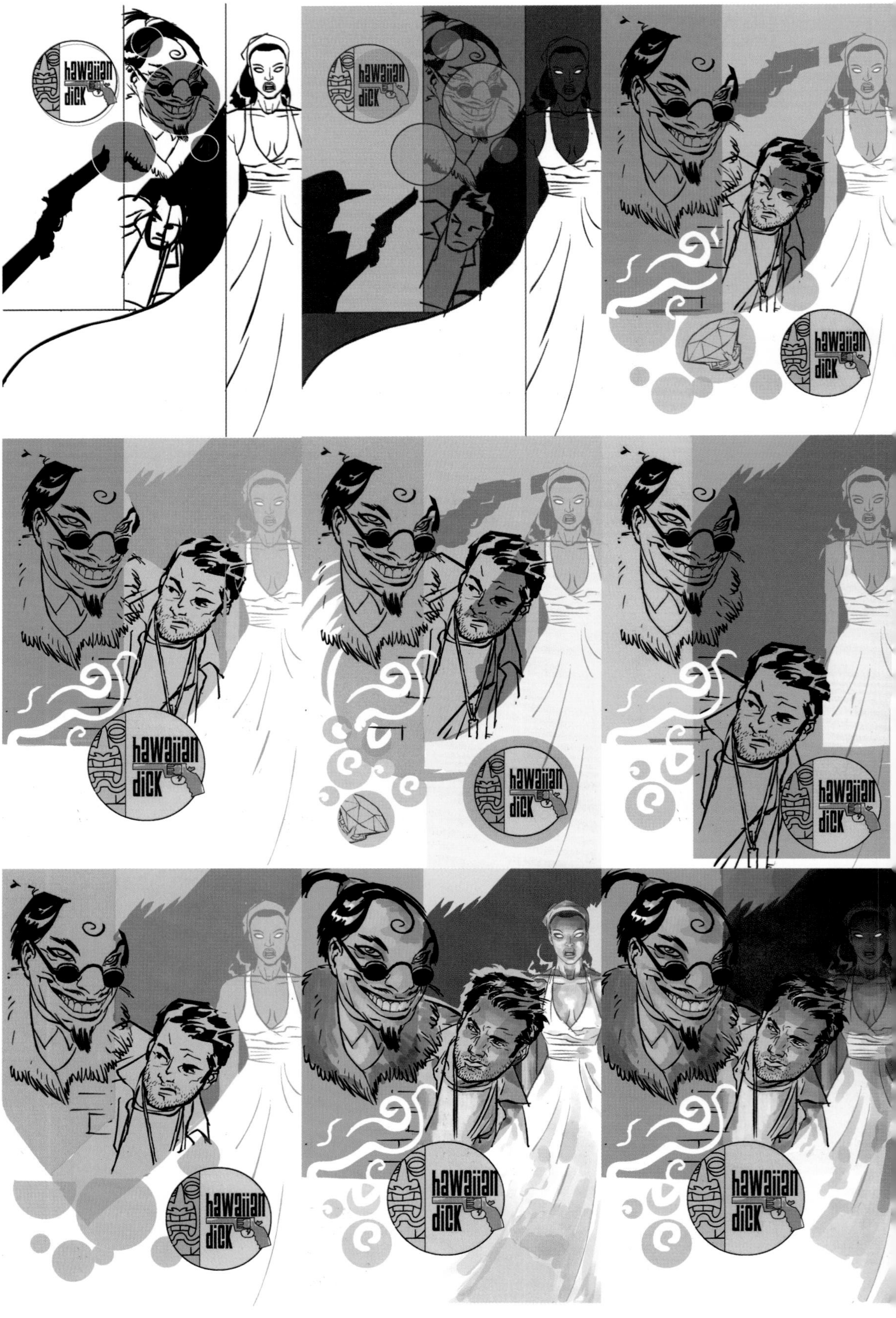
hawaiian dick
hawaiian dick
hawaiian dick
hawaiian dick
hawaiian dick
hawaiian dick
hawaiian dick
hawaiian dick
hawaiian dick

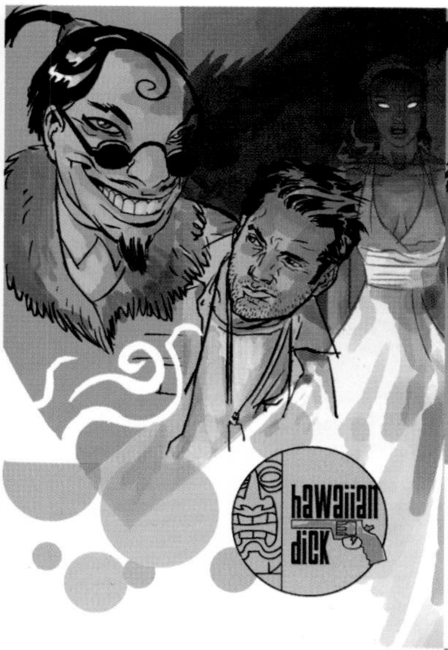
hawaiian
dick
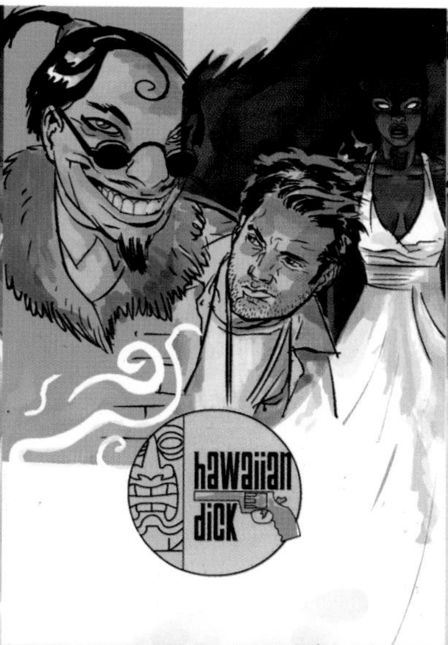
hawaiian
dick
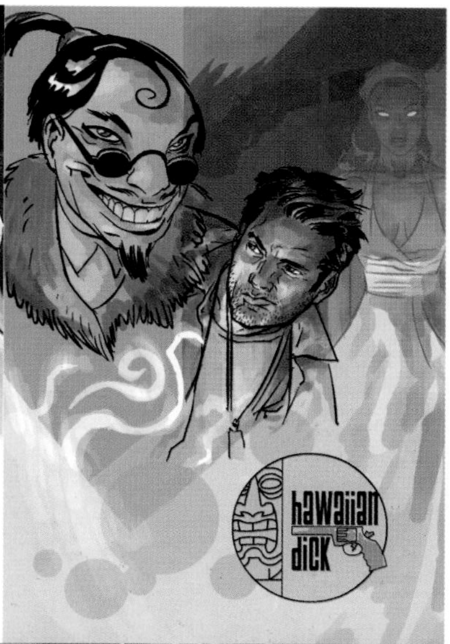
hawaiian
dick
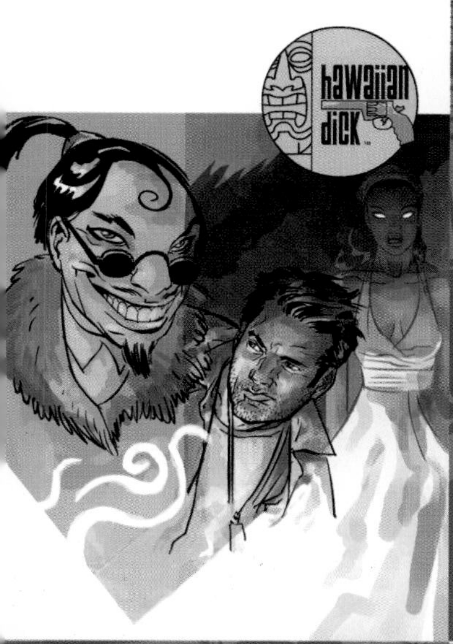
hawaiian
dick
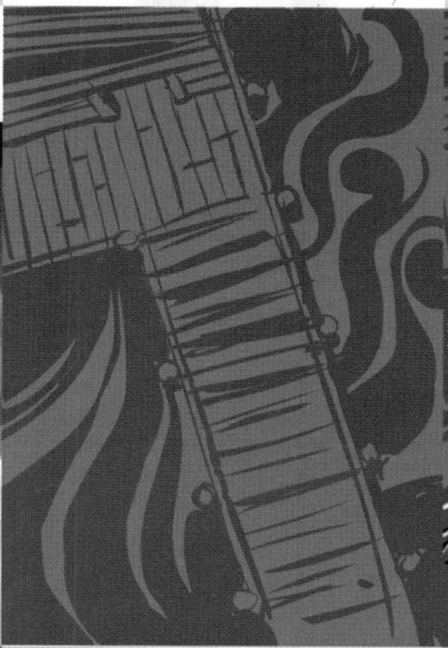
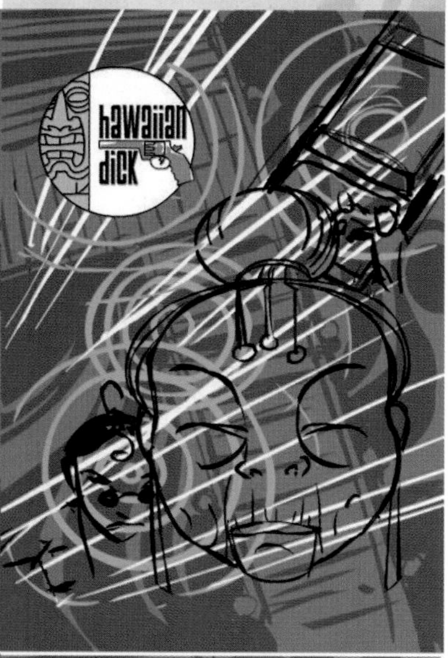
hawaiian
dick
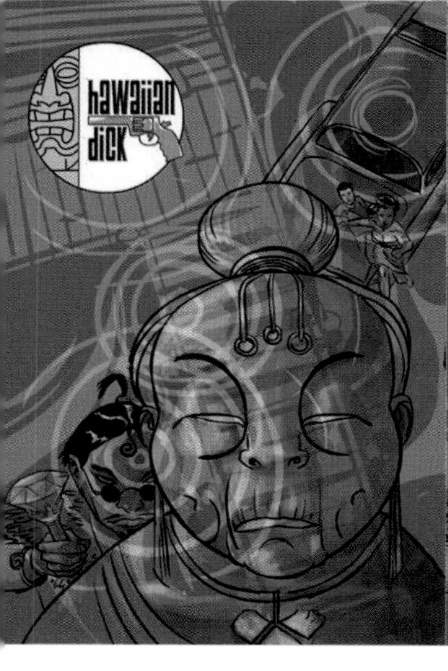
hawaiian
dick
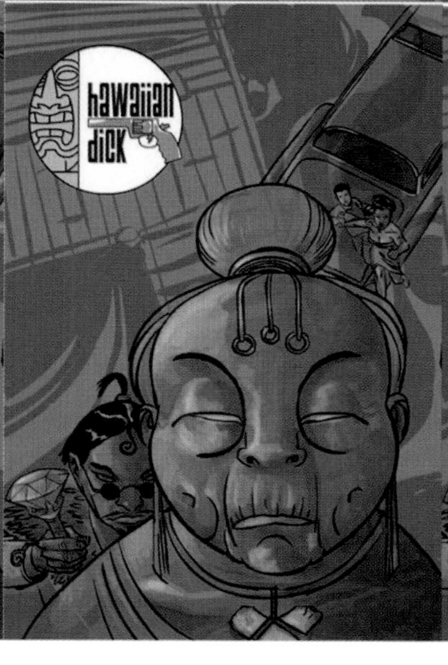
hawaiian
dick
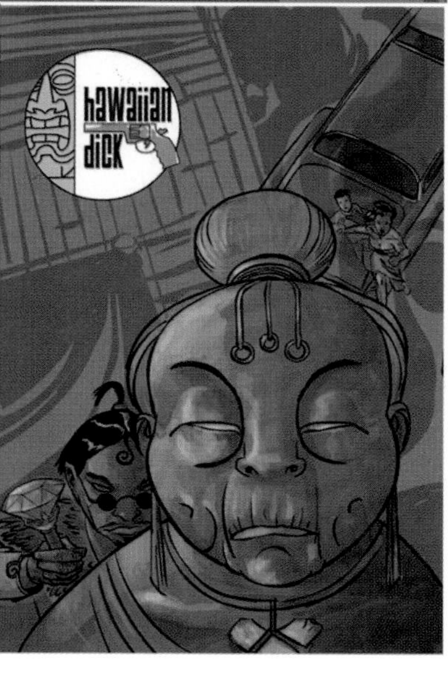
hawaiian
dick

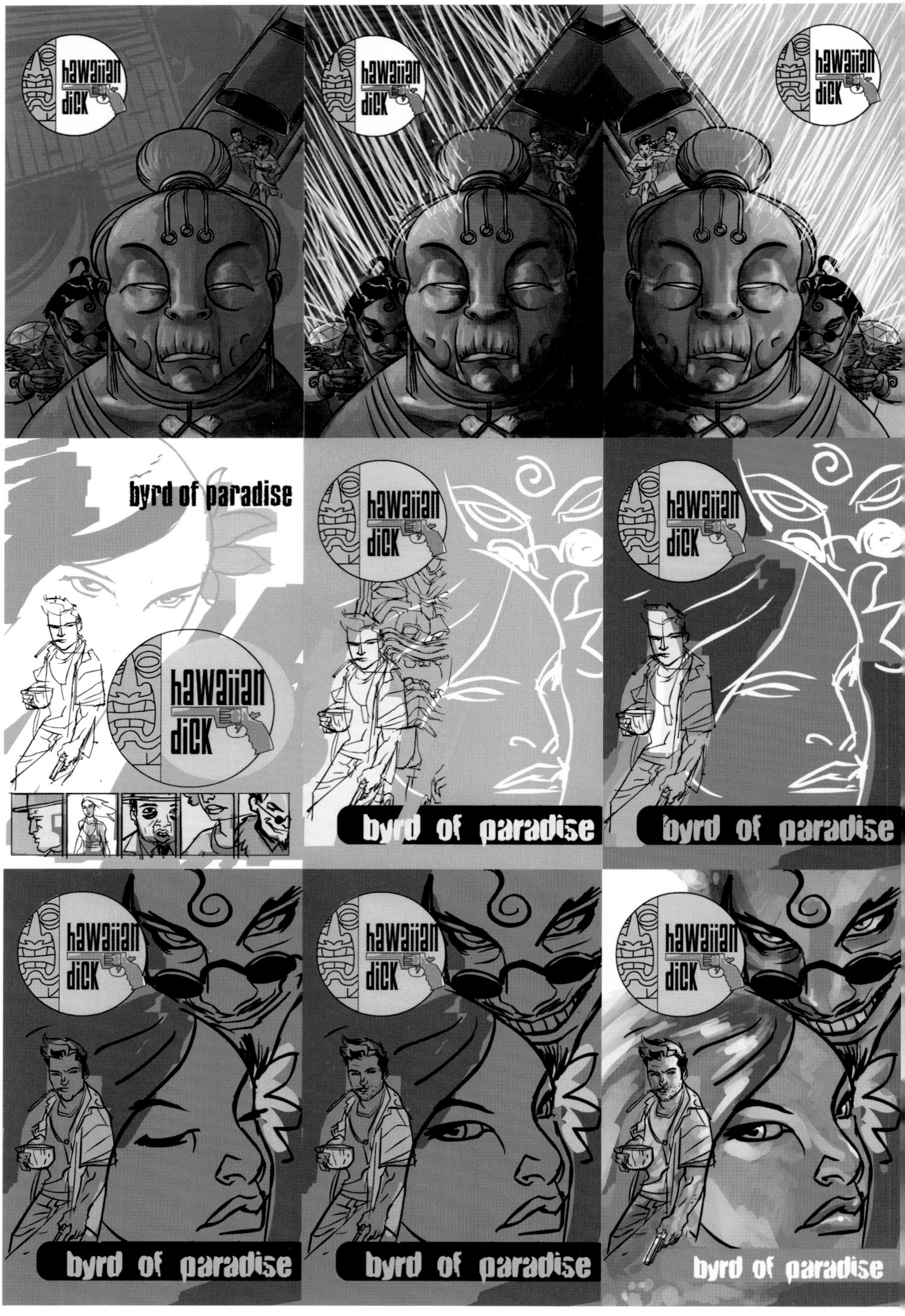
hawaiian dick
hawaiian dick
hawaiian dick
byrd of paradise
hawaiian dick
hawaiian dick
byrd of paradise
hawaiian dick
byrd of paradise
hawaiian dick
byrd of paradise
hawaiian dick
byrd of paradise
hawaiian dick
byrd of paradise
hawaiian dick
byrd of paradise

Sketches for unused cover designs

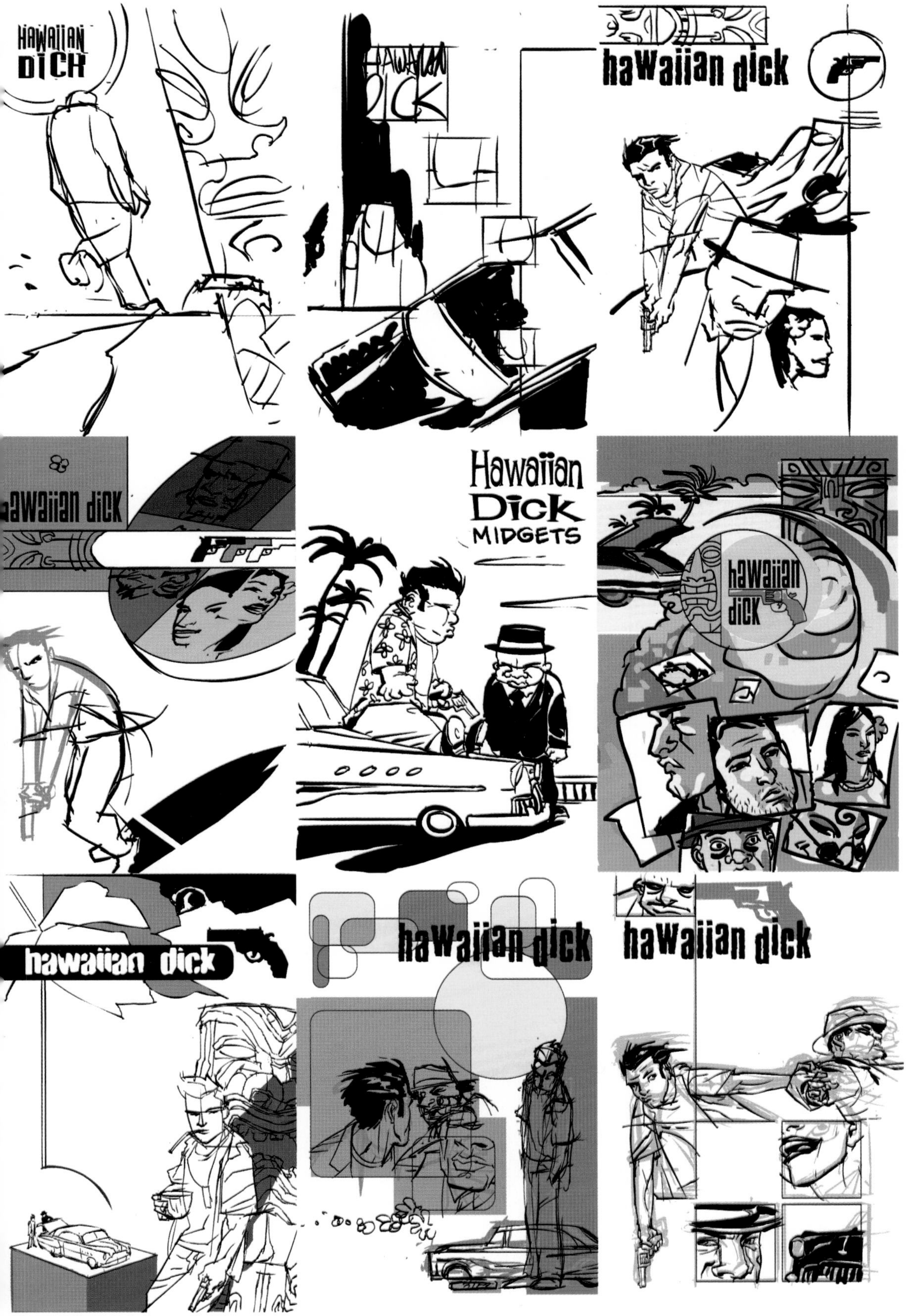
HAWAIIAN DICK
HAWAIIAN DICK
hawaiian dick
hawaiian dick
Hawaiian Dick
MIDGETS
hawaiian dick
hawaiian dick
hawaiian dick
hawaiian dick

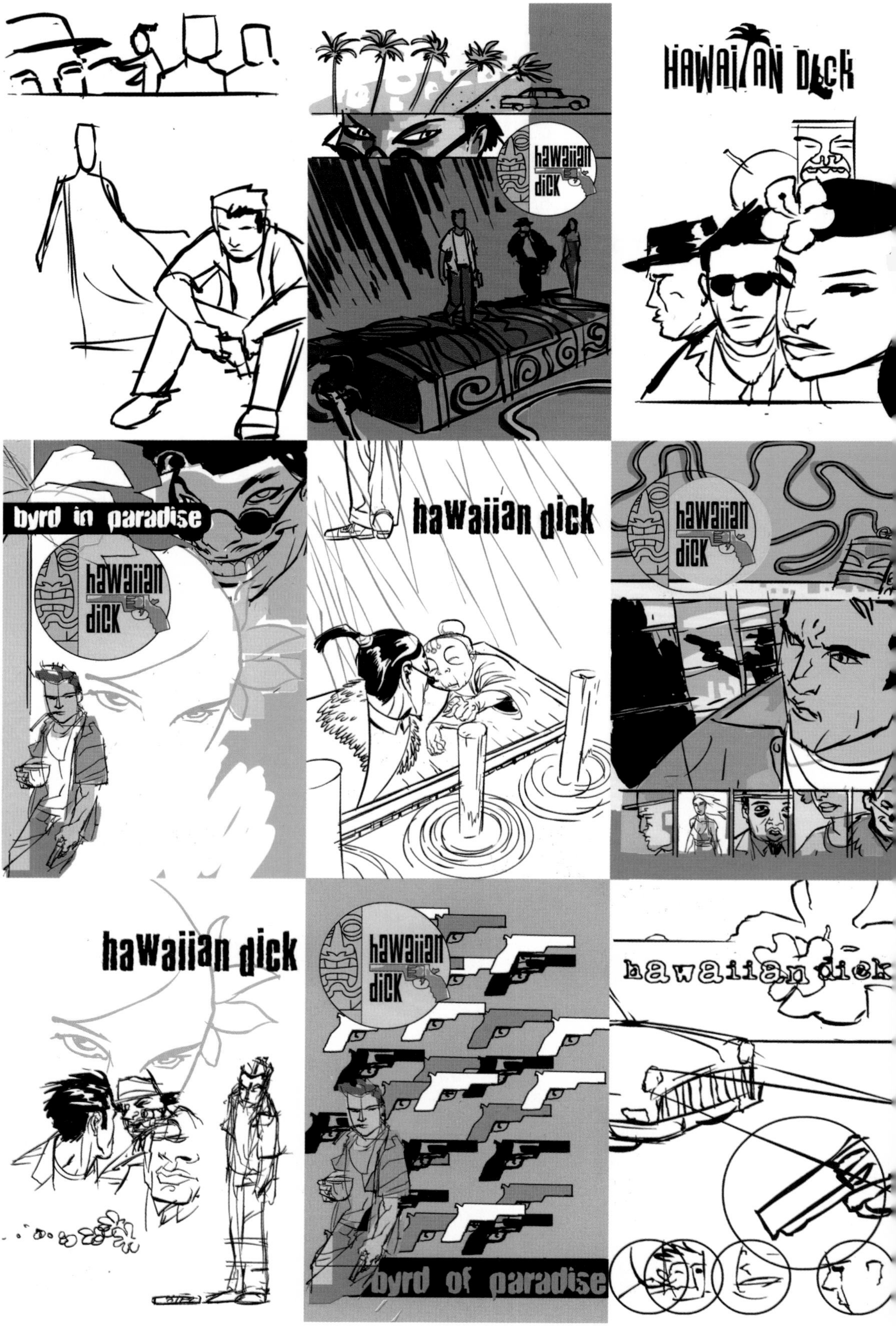

hawaiian dick
HAWAIIAN DICK
byrd in paradise
hawaiian dick
hawaiian dick
hawaiian dick
hawaiian dick
hawaiian dick
hawaiian dick
byrd of paradise
hawaiian dick

Unused cover concept for issue 2

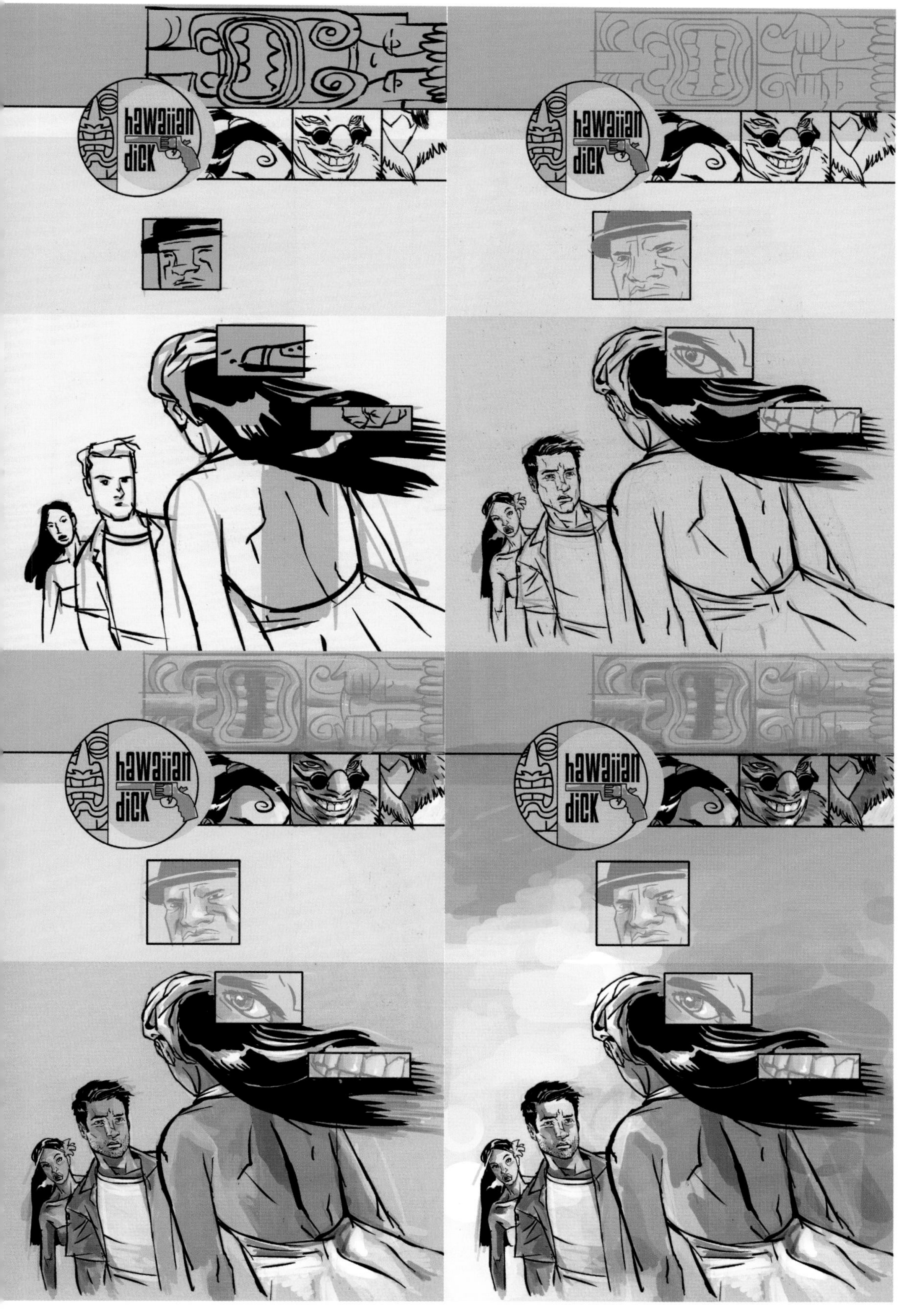
hawaiian dick

Mock-cover used for initial pitch.

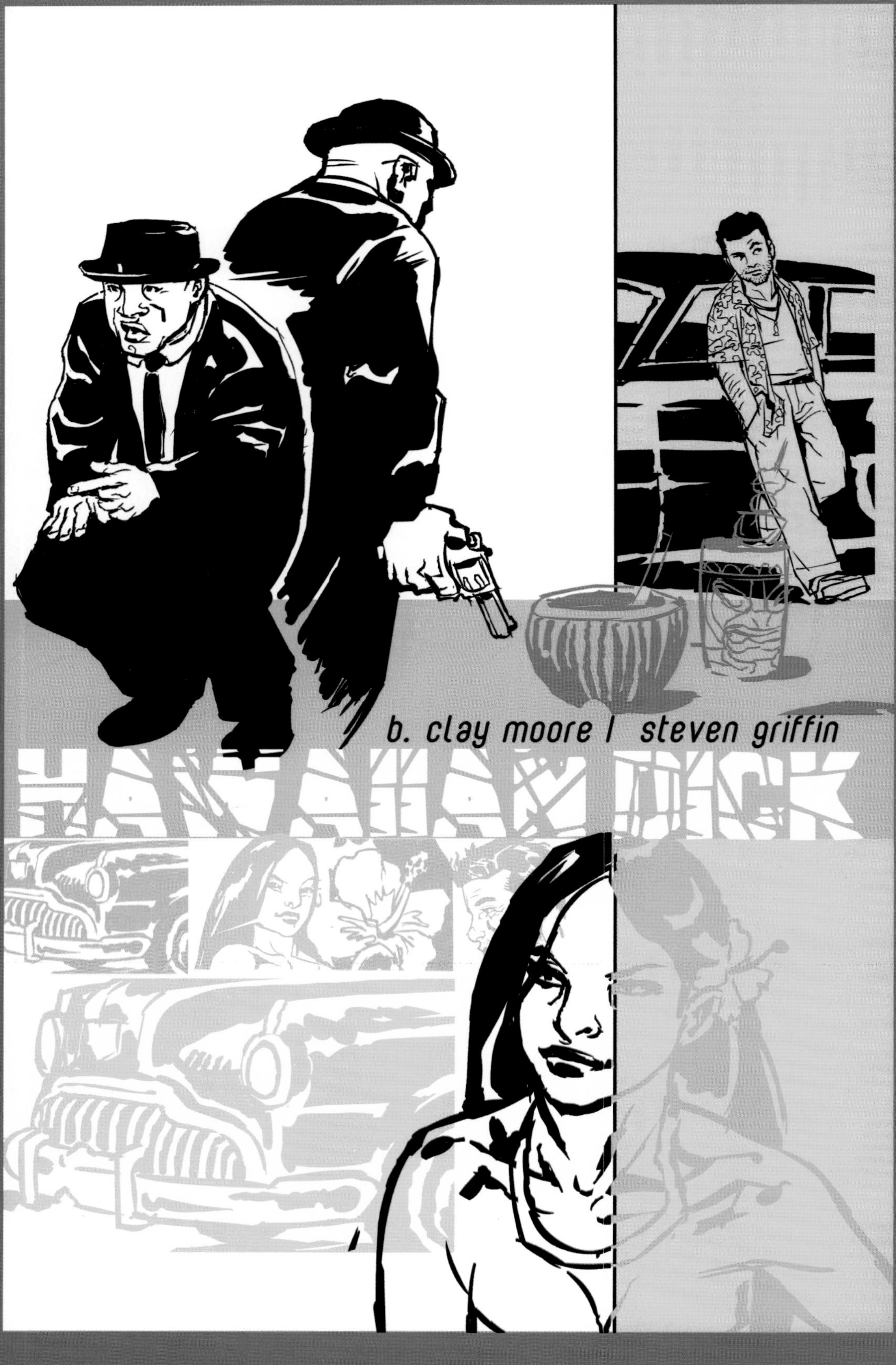
b. clay moore / steven griffin
HAWAIIAN DICK

Early Byrd piece. Unused.

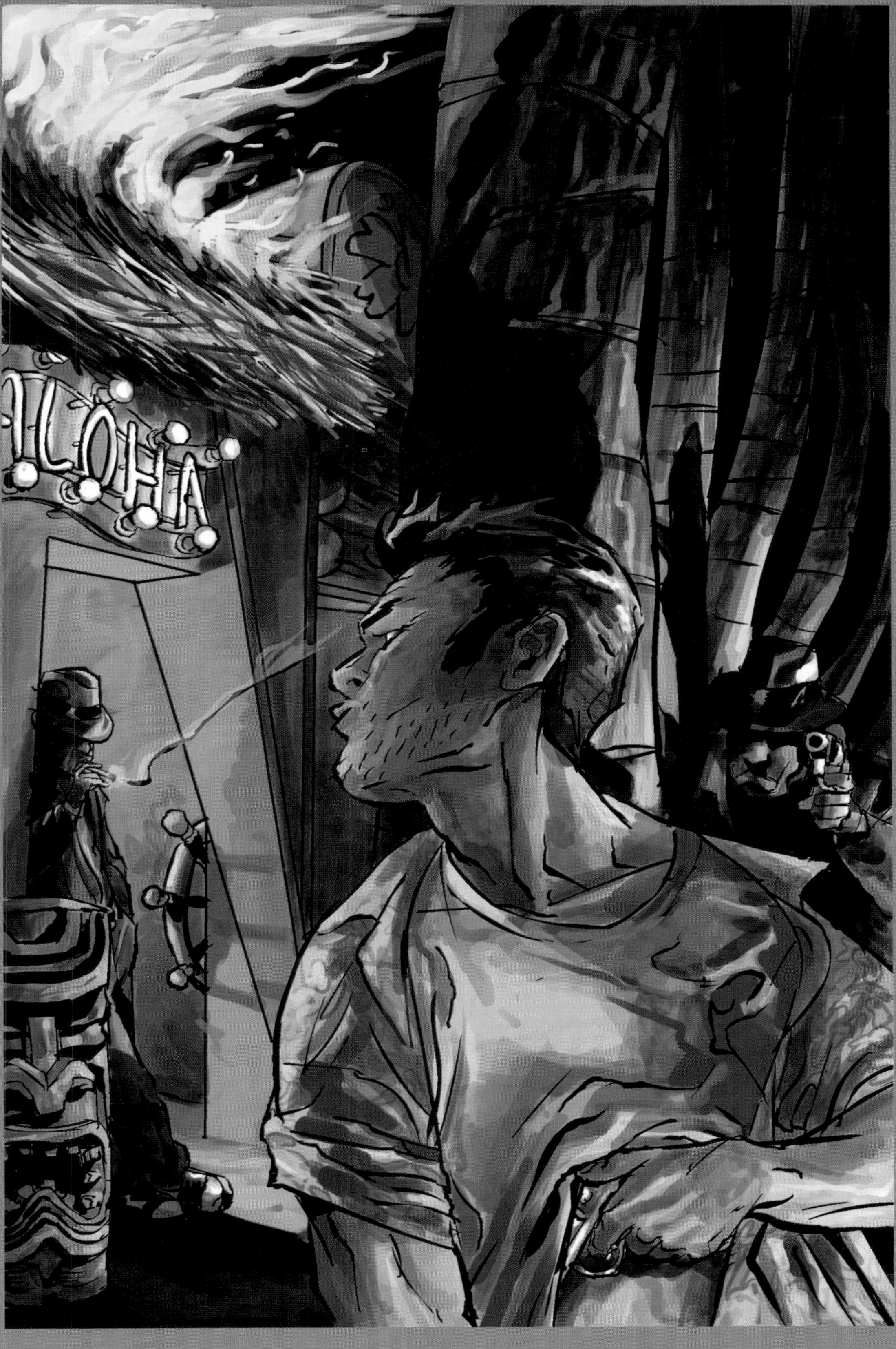
LOHA

Early cover design. Used for promotion.

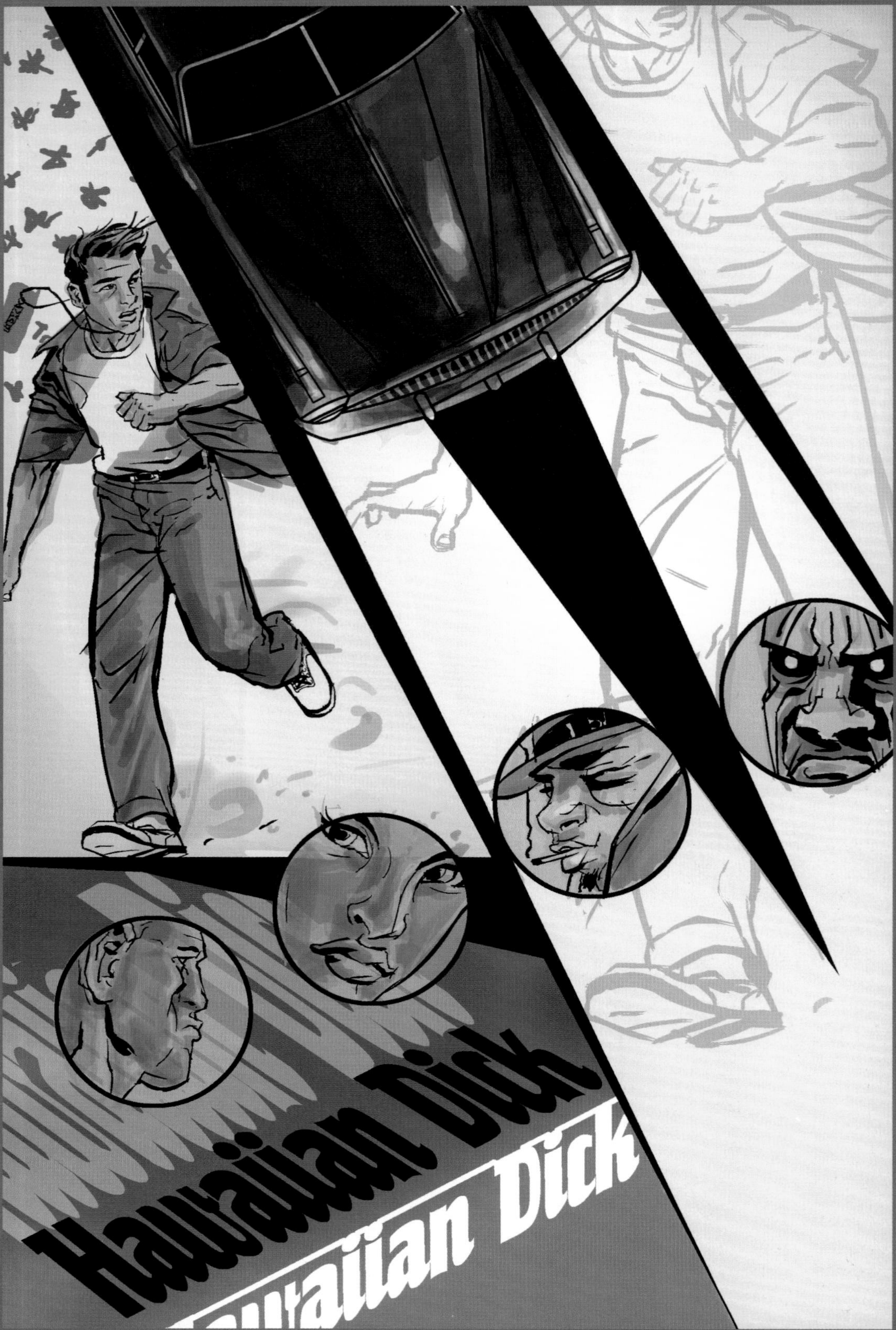
Hawaiian Dick
Hawaiian Dick

THE OUTRIGGER DRINK MENU

Tropical delights
served cooler than an
island breeze.

1. Mai Tai

This is the original Mai Tai formula from 1944, invented by Trader Vic's. You'll notice its ingredients do not include any juices (besides lime juice), which is the way all true Mai Tais are made.

Ingredients:

2 oz. 17-year old J. Wray & Nephew Rum over shaved ice.
1 fresh Lime
1/2 oz. Holland DeKuyper Orange Curacao.
1/4 oz. Trader Vic's Rock Candy Syrup.
1/2 oz. French Garier Orgeat Syrup

Cut the lime in half and squeeze juice over shaved ice. Add the remaining ingredients. Shake vigorously.

Garnish with a lime shell and a sprig of fresh mint. Serve with straws.

"... I gave two of them to Ham and Carrie Guild, friends fro Tahiti, who were there that night.

Carrie took one sip and said, "Mai Tai - Roa Ae". In Tahitia this means "Out of This World - The Best." Well, that wa that. I named the drink "Mai Tai."

"...In 1953 the Mai Tai was brought by me to the Hawaiia Islands, when I was asked by the Matson Steamship Lines t formalize drinks for the bars at their Royal Hawaiian, Moan and Surfrider Hotels. Any old Kamaaina can tell you abou this drink and of its rapid spread throughout the islands."
--Trader Vics

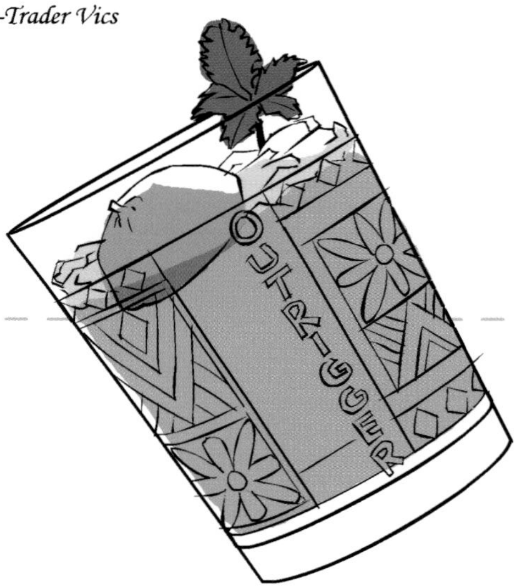
OUTRIGGER

2. Leilani Volcano

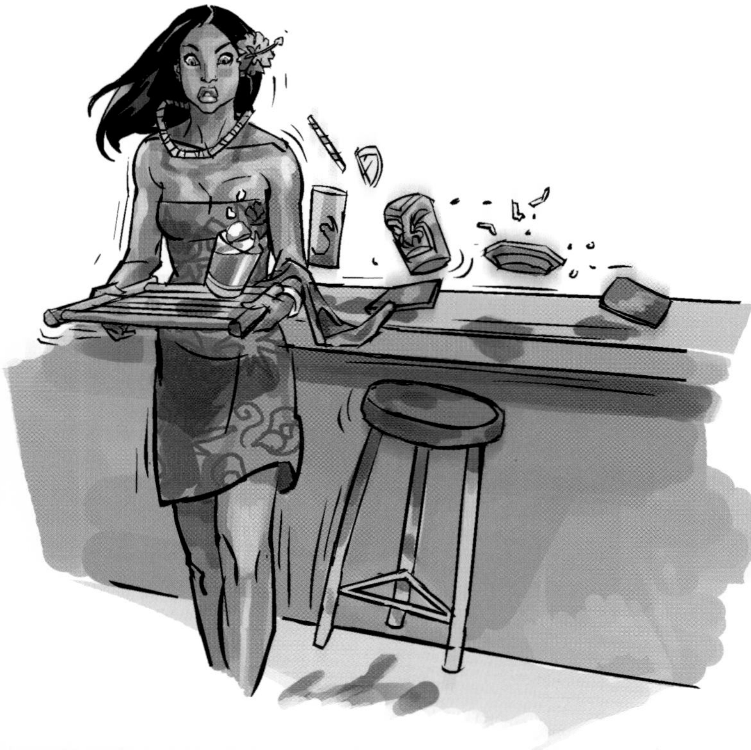

Ingredients:

4 oz. Light Rum
2 oz. Pineapple juice
Juice of 1 Lime
1 oz. Papaya juice
1 tsp. sugar

Shake with ice. Pour over ice in a large Tiki Mug of Hurricane glass. Prepare for tastebud to erupt.

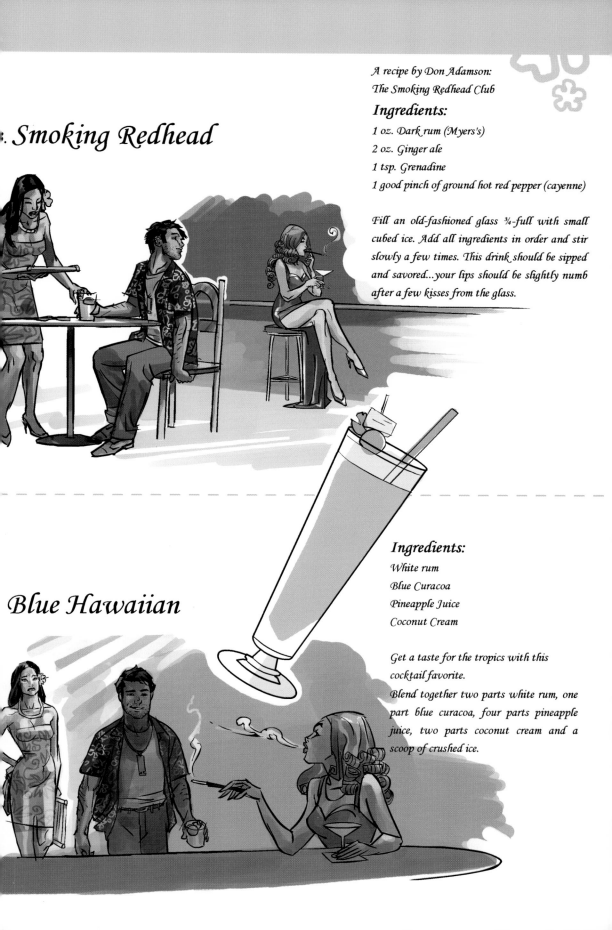

Smoking Redhead

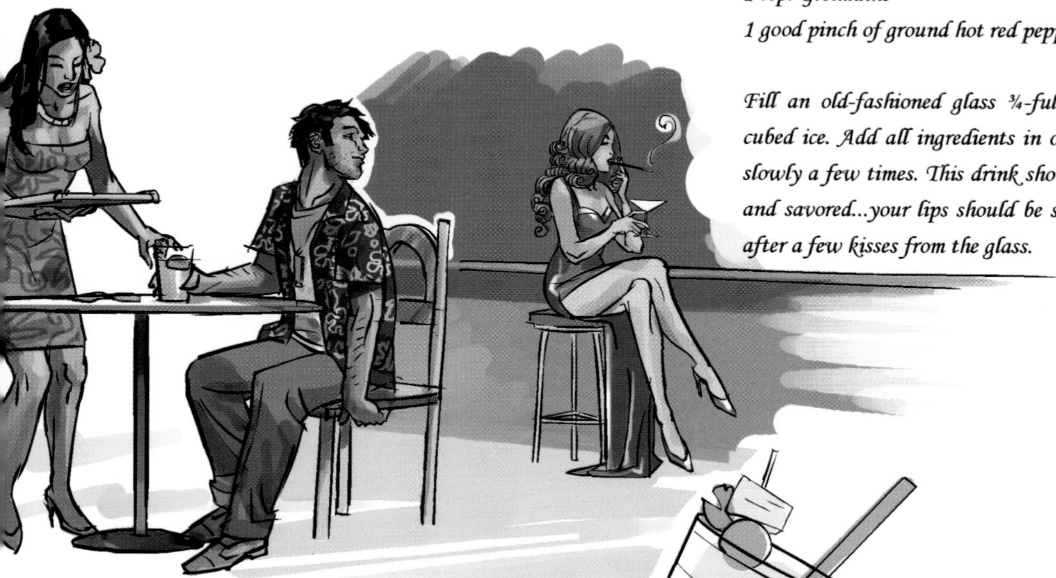

A recipe by Don Adamson:
The Smoking Redhead Club

Ingredients:

1 oz. Dark rum (Myers's)
2 oz. Ginger ale
1 tsp. Grenadine
1 good pinch of ground hot red pepper (cayenne)

Fill an old-fashioned glass ¾-full with small cubed ice. Add all ingredients in order and stir slowly a few times. This drink should be sipped and savored...your lips should be slightly numb after a few kisses from the glass.

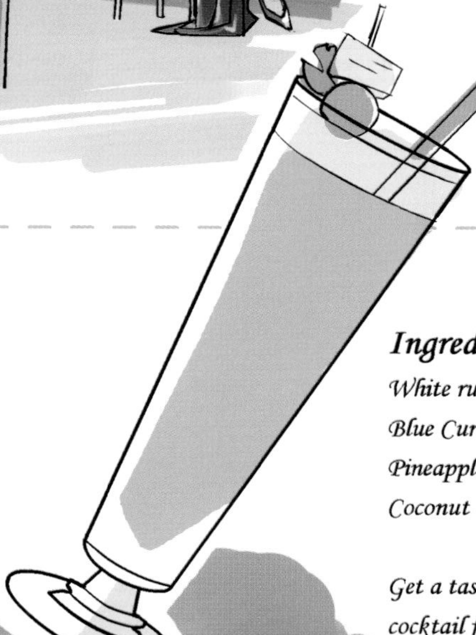

Blue Hawaiian

Ingredients:

White rum
Blue Curacoa
Pineapple Juice
Coconut Cream

Get a taste for the tropics with this cocktail favorite.
Blend together two parts white rum, one part blue curacoa, four parts pineapple juice, two parts coconut cream and a scoop of crushed ice.

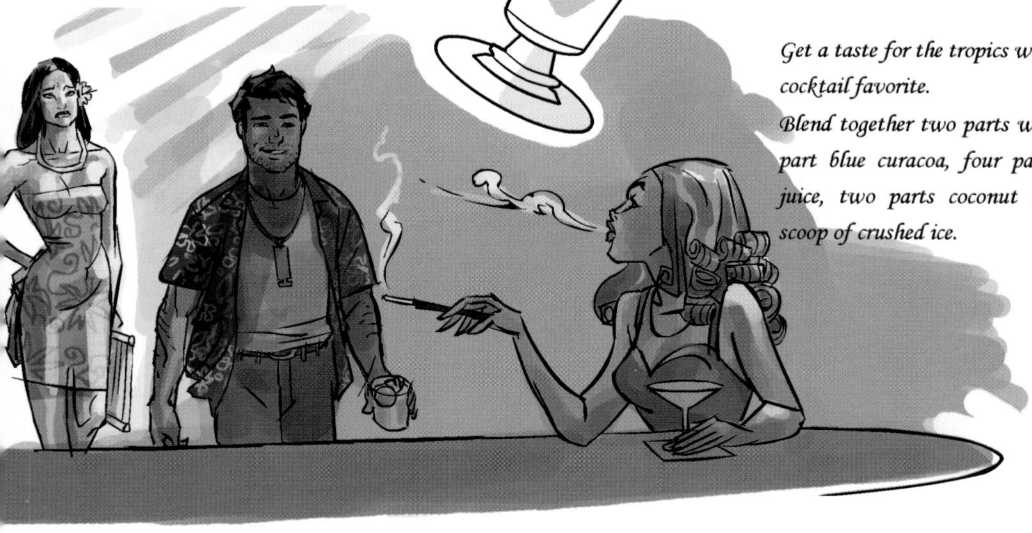

5. Molokai Mike

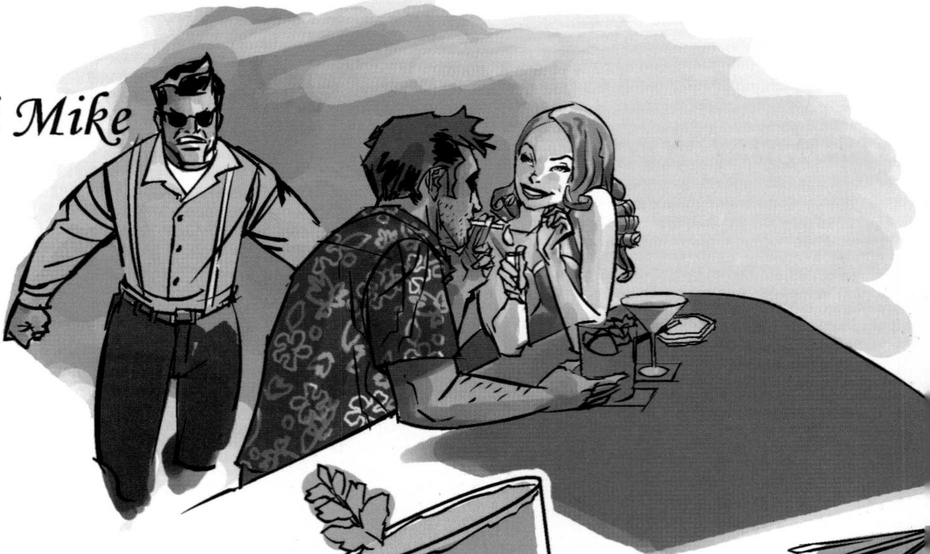

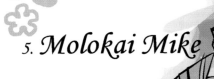

A Trader Vic's recipe.

Ingredients:

1 oz. Lemon Juice
1 oz. Orange Juice
1/2 oz. Orgeat syrup
1/2 oz. Brandy
1 oz. Light rum
1/2 oz. Rhum Negrita
Dash of Grenadine

Blend lemon juice, orange juice, orgeat syrup, brandy, light rum and one small scoop of crushed ice. Pour into glass, half filling. Then blend Rhum Negrita, a dash of grenadine and a half scoop of crushed ice. Pour slowly into top half of the glass.

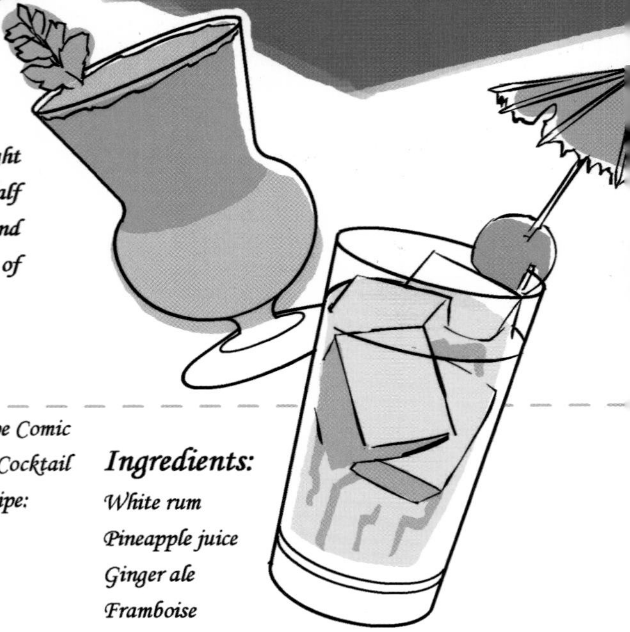

The swanky San Francisco comic book hangout - the Isotope Comic Book Lounge, conducted the official Hawaiian Dick Cocktail competition, the prize going to Meriko Borogove for her recipe:

6. Bruised Kidney for a Hawaiian Dick

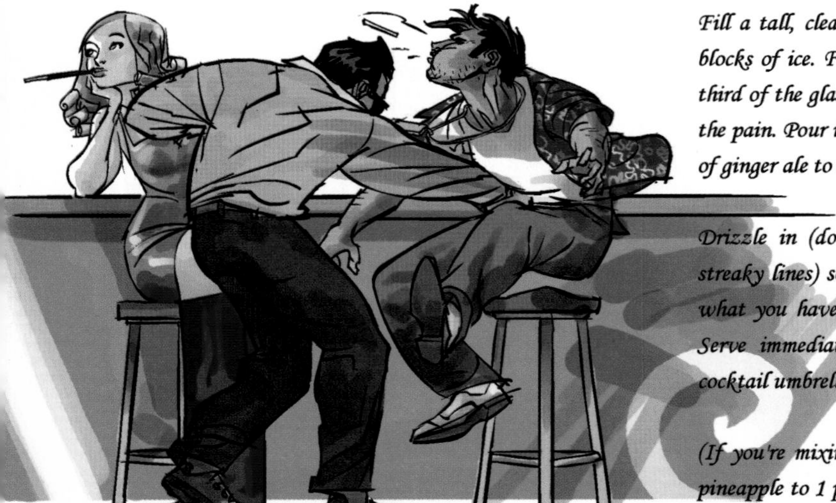

Ingredients:

White rum
Pineapple juice
Ginger ale
Framboise

Fill a tall, clear glass with ice. For best results, use big blocks of ice. Fill the glass full. Add some white rum. A third of the glass full will do - unless you're trying to kill the pain. Pour in a bunch of pineapple juice. Add a splash of ginger ale to the top. Stir up the drink.

Drizzle in (down the sides of the glass, for optimum streaky lines) some framboise (or creme d'cassis, if that's what you have, or some other dark, sticky, red liqueur). Serve immediately, garnished with a slightly battered cocktail umbrella. Maybe with a cherry.

(If you're mixing up a big pitcher of the mixer, 4 parts pineapple to 1 part ginger ale seems about right. I always booze to taste for the lucky recipient.).

7. Tango

Throw together two parts gin, one part sweet vermouth, one part dry vermouth, a couple of dashes of orange curacao and a dash of orange juice. Shake it up.

Ingredients:

Gin
Sweet vermouth
Dry Vermouth
Orange Curacao
Orange Juice

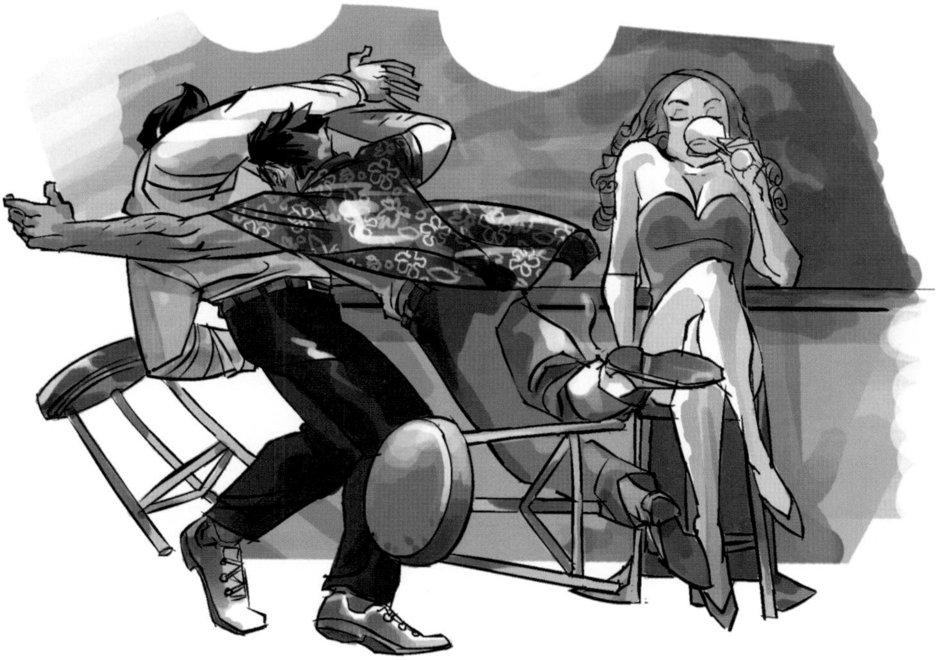

8. Stinger

Ingredients:

Brandy
White crème de menthe

Stir two parts brandy with one part white crème de menthe. A spectacular blend, just the thing to make your troubles go away. Serve straight up or on the rocks.

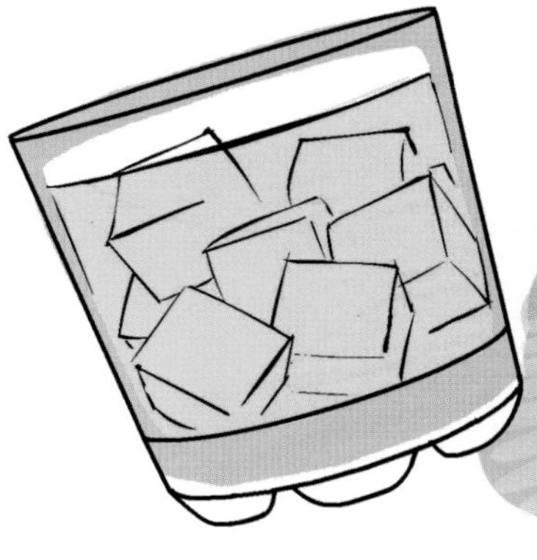

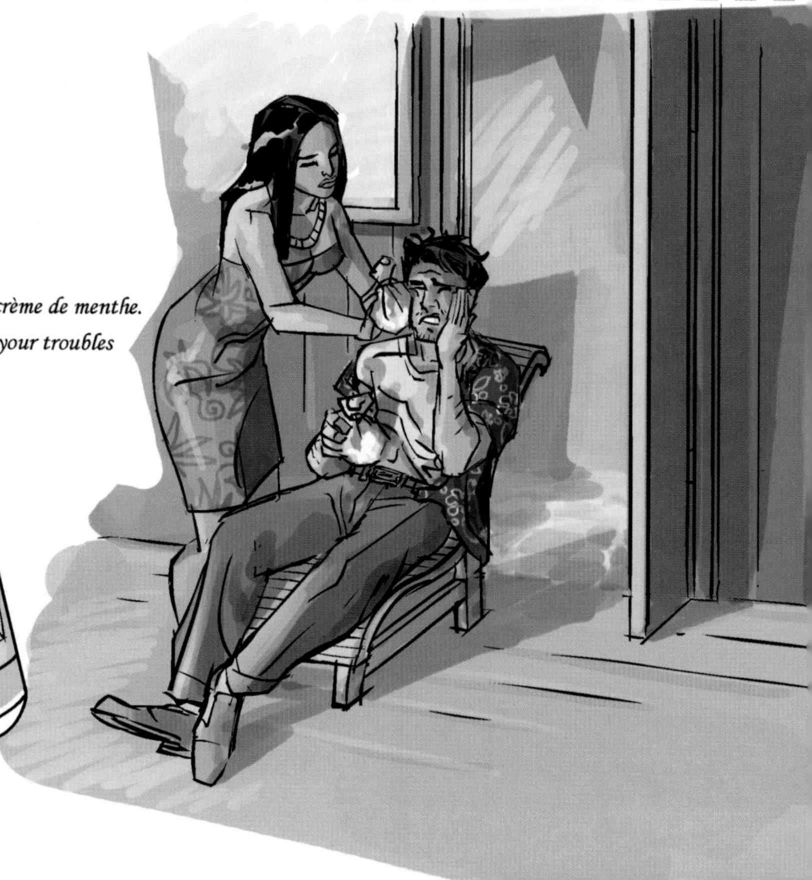

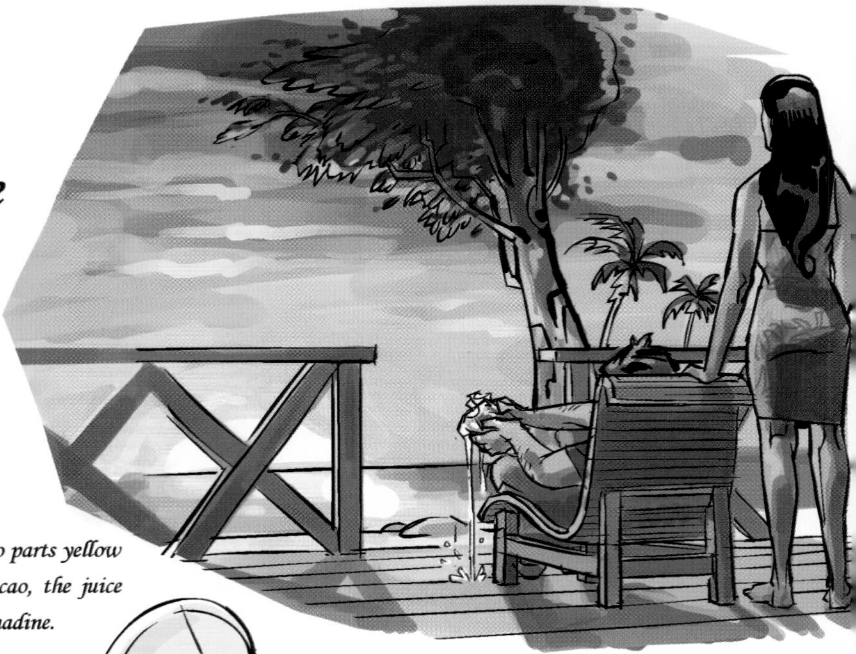

9. *Palm Breeze*

Ingredients:

Dark rum
Yellow Chartreuse
Crème de cacao
Fresh lime
Grenadine

Combine three parts dark rum, two parts yellow Chartreuse, one part crème de cacao, the juice from half a lime and a dash of grenadine.

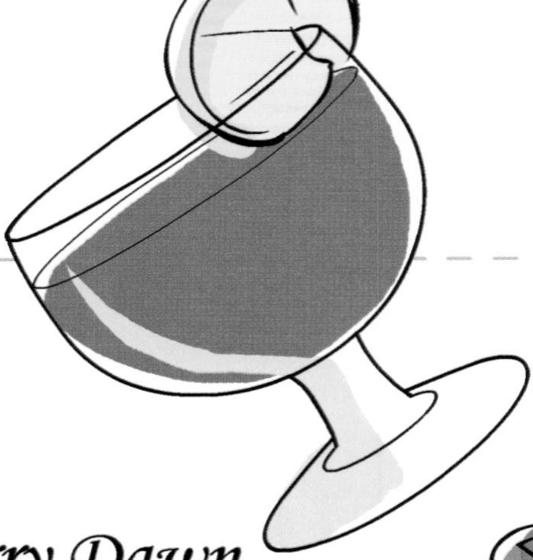

10. *Strawberry Dawn*

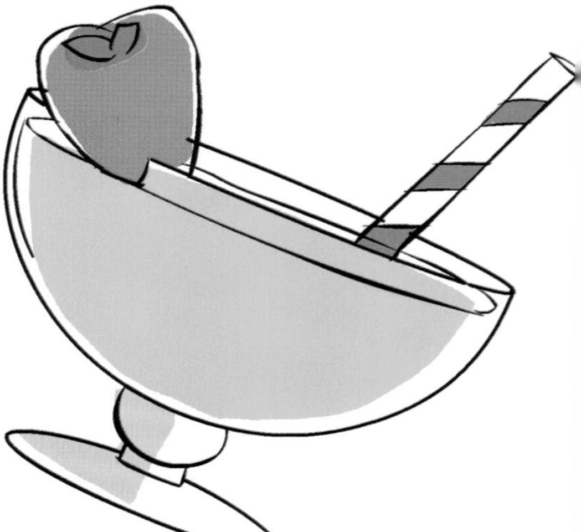

Ingredients:

Fresh strawberries
Gin
Coconut cream

Blend one part gin with one part coconut cream, three strawberries and a couple of scoops of crushed ice.

For best results, do not blend for too long or the drink becomes over-diluted.

Serve in a large, bowl-shaped glass with a strawberry on the rim. Drink through short, fat straws.

ART
GALLERY

Kalman Andrasofszky

Rick Cortes

Hector Casanova

Brian Frey

Azad

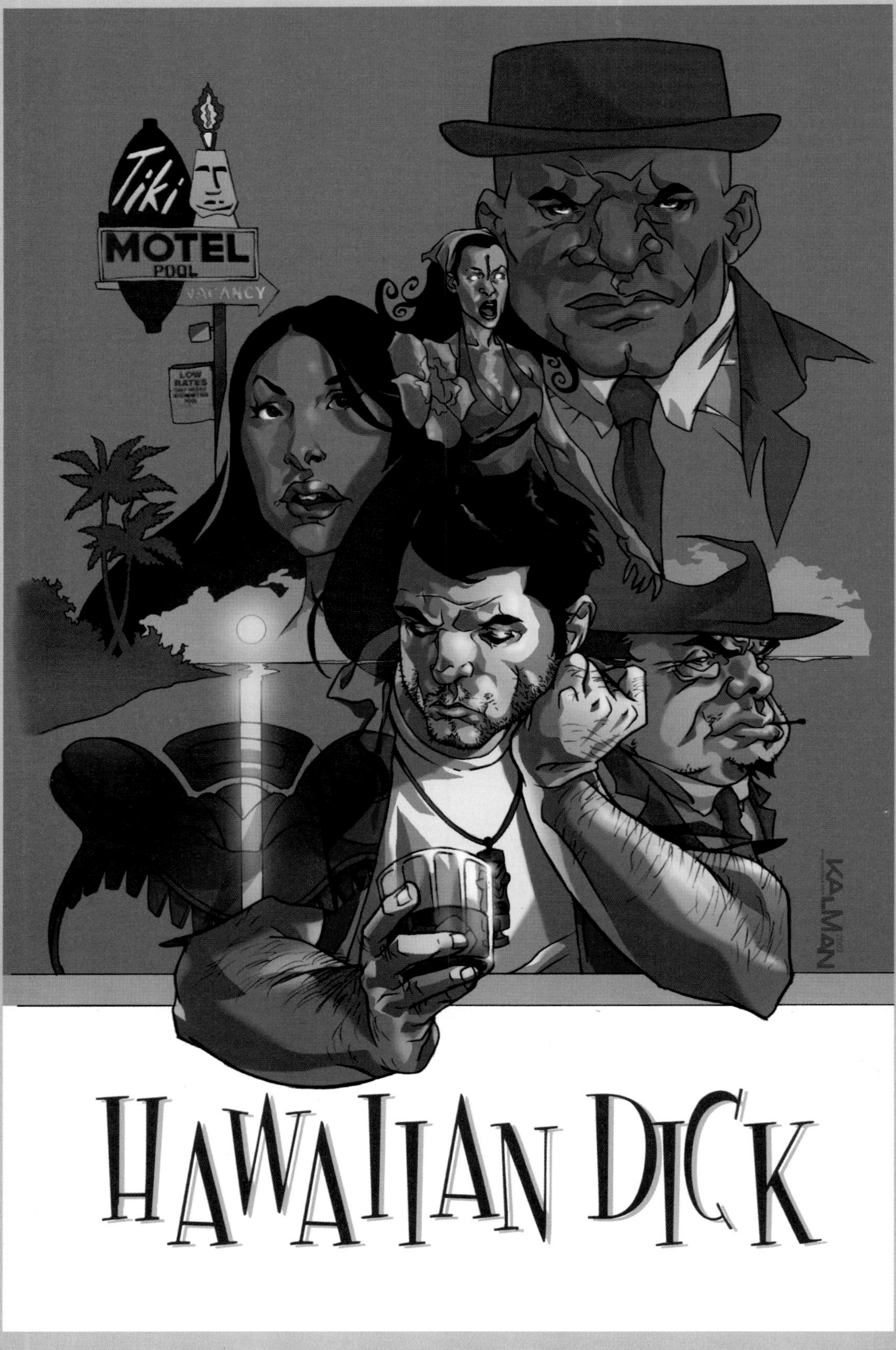
Tiki
MOTEL
POOL
VACANCY
LOW RATES
KALMAN
HAWAIIAN DICK

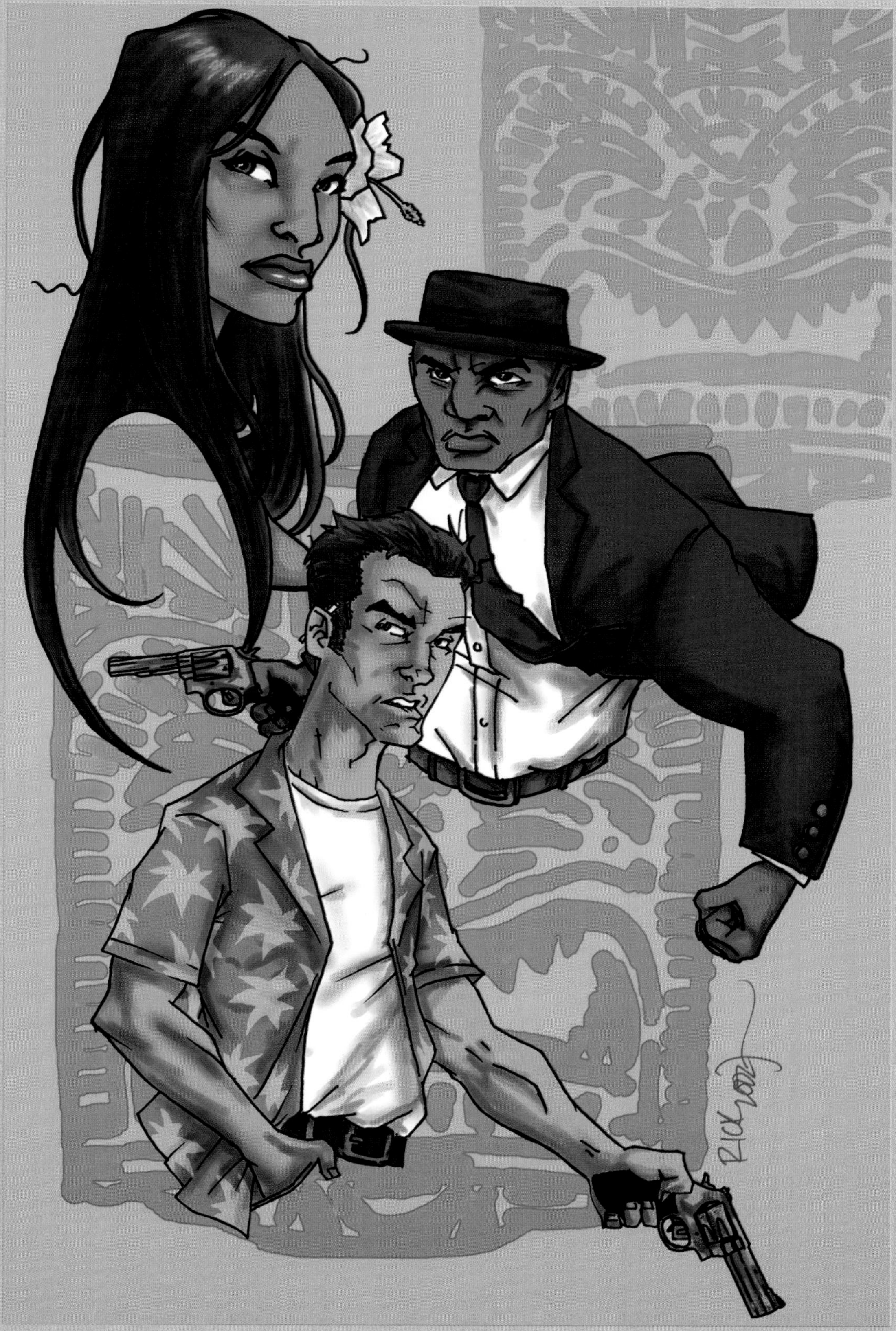

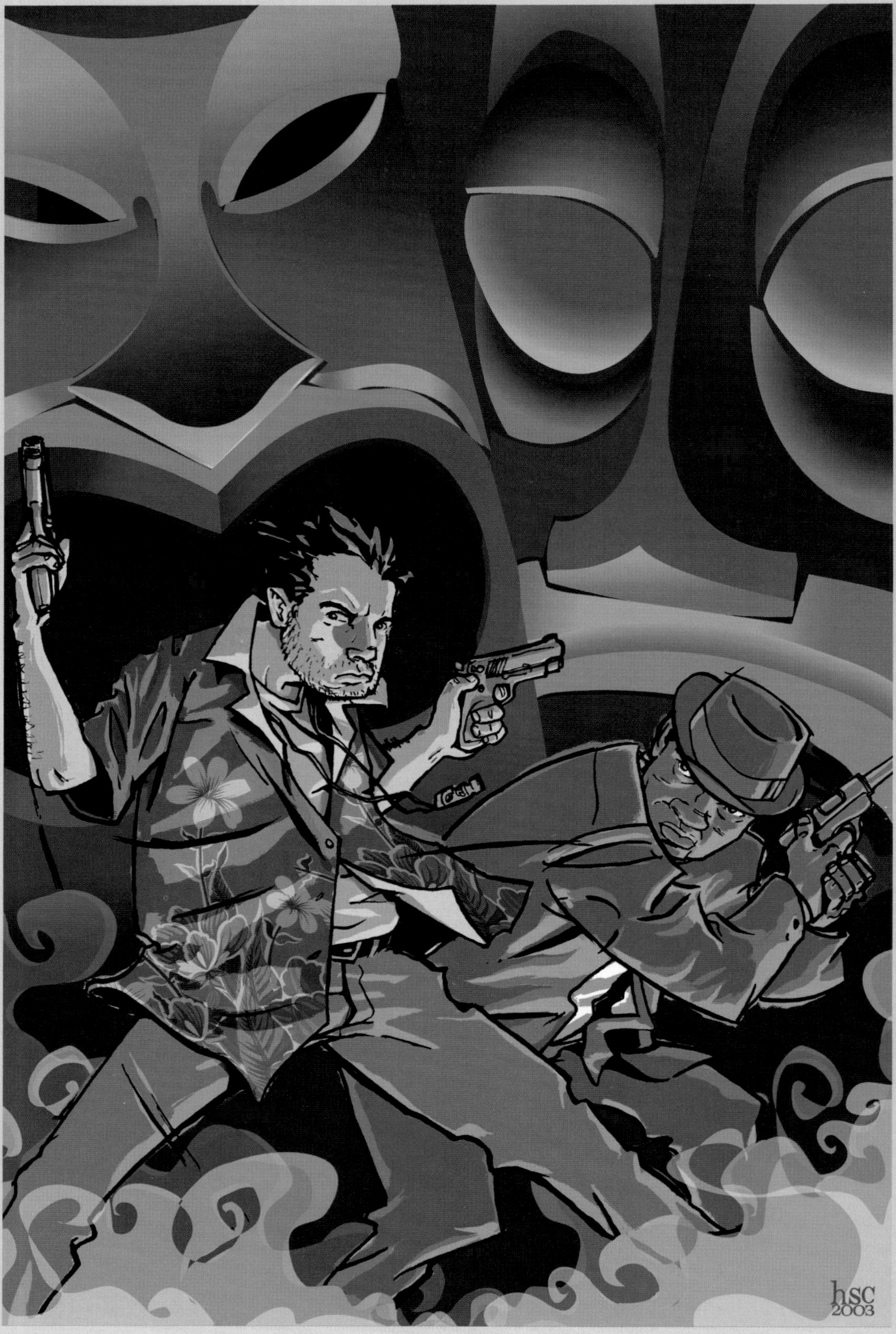
hsc
2003

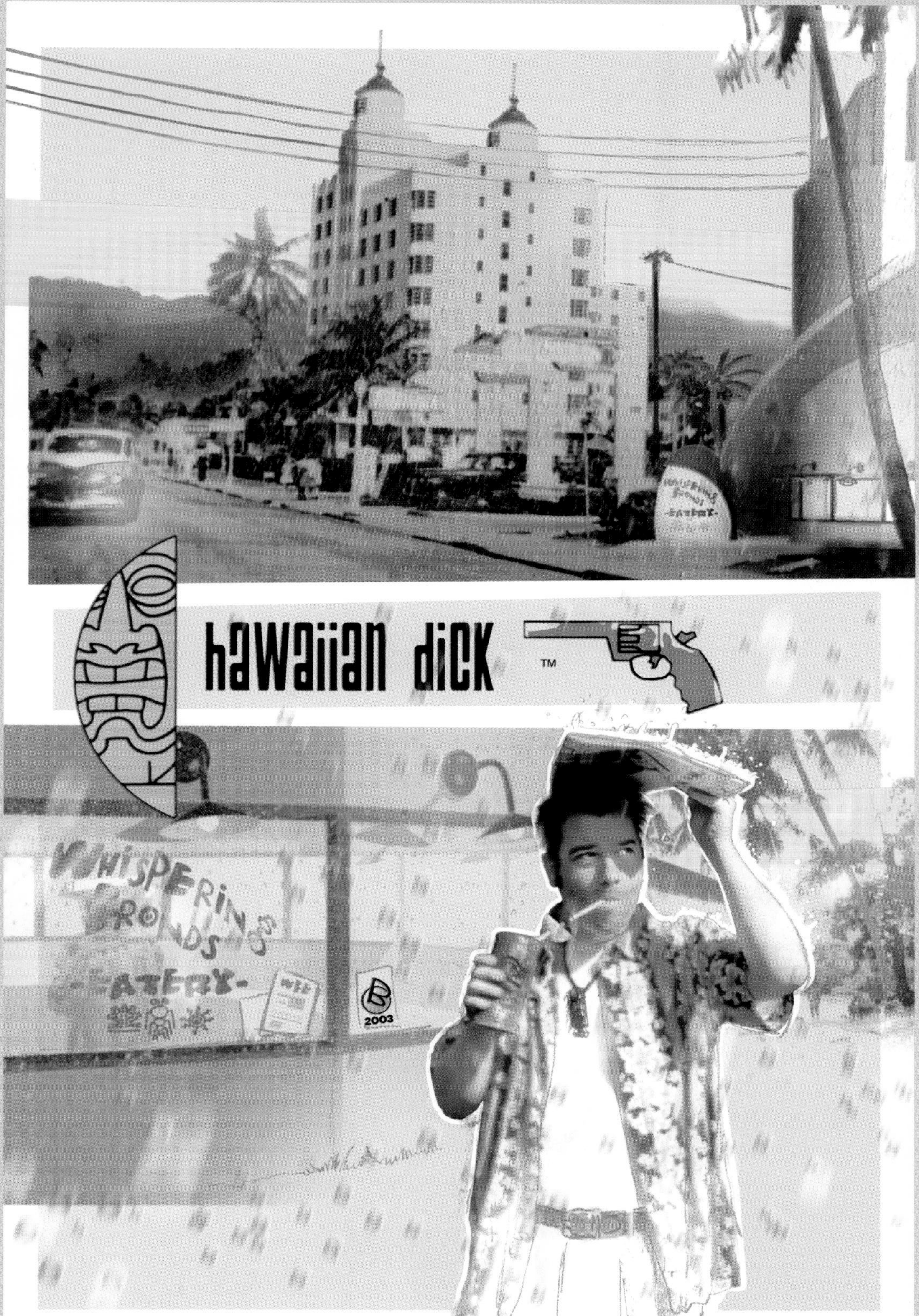
Whispering Fronds
-Eatery-
hawaiian dick
™
2003

In an effort to cash in on the success of "Hawaiian Dick", Azad underhandedly resolicits "Sammy:Tourist Trap" with a "Double-Entendre" in the title:

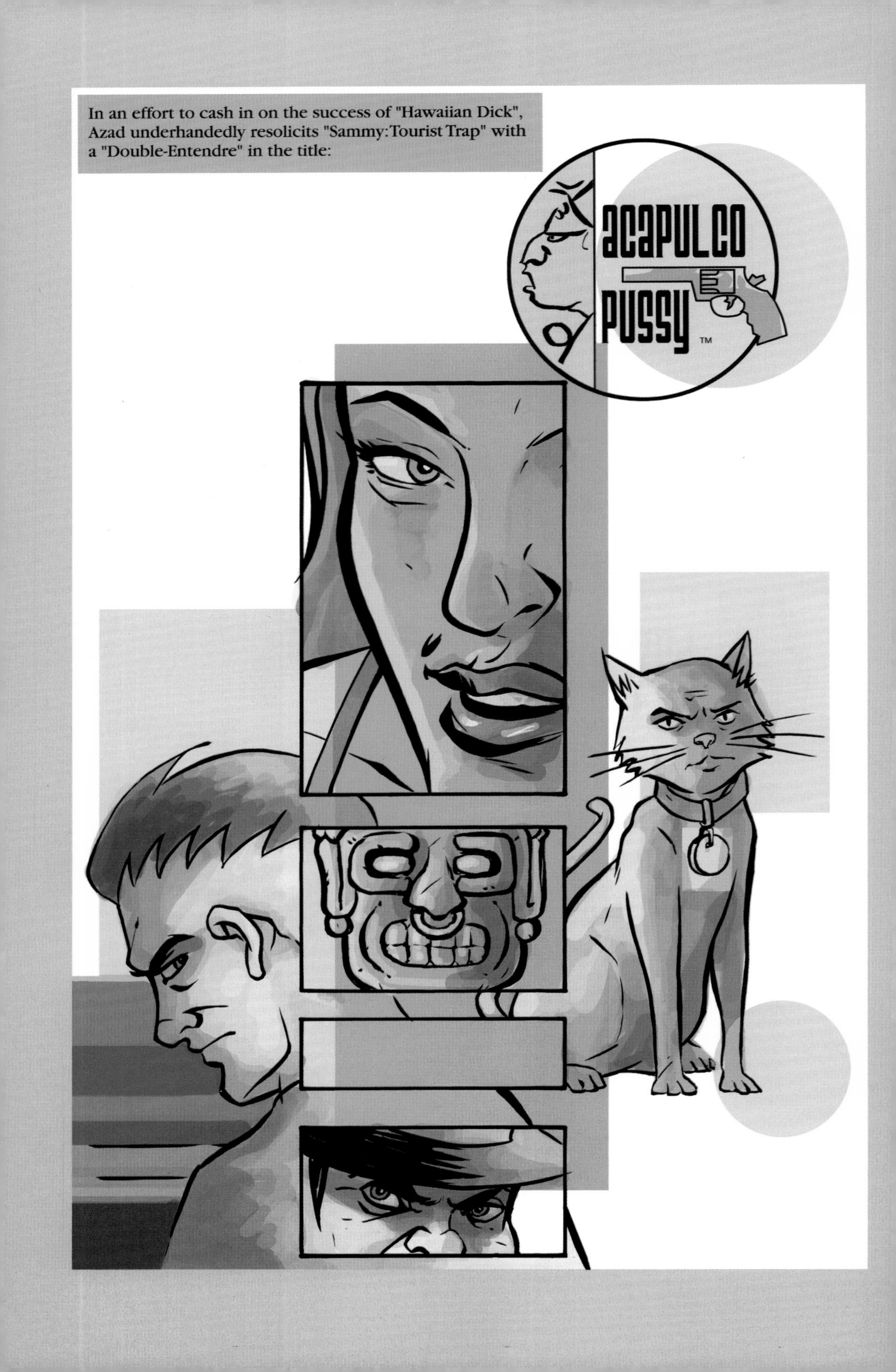
ACAPULCO
PUSSY
TM

NOW THAT THE MYSTERY IS SOLVED...AN AFTERWORD
by Jamie S. Rich

I like to think of Hawaiian Dick as a gateway comic.

It looks all soft and easy and harmless, and it reads like a dream
and makes you feel real good, but really, it's just easing you into
the harder stuff.

The comics world is rather stuck at the moment. This is probably
the umpteenth essay you've read that says this, but really, not
enough people are getting it, so I'll say it again. Comics
development was arrested somewhere in its adolescence (making the
comic book industry the Robert Cohn in this Sun Also Rises world of
ours), condemning the art form to an endless cycle of guys in
garish costumes beating each other up. That's what most people
think of when they think of comics. That's even what most fans
think of when they think of comics, so stuck in this groove are we.

But it's not the whole truth. There is a bigger picture. There is
more to this world than guys in fetish gear wearing their underwear
the wrong way.

There is Hawaiian Dick.

Hawaiian Dick is good.

Hawaiian Dick is so good, that the sort of people who turn up their
nose to four-color adventures like they would to rancid cheese
would actually read this and think, "This is pretty good."

It's so good that even though I edit for and co-own a competing
publisher, I am writing this little afterword gratis. I have no
problem saying this book is good. And if I didn't have shelves upon
shelves of my own books to show people to convince them comics are
a vibrant and exciting medium, I'd give them Hawaiian Dick. Why?

It's like I said. It's a gateway comic. Genre-wise, it has as much
to do with detective movies and old school ghost stories and cool
retro-TV shows with Jack Lord as it does your standard funnybook.
It's more mainstream than the comics mainstream, a concept that is
still in its infancy, but one that we at Oni Press get behind. The
pervert suit books from the Big Boys may be mainstream comics, but
in the real world of mass media and popular entertainment, you're
more likely to find a Hawaiian Dick lighting up the charts then

you are a Fisticuffs Fella. (And yes, there are exceptions, but save 'em. I probably know more of them than even you.)

The fine folks that created Hawaiian Dick didn't sit around thinking, "Can I do a comic book just like they did when I was a kid?" Instead, B. Clay Moore and Steve Griffin sat around and asked themselves what kind of story they wanted to tell, knowing all along that any idea they had would be something that comics could handle. It's a big art form. It can do anything.

Which you've likely seen. Since I am the caboose on this here caravan, you've probably already sunk your teeth into Byrd of Paradise and gotten a good taste of it. So, this next bit will be preaching to the choir, but for those of you who came in the back way and need to be convinced to flip over to the beginning, here is where I tell you why this book works so well.

It's all a matter of Chemistry. B. Clay Moore is the story compound. He brings the initial verve, that first inhale, lacing it with good characters and a strong narrative voice, and a willingness to put a twist in when he thinks you're losing a little of the buzz. Steve Griffin is your artful rolling paper. He takes Clay's compound and shoves them inside an appealing package. He makes sure those characters express the right things on their face, makes sure they have a world to walk around in, and splashes color all over it so that the reader trips good and hard.

Light it up, and you've got some Hawaiian Dick. Put this graphic novel in the hands of your favorite anti-comics curmudgeon and watch them lose their inhibitions. They'll start thinking in panels and word balloons, and the next thing you know, they'll have a secret stash of sequential literature on their bookshelves. And they'll have Moore and Griffin to blame. The first taste seemed so smooth, but soon everyone will be a comic book junkie.

Jamie S. Rich,
in da mudd
June, 2003

Jamie S. Rich is the writer of Cut My Hair, a novel with illustrations (as opposed to this, which is an illustrated novel). He is also the editor in chief of Oni Press, themselves a fine publisher of illustrated novels. He is currently working on The Everlasting, a novel with no pictures whatsoever. You can visit him at confessions123.com.